STARTING OVER

A BROOKINGS LATIN AMERICA INITIATIVE BOOK

The Latin America Initiative at Brookings focuses on the most critical economic, political, and social issues facing the region. The books in this series provide independent analysis for a modern Latin America.

Titles in the series include:

Javier Corrales and Michael Penfold
*Dragon in the Tropics: Hugo Chávez and
the Political Economy of Revolution in Venezuela*
2011

Albert Fishlow
Starting Over: Brazil since 1985
2011

Abraham F. Lowenthal, Theodore J. Piccone,
and Laurence Whitehead, eds.,
Shifting the Balance: Obama and the Americas
2011

A BROOKINGS LATIN AMERICA INITIATIVE BOOK

STARTING OVER

BRAZIL SINCE 1985

ALBERT FISHLOW

BROOKINGS INSTITUTION PRESS
Washington, D.C.

The Library of Congress has cataloged the hardcover editon as follows:
Fishlow, Albert.
    Starting over : Brazil since 1985 / Albert Fishlow.
      p.   cm.
    Includes bibliographical references and index.
    Summary: "Explains how the changes that Brazil has undergone over the last twenty-
five years have transformed the social, political, economic, and diplomatic realms in that
country and will affect its future, and especially influence the new presidency of Dilma
Rousseff"—Provided by publisher.
    ISBN 978-0-8157-2143-7 (cloth : acid-free paper)
    1. Brazil—History—1985– 2. Brazil—Economic conditions—1985– 3. Brazil—Social
conditions—1985– 4. Brazil—Politics and government—1985–2002. 5. Brazil—Politics
and government—2003– I. Title.
    F2538.3.F555 2010
    981.06'4—dc23   2011019462

    ISBN 978-0-8157-2541-1 (pbk. : alk. paper)

Digital printing

Printed on acid-free paper

Typeset in Sabon and Strayhorn

Composition by Cynthia Stock
Silver Spring, Maryland

To Harriet

Contents

Preface to the Paperback Edition

Two years have passed since *Starting Over* first appeared. In mid-2011 Brazil was a great favorite of all the international financial institutions and of the UN as well. The country managed to recover from the Great Recession with a soaring annual growth of 7.5 percent and was touted to slow down a bit to a continuing rate of 5 percent or so, placing it among the BRIC global leaders. Internationally, Brazil was extending its reach from Haiti to the troubled Mideast, and contending for a seat on the Security Council.

Today, there has been a 180-degree shift. The country has failed to sustain the high growth rate of prior years. In 2011 expansion was only 2.7 percent, falling to 0.9 percent in 2012, with less than 2.5 percent likely in 2013. That is the key Brazilian story. Several causes contributed. Favorable terms of trade began to turn the other way in the feeble global economy, and exports grew little. A large Central Bank decline in real interest rates was unable to rally investment very much. Investment now stands at around 18 percent, much lower than other Latin American countries, not to mention India and China. Personal consumption expanded at a higher rate than national income, benefiting from increasing personal credit flowing to a progressively larger lower middle class. Increasingly greater government intervention through reduced taxes on consumer durables and automobiles and cheaper credit through the National Development Bank were not enough to counter the tide.

Inflation did not fall in response, but continued well above the targeted 4.5 percent set for the Central Bank. Instead of really cutting back, the government's commitment to a primary surplus—excluding its interest obligations—was more in name than in fact. Improvisation occurred on all sides, extending even to the delayed accounting of petroleum imports. Unemployment rates remained low, and minimum wages continued to go up, increasing pension payments and helping to sustain demand.

In 2013, as inflation began to exceed 6.5 percent, new efforts to reduce energy costs occurred, and public sector prices were kept constant to avoid further acceleration. Even an empowered Petrobrás was forced to cut back its substantial investment to develop the new pre-sal oil resources as its revenues—in the absence of permitted domestic price increases—fell short of expenditures.

The Central Bank, recognizing that domestic demand exceeded supply and that the country had been constrained by years of inadequate public investment in infrastructure, including roads, port facilities, airports, and urban areas, as well as modernization of the manufacturing sector, began to raise interest rates. As projections of growth fell in Brazil's principal market, China, and Argentina's commitment to import substitution led to additional loss of sales, despite Mercosul, exchange rates rose in response.

President Dilma Rousseff, elected as Lula's successor, managed economic policy from the very beginning. At the outset of her administration, Brazil was projected to grow at extraordinary rates through 2022, two hundred years after independence from Portugal. But as prospects progressively diminished, her efforts redoubled. She was a technocrat, never elected to public office before, and was persuaded that a larger and more active state was the right response. Dilma showed little disposition to interact with Congress, her thirty-nine cabinet members, or, for that matter, with private business executives. But she was insistent about fighting corruption within the executive branch, sacking numerous ministers accused of confusing private gain with social responsibility. She expanded *Bolsa Família* from the very beginning, hoping to diminish poverty even more. Despite the disappointing aggregate results, her popularity matched that of her predecessor.

Congress never played a major role in drafting legislation. The *medida provisória,* allowing the executive to announce legislation that Congress could subsequently ratify or mildly alter—few proposals were defeated—

substituted for congressional action. Advances were made in legislation governing land rights in the Amazon, and more recently in provision for port expansion, but accomplishments were modest. Instead, Congress focused on the future, seeking to increase the allocation of profits from pre-sal oil development to recipient states and municipalities that they represented. Interestingly, polls consistently report political parties—Brazil has more than twenty-five—and the legislature as the most corrupt institutions within the country.

The Supreme Court surprised Brazil by its decision in 2012 to uphold guilty verdicts for leaders of the PT (Workers' Party) and other political parties involved in the 2005 *mensalão* scandal. Regular payments to congressmen ensured support. Although justice is proceeding slowly, it seems to advance. Few expected such an outcome. Popular reaction has been positive: the courts, and more broadly, the Ministério Público as well, improved in public regard.

Suddenly, in early June 2013, the Brazilian street came alive. This was not the first time. In 1984 demonstrators had demanded immediate direct presidential elections. That was not to be, but military rule soon ended. In 1992 pressure was exerted to impeach President Collor, and Congress soon acquiesced. In 2013 the initial, and modest, demand was for retraction of the nine-cent increase in municipal bus fares just put into effect. What had aroused this angry opposition? Long commute times in expanding urban areas, made worse with government efforts that encouraged automobile sales.

All politicians were surprised by the growing discontent in evidence. At least three ancillary factors magnified public concern. One was the initial violent response from the police to largely orderly marches. Some people were hurt, including members of the press, and opposition grew. Another was the imminent congressional legislation reducing the influence of the Ministério Público, regarded as an independent and important voice by many. The MP stood against corruption: that was becoming the central rallying cry of the crowd. The third trigger was the Confederation Cup, a set of international soccer matches being held around the country preliminary to the World Cup a year later. Resources spent on new stadiums, much beyond early cost estimates, became a highly visible issue, as were the large sums committed to the Olympic Games in 2016. Spending for better education and health services soon became a banner cause.

Dilma responded early on, recognizing the legitimacy of the protests and seeking to channel them favorably. But, as the *New York Times* reported on July 14, "Brazilian President's Attempts to Placate Protesters Backfire." An initial proposal for a constitutional assembly to take up fundamental political reform in time for the 2014 election soon gave way to a complicated plebiscite, and that in turn has moved to congressional consideration in coming months. More money for education and health care is not available, just when the Central Bank is trying to reduce demand, so the solution is to promise the presumed profits from pre-sal oil reserves in the distant future. Only the generalized furor surrounding U.S. National Security Agency activities in Brazil, and congressional recess, has provided temporary relief. Meanwhile, Dilma's popularity has declined precipitously, and she—or perhaps even Lula—faces a competitive presidential campaign that has already begun, more than a year before the election in October 2014.

Political reform to go along with the introduction of the *real* in 1993 has been a long-standing issue. So too, has been the need for government saving—instead of public deficits—to finance greater investment in infrastructure, primary and secondary education, and public health. Transferring some of the money from public pensions to better training of the young makes good sense. Finding solutions to these concerns is hardly easy in a more middle-class and participatory Brazil. In the present global world, Brazil also will want to pursue international leadership both by South-South interaction and a better relationship with the North.

These ideas are not new, but have evolved over the years since 1985. *Starting Over* places these proposals within their historical base.

Acknowledgments

I am grateful to Mauricio Cardenas, director of the Brookings Latin American Initiative, for his many suggestions and his active engagement in moving the manuscript to publication. Everyone at the Brookings Institution Press has been helpful as the final form of the book took shape. To Columbia University and SIPA, I owe thanks for partially underwriting this volume. Over my recent years there in the Institute of Latin American Studies and the Center for Brazilian Studies, Tom Trebat has been central, offering administrative and intellectual help. Discussions with Alfred Stepan, Vicky Murillo, and faculty visitors from the region have contributed as well. I note especially the administrative assistance of Teresa Aguayo and Eliza Kwon-Ahn. They have helped well beyond the ordinary, not only on this project, but on several others.

I have accumulated many debts since I first visited Brazil in 1965. Were I to list here all of my students and colleagues to whom I am indebted, the list would be substantial. The contributions of my master's and doctoral students from Brazil have been central. These students have become personal friends and valued tutors, as have other Brazilians from all professions whom I have had the good fortune to meet and learn from. Colleagues at Berkeley and Yale, and elsewhere, also have had a positive influence. I acknowledge specifically only my personal friends, Faith and Jerry Jaffe and Molly Poag, whose presence has been important to completion.

Last to acknowledge is my family. They will find that order totally appropriate. Over the years, my three children, their spouses, and nine grandchildren have come to accept and understand my commitment to Brazil, and my consequent frequent absences, both physical and mental. To my wife, Harriet, I dedicate this book, as I did my first more than forty-five years ago. (That first volume dealt with railroads in the United States before the Civil War—quite a different subject.) Without her wise and generous support in so many ways, neither volume—nor my intervening evolution southward—would ever have been possible.

1

Introduction

Brazil has undergone transformative change since its return to civil rule in 1985. The country has started over. As electoral participation has widened, politics has altered. Effective economic policies have become permanent, and economic advance has become more widespread and consistent. With rising income a healthier and longer life is available to a much broader swath of the population, and there is increased opportunity for social advancement. And Brazil's foreign policy has assumed greater importance within a multipolar world.

The Economist featured Brazil in its issue of November 14, 2009. According to the final words both of the lead editorial and the special report, "Its take-off is all the more admirable because it has been achieved through reform and democratic consensus. . . . What makes the country so exciting at the moment is that, thanks to its newfound stability, Brazil's better self now has a much greater chance of prevailing."[1]

This advance was neither continuous nor without occasional good fortune. At times, the challenges facing the new civilian regime seemed beyond its capability to respond. Nor did the "New Republic" begin with a tabula rasa. The past did not just disappear; rather, its influence gradually eroded over time, as reforms were implemented and a new generation exerted its influence.

Initially, after 1985 the prime emphasis was on a new constitution, which was accompanied by political party multiplication and realignment. Emergence from decades of political constraint under military dictatorship was the main concern, in part because a competent technocracy had dealt with the economy, and not altogether badly. Coping with burgeoning inflation had secondary significance; it is not accidental that both Argentina and Brazil failed the first time around in this battle. Other priorities took precedence.

The Constitution of 1988 established the basis for the New Republic. A strong executive emerged and remained central to subsequent events. Social principles were enacted, if not immediately implemented. Universal claims to education, health care, and retirement benefits were henceforth legitimate demands upon the state. But these could not be realized until inflation had been successfully eliminated. Brazil finally succeeded in doing so with the Real Plan in 1994. Thereafter, the currency unit has stayed the same, a sharp difference from the previous constant elimination of zeroes and frequent name changes.

Freed from these inflationary shackles, the Cardoso years saw much constitutional amendment to better provide an institutionalized basis for moving forward. This was especially the case within the social area: original rights required modification before they could be effectively implemented. In addition, privatization and globalization entered in a decisive way as the economy finally began to grow. International affairs assumed greater importance: Brazil exerted leadership in Mercosul (a customs union of neighboring states), considered the possibility of membership in a new continent-wide Free Trade Agreement of the Americas sought by the United States, reached out to the European Union, and launched an organization of all South American nations.

But in the wake of crises in Asia and Russia, Brazil had to devalue its currency and seek assistance from the International Monetary Fund (IMF) and World Bank. Economic matters again assumed priority. A new macroeconomic policy was implemented and has continued into the present: inflation targeting, a primary fiscal surplus, and a floating exchange rate with an open capital account. Slowing economic growth, rapidly rising taxes, and soaring public debt altered domestic politics definitively: Lula and the Workers' Party (PT) emerged as clear winners in 2002. International capital markets then became extremely worried about future policy, as a sharply devaluing *real* showed.

Their fears were unfounded: the Lula administration retained the preestablished economic framework, including the IMF program. There was no renunciation of public debt. Instead, in the midst of this

continuity—unwelcome to Lula's supporters—the government emphasized social policy. There was larger investment in a conditional cash
transfer program, Bolsa Família, incorporating approximately a fifth of
the population. Education received attention, as did the universal health
system. The burgeoning social security system with its continuing deficit
was managed. A highly unequal income distribution has continuously
improved. At the same time, greater independence emerged in foreign
affairs: Brazil ended its engagement in the Free Trade Agreement of the
Americas and devoted greater attention to South-South relations.

World economic expansion—leading to global growth rates not seen
since the 1970s—included Brazil after 2003. Exports and prices of primary products rapidly rose. Amid rapid expansion of trade with China,
there was much talk of delinking from the slower growing developed
countries. All that ended with the global economic collapse in the last
quarter of 2008. Brazil, benefiting from its high level of international
reserves, reacted well to this challenge. Compensating fiscal and monetary policy produced economic growth in 2010 of 7.5 percent. Additionally, discoveries of large petroleum reserves below the offshore salt
barrier, with promises of an immense surplus in years to come, have provided a new boost. The eternal land of the future has finally transformed
into the land of the present.

How was it possible for Brazil to move from its authoritarian past to
its lively democratic present over this interval, advancing not only politically but also economically, socially, and diplomatically? Three factors
played a role.

First is a pattern of sequential advance. Politics took initial precedence,
with concentration on preparing a new constitution as a framework for
the New Republic. In that effort, numerous independent political parties arose. But there was not the policy coherence required to end inflation and pursue economic growth. That only happened with the Real
Plan and with subsequent macroeconomic adjustment of the economic
model in 1999. Resumption of economic expansion, in turn, enabled
more effective social policies by ensuring needed resources. Brazilian foreign policy became more prominent at the last stage of this process, once
domestic achievements had occurred and became more institutionalized.

Second, of these multiple objectives, regaining economic growth
quickly came to dominate. There was an impressive prior record of
achievement to match: not only the "Brazilian Miracle" from 1968 to
1973, but earlier as well. Ending inflation alone was not enough. This

economic priority impelled a permanent increase in the size of the public sector but allowed privatization and emphasis upon expansion of foreign trade to proceed. Brazil modified budgetary rules to ensure a continuing primary surplus. Growth fully resumed only in the Lula years: the Program for Accelerated Growth, launched after his reelection in 2007, was a dominant factor in the recent electoral campaign.

Third, over the preceding twenty-five years, the outside world changed from a negative to a positive force, assisting Brazilian transformation. In the 1980s Brazil was afflicted by the debt crisis and eventual default. From the mid-1990s on came a sequence of economic problems: Mexican devaluation, the Asian crisis, Russian default, U.S. recession, and Argentine collapse. But thereafter, the terms of trade considerably improved, by some 34 percent since 2000 as commodity prices rapidly increased. Rising income exceeded gains in production. As the source of global income growth has increasingly shifted to the BRICS (Brazil, Russia, India, China, and South Africa), Brazil has been able to extend its diplomatic outreach.

The successive chapters of this volume treat four aspects of Brazil's transformation over the past twenty-five years: politics, economics, social policy, and international affairs. Each of them attempts to explain the changes observed in Brazilian policy. Quantitative tables abound, aiding the arguments advanced.

A final chapter looks ahead. The election of President Dilma Rousseff of the PT in 2010 was almost inevitable. She was the immensely popular Lula's personal choice. Continuing is not an easy task. Despite past gains, issues remain, and important decisions will have to be made. Already, immediately after inauguration, the new administration committed itself to fiscal restraint for 2011, and the central bank has begun to react to rising inflation by raising interest rates. But other long-standing questions also require attention, as Dilma has already acknowledged. In her speech opening the National Congress, she included several of them, but not fully.

In the political area, efforts will reemerge to alter voting regulations and strengthen the role of parties within the congress. Brazilians chose representatives from among more than twenty political parties in the recent election, and such a wide array hampers development of a stronger and more independent legislative branch. Although there is a pro-government majority greater than the 60 percent required for constitutional amendment, signs already emerge of discontent.

In the economic sphere, the high domestic real rate of interest, and the consequent assortment of offsetting subsidies granted to domestic industry, will have to be confronted. Brazil's interest rate will rise this year. A reason is the persistent fiscal deficit, despite a level of government receipts that approximates 38 percent of gross domestic product. The primary surplus is positive because government interest payments are excluded.

Socially, despite considerable expenditures, education and health compare unfavorably with the situation elsewhere. Large governmental outlays for pensions threaten future fiscal stability. The success of Bolsa Família and a surging lower middle class are quite positive developments, but in the absence of additional reforms, those advances may encounter setbacks if economic growth falters.

Within international affairs, there is now a greater Brazilian presence, bilaterally and regionally, as well as increased involvement in a variety of global issues relating to the environment, atomic energy, the World Trade Organization, and others. Making the recent South-South orientation compatible with closer relations with the United States and Europe will be an ongoing challenge.

2

Political Change

Constitutional change dominated the agenda following the return to civilian government. The new National Congress, elected in November 1986, served simultaneously as the Constituent Assembly with direct responsibility for promulgating the constitution. That effort required almost two years before completion and enlisted Brazilian society in all its modern diversity. Extensive participation by the public, as well as by nongovernmental organizations, was encouraged. On the other side, lobbies representing various economic interests were always present, ready to exert their influence on virtually every subject.

Radical change, although advocated by some, did not occur within the traditional three areas of governance. Attempts to substitute a prime ministerial form of governance failed. The executive branch retained its traditional presidential form and continued to possess considerable powers. The position of the congress was strengthened somewhat but less than had been anticipated. A modestly more independent judiciary emerged but was soon caught up in a mass of cases.

Mandated constitutional review five years later did not alter the document significantly. Only five amendments, out of some 30,000 proposals, were approved, despite requiring only a majority vote. Later, as basic reforms mounted during the Cardoso years, reluctance to alter original principles disappeared. There was a clear reason: almost all significant economic legislation required constitutional modification. A 60 percent majority vote, twice within the Câmara dos Deputados (the Chamber of Deputies, or lower house) and the Senado Federal (the Federal Senate, or upper house), required negotiation before additional change could occur. More than sixty amendments have since been passed.

This chapter focuses on three aspects of political change in Brazil. The first is the Constitution of 1988 and its principal consequences. Another topic is the inherent, and ongoing, struggle between centralization and decentralization of authority and resources. The final subject reviewed is the rise of independent regulatory authority over the past fifteen years.

Constitution of 1988

This section examines the particular powers extended to the executive, legislative, and judicial branches. The final document did not conform to initial expectations.

Executive Powers

The precise form executive power should take was a leading issue in the constitutional debate.[1] Its importance was heightened by José Sarney's unexpected assumption of the presidency after the death of president-elect Tancredo Neves in 1985. Early on, within the Constitutional Studies ("Arinos") Commission, a number of academics and others had argued for something like the French framework: a joint executive with both a president and a prime minister. Within the Constitutional Convention, too, there was a clear majority initially committed to this sharing of responsibility, and early versions of the draft documents distributed throughout 1987 all contained a provision establishing such apportionment of powers.

A leading reason was the historical moment: formerly authoritarian governments were returning to the fold of civil regimes, not only in Latin America but also in Eastern Europe. The distinguished Spanish academic Juan Linz argued for greater legislative engagement. Presidentialism meant a rigid structure where, after an election, the minority would have little weight. Hence there would be temptation to rely on extralegal coups d'état. There also was the potential for sheer immobility due to lack of legislative support, just when immediate responses might be required.

On the other side, the United States' favorable experience always is cited in favor of a presidential system. Both accountability and identifiability, requisites of a functioning democracy, could be found in a chosen leader more readily than one selected ex post. That is especially the case where there are a large number of individual political parties within the legislative body, as occurs in Brazil.

These opposing intellectual positions continue to flourish. Specific empirical findings vary, and results depend much upon which countries are included in a given study as well as on the period of the sample. Neither model is overwhelmingly endorsed. But the practical outcome in Brazil decisively favored a presidential system, contrary to early tendencies.

However, the dispute over the shape of the presidency was even more complicated: it centered on both the length of Sarney's term and the range of powers the executive would receive. As debate continued through successive constitutional drafts, Sarney won the day by actively entering the fray in favor of a presidential system as well as a full five-year term.

That he accomplished his goal is testimony to two political trends at the time. One was fear of the Left and an associated populism that seemed on the rise. Not only military leaders but also business leaders and centrist politicians strongly opposed an immediate election in 1988 for fear that Leonel Brizola, leftist ex-governor of Rio de Janeiro, might capture the presidency. At a moment when Alan Garcia had been elected president in Peru, and Nicaragua remained in the hands of the Sandinistas, these were troubling concerns to many. A second element was strong national sentiment in favor of a presidential structure. The national press, joined by popular—if partially uninformed—opinion, preferred the historical system to something European in origin.

When the crucial votes were tallied at the Constitutional Convention, first for the presidential form of executive and second for the length of term, the victories were greater than had been anticipated: 343-213 in favor of the first; 304-223 for the second. Most support came from the poorest and disproportionately represented states. From the political parties then leaning to the Left, 132 votes were positive for retaining the traditional executive, whereas only 81 favored a five-year term. This difference in the two results is a measure of the Left's interest in an immediate presidential election.

Sarney won on these two decisive issues. The Centrão, a group of legislators organized with his support, many emanating from the Liberal Front Party (Partido da Frente Liberal, or PFL), was key to the outcome. However, the presumed center did not do nearly as well on a range of social topics. On substantive matters involving claims of individuals for state services, the constitution took a more radical turn, as discussed below.

This was not the final word. A national referendum recording preference for presidentialism or parliamentary rule was held in April 1993. After President Fernando Collor's inability to end inflation and his impeachment, one would have anticipated support for a parliamentary alternative. The Brazilian Social Democratic Party (Partido da Social Democracia Brasileira, or PSDB), formed in 1988 in the midst of the constitutional debate, was the lone political party favoring change. The Brazilian Democratic Movement Party (Partido do Movimento Democrático Brasileiro, or PMDB), the PFL, and the Partido Democrático Trabalhista (Democratic Labor Party, or PDT) all came out for a presidential system. So did the PT, although its militants were somewhat divided. Such positions favoring the status quo were influenced by the forthcoming election, where each party had presidential hopes. In the end, some two-thirds of the electorate voted to retain the Constitution of 1988. That ended the matter: no one has again seriously proposed the parliamentary option in Brazil.

Sarney not only won presidential continuity, but Brazil also gained a strong executive branch. The *medida provisória* (provisional measure) is the principal reason. That instrument granted to the president "supposedly emergency powers" to enact laws temporarily and subsequently became a centerpiece of Brazilian governmental operation.

Although limited in principle to actions immediately required and valid only for thirty days unless authorized by the National Congress, these could be continuously reissued—with insignificant change (until Constitutional Amendment 32 passed in 2001). The medida provisória (MP) became the principal source of economic and administrative measures instituted.

The number of MPs was significant. During the eighteen months after approval of the constitution, Sarney issued 125 MPs, excluding reissues. Collor managed to issue 89, the great majority within the first year of his shortened presidency, before legislative opposition forced his exit. Itamar added 142 MPs, with the total number of reissues mounting rapidly to 363.[2] Cardoso's two terms involved more than 300 new MPs (and reissues of more than 4,500), while Lula's period saw an increase to 521. After Amendment 32 passed, many more of these turned into legislation than before. With the requirement that congress now consider any MPs within forty-five days, and the termination of presidential authority to renew them, many legislative sessions could not be held and were canceled until the requisite vote.

A recent study examines the executive preference for MPs. Were they used as an opportunity to bypass legislative authority, owing to its lack of support, or were they a willing delegation of power to the executive? The answer suggested seems reasonable enough: in the years before the success of the Real Plan, the interpretation favors presidential attempts to overcome a contrary public and legislative environment.[3] Subsequently, the delegation became more a matter of congressional acceptance.

This allocation of authority, even as later modified, has turned out to be an essential component of the Brazilian presidency. "In sum, the medidas provisórias became a powerful and deciding instrument in the hands of the executive because they allowed it to change the legal status quo of the country in unilateral form."[4] The president also had other effective instruments: ability to reward supporters with governmental positions, allocate revenues to allied states and municipalities, and reward allies in myriad other ways.

There also is presidential need for a dependable administration super-majority within the congress. This stems from the required three-fifths vote, twice in each house, to ratify constitutional amendments. Thus effective policy depends upon corralling the requisite majority. Elected representatives of the winning president's party within the Câmara and the Federal Senate never get beyond a mere fraction of needed support. Typically, they come to a fifth of the total membership. Other political parties have to be brought along, and that has meant cabinets of close to forty members and second-rank appointment privileges to entice the many additional parties required for viable coalitions. Nor are such efforts always enough: Dilma's selection of a higher proportion of PT ministers has already riled the allied PMDB to the point of organizing a separate bloc within the Câmara.

Congressional Responsibility

What had been intended at the outset as a document augmenting legislative authority entailed only a modest advance. There were significant new powers related to preparation of the annual budget. The president could make proposals, but the congress had the ability to amend them. In addition, congress was allowed to participate in the Tribunal de Contas, the judicial auditing authority. Such changes increased legislative voice, but the result was not always positive. For example, due to wide-ranging corruption charges, the Budget Committee of the Câmara underwent a full-scale investigation at the end of 1993.

Furthermore, internal rules weakened the legislature's strength. Seniority played no role in assignment of committee chairmanships, and little weight was given to specific expertise. Only a small proportion of members was actively involved in the decisionmaking process. The *baixo clero,* the excluded members, were called in from time to time when formal votes were required, contributing in turn to the use of presidential patronage to secure needed majorities or the even more difficult three-fifths majority vote required for constitutional amendment.

Strong party structure has not been a feature of Brazilian political life, and with the continuing multiplication of separate entities, their number grew from five after 1983 to the nineteen represented in the congress in 1991. None came close to majority status after 1986. Currently, the number of parties with seats has even slightly increased.

Political parties, moreover, were unstable in membership: one in three legislators switched in affiliation when the congress first met after the election. That was in response to the executive's effort to create a working majority. Changes went beyond marginal shifts; some were more extreme. Now, after the 2007 court ruling in favor of party rather than individual ownership of a seat, that practice has altered. More stable coalitions of the smaller parties have begun to occur.

Constitutional electoral rules contributed to this proliferation of parties. Brazil opted for proportional representation in the Câmara while imposing a simple plurality in the Federal Senate. This arrangement appeared in virtually all of the many constitutional drafts. An open, state-wide system served for choosing members of the lower house: any party could have an unlimited number of candidates, unranked by priority. Individual votes are summed by party, or by coalition when relevant, and those candidates with the necessary total—after continuing reallocation of excess votes cast for those already elected—are chosen. In populous states this arrangement led to an emphasis on local areas of support as an assurance of success, further weakening party identity.

One consequence of the enormous size of the ballot was the large number of blank and null votes, amounting to as much as 40 percent of the ballots cast. Brazilian voters have difficulty knowing who their congressional representatives are, as a number of opinion polls some time after the election regularly show. And not only that: "Candidates for federal and state deputy cultivate personal reputations, but voters do not remember for whom they voted."[5]

Getting to change is not easy. The most contentious issue is moving to a closed list. This has been under discussion for more than fifteen years. Instead of choosing among individuals—around 6,000 in the 2010 election—one would select by party; in turn, party conventions would specify candidates in preferential order. Proportional representation would continue, along with possible specified districts within states. So far no changes have been implemented—who would want to change rules that have worked to one's advantage? Lula has indicated a personal interest in achieving reform now that he has left office. It may take his involvement to move matters along.

Some have argued that a legislative career is not of central interest. Other executive positions, such as mayor and governor, are preferred paths of political advancement. David Samuels puts it plainly: "Political careerism among Brazilian legislators is largely focused on positions outside the Chamber, and mainly at the subnational level."[6] In part, that also operates as a result of voter choice. The rate of reelection to the lower house (the Câmara) has been lower than in other countries, and that is also true of the upper house (the Federal Senate). For instance, in 2010 in the United States, two incumbents in the U.S. Senate lost and twenty-one were reelected. In that same year, only seventeen of twenty-seven incumbents from the Brazilian senate were reelected. In the lower house, a parallel although lesser difference holds.[7] Not all of these candidates are political novices: there is great circulation, with politicians changing positions frequently.

Unlike elsewhere, the Brazilian congress is not yet a permanent political home. With term limits operative on executive positions, sometimes there are returnees. Still, the degree of inexperience within the legislative branch handicaps its ability to play a positive role in conjunction with the executive, the more so when issues become technical in nature. Few members regularly follow the details, although improved administrative support is beginning to make a difference.

Regionalism adds to this problem by distorting popular choice. The Federal Senate is composed of eighty-one members, with three chosen by each state. The body is unrepresentative by design. This lack of proportionality to population is not surprising within a bicameral system; other countries share the same characteristic. Yet the circumstances in Brazil are extreme. Taken together, the states of the north, center–west, and northeast possess more than three quarters of the seats but contain only a third of the population, and generate an even smaller share of national income.

Such bias extends to the Câmara. Brazil grants minimal participation to small states, and limits the number of representatives from large states. There is a total membership of 513. Roraima has 8 deputies instead of the single one its size merits, whereas São Paulo has 70 deputies instead of the more than 110 that its population alone would indicate. On a total basis, the three regions mentioned above again account for a disproportionate amount—more than half—of the total membership. This allocation punishes the more developed south and southeast regions of the country. Particular parties, like the former PFL (now Democratas), have benefited in the past; now it is the PT that is beginning to reap the advantage.

Legislative performance in recent years has shown improvement, even without far-reaching reform, and a strong press has helped to publicize the more than occasional corruption. Congress is organized around the largest seven parties, responsible for 80 percent of the national vote. Are these evolutionary changes enough?

Scholarly opinion differs. A growing group sees advance, giving weight to changes within political parties and to structural evolution within the legislature as well as the executive. The leading proponents of this assessment are Argelina Figueiredo and Fernando Limongi, whose contributions have elicited a series of followers.[8] In their view, internal structures and norms operative within the National Congress result in productive interaction with the executive. Parties are therefore the significant elements, not individuals. Moreover, "behavior on the legislative floor is predictable and consistent, thus engendering governability. In this revisionist view, there is no institutional malaise in Brazilian institutions."[9]

There is an older viewpoint, based in part upon insights by Barry Ames and Scott Mainwaring, suggesting a less positive conclusion. There is lack of party discipline and fragmentation in the legislature, making impossible shared participation. "Even if we accept certain differences in presidential style, Brazilian legislators . . . during the democratic period have tended to support the government to retain access to the sources of pork. . . . The political class in Brazil is largely autonomous in its ability to frame issues and shape the nature of party and legislative politics."[10] This interpretation is shared by many who are pursuing changes in electoral rules.

The public in Brazil, as in many other countries, gives its congress and political parties low marks. Moisés and Meneguello, in a recent interview about their project sampling popular opinion, state it this way: "A growing preference for a democratic regime is accompanied by lack of confidence in representative institutions."[11] Furthermore, 30 percent of their sample believed democracy can function very well without the congress. The number rejecting congress amounted to 72 percent in 2006, and those rejecting political parties came to 81 percent. Not surprisingly, these responses undergird support for enforcing party fidelity and reforming campaign finance as a way of establishing institutional rules.[12]

I draw a more positive conclusion. The corruption disclosed in 2005 surrounding the *mensalão* crisis was a moment for negative judgments about politics in general, and the PT in particular.[13] That seems to have passed. Less party switching occurred after the presidential election in 2006 than earlier, and now, after a contrary judicial decision, it has become an exception. There seems to be a progressive, if irregular, advance in congressional performance since the advent of democracy more than twenty-five years ago.

These opposing interpretations are beginning to converge. Together they provide an understanding of the combination of current pressures— internal and external—influencing legislative decision—or as is frequently the case, indecision. Perhaps the judgment of Nelson Rojas de Carvalho is the right one: there is "no premise of theoretical exclusiveness when one comes to understanding the analysis of our Congress."[14]

Judicial Review

The Constitution of 1988 restored the powers of the judiciary, and then some.[15] The provisions, forty-three articles in all, were largely assembled by judges and attorneys on their own, without much external discussion or extensive debate. As a result, "They accord the Brazilian courts more political and operational autonomy than anywhere else in Latin America."[16] In the United States, selection of judges at state and municipal levels is largely a matter of electoral choice. In Brazil judges begin their career by means of quite competitive examination.

One characteristic of the judiciary was constitutionally ensured independence. Article 99 guaranteed the financial autonomy of the judicial system—budget requests went to congress without executive intervention —and actual expenditures increased. Salaries likewise rose, as did construction costs for facilities. Not all requests won approval. There was negative response on more than one occasion, not only within congress and the executive but even among the broader public.

There was also a restructuring of the federal judicial system. The new Superior Tribunal de Justiça (Superior Tribunal of Justice) enabled the Supremo Tribunal Federal (supreme court) to focus on constitutional issues, serving in its place for final civil and criminal case appeals. At the local level, innovative facilities—parallel to small claims courts within the United States—were introduced to expedite cases of limited financial value. These modifications improved the access to and speed of minor proceedings.

Another change incorporated a more important and independent status for the Ministério Público (Public Ministry). Formerly linked to the Justice Ministry, the federal prosecutor's office would now stand apart, serving as an intermediary in the areas of collective and social rights. The constitution had granted rights to education, health, social security, and other services to all citizens. Now there would also be a mechanism available to enable potential beneficiaries to claim their rights.

Such cases began to account for the largest number of public civil actions in the courts. Not all judges were pleased; many preferred a narrower definition of those with legal status. "If before, programmatic norms had to be invoked by society in the political realm, today, in accord with the Constitution, they can be, and have been, taken to the courts as the principal task of the *Ministério Público*." Or to put it another way, "The *Ministério Publico* moved from being a defender of the State to being a defender of society."[17]

After constitutional reform, the rising volume of cases exceeded all expectations, putting pressure on the judiciary. Between the years 1988 and 1991, the number of federal cases expanded from 193,709 to 725,993, making the task of immediate resolution impossible. The burden on the supreme court grew rapidly to 60,000 cases a year, while that of the Superior Tribunal de Justiça amounted to 5,000 cases a week. And there were the additional cases taken on by two other special branches of the Brazilian judiciary: the Tribunal Regional Eleitoral (Regional Electoral Courts) and the Tribunais Regionais do Trabalho (Regional Labor Courts). In the former the number of processes grew from 10,000 in 1989 to more than 30,000 in both 1992 and 1994; in the latter cases expanded to about 1,500,000 a year in the early 1990s.[18]

The power of the medida provisória permitted the executive to emerge the stronger partner compared with the legislature. Almost reflexively, the judiciary became a compensatory agent, responding to constant appeals to rule against measures taken by the president. The constitution extended access to the *ação direta de inconstitucionalidade* (ADIN; direct action of unconstitutionality) to eight other political units, apart from the attorney general; these included the president, the two national legislative branches, the twenty-seven state legislative assemblies, all governors, political parties with congressional representation, labor unions, and other interests. The number of appeals increased to over 150 by 1989. Thus one suddenly had the problem of "judicialization of politics": the courts immediately became central agents in the political battle among established interests.[19] The supreme court had final authority; its decisions could not be appealed.

Political intervention also occurred as a result of *liminares* granted by lower courts. These injunctions halted executive actions and were used to oppose the process of privatization beginning in 1991. Within a large federal system, it was not difficult to find sympathetic judges to impede auction sales that had been programmed. Delay was virtually assured, and with it came strikes and public demonstrations in opposition to selling off state assets for what was asserted to be a pittance.

Within the legal profession, intellectual differences emerged. On the one side were those who perceived the constitution as a basis of new powers for the judiciary. The courts could contest the authority of the executive and legislative branches, and exert their authority.

> The "complicated intimacy" of the state of law with the social welfare state is evidenced by the need for new categories of interpretation. . . . In a state of affairs with these characteristics, to categorize the law as capable of a literal, focused, bureaucratic, or Weberian rational-legal framework, is an abstraction. . . . There is a demand for a new conception of legality—perhaps more flexible and fit to the dynamic of post-modern societies."[20]

On the other side, there was a more conservative view, analyzing the law narrowly as written, without seeking to go beyond to new circumstances and applications. This classical interpretation stood against legal activism, with its potential for eroding the credibility of the justice system. Politicization of the judiciary would be cumulative and uncontrollable, and ultimately hinder the very functioning of a civil society the judicial system was intended to foster.

There is little question about which side won. Within a decentralized system, with magistrates who believed social circumstances could outweigh the written law, cases multiplied. Justices did not hesitate to express their views publicly, and these were disseminated widely by the press. Most of the early victories were gained by the private sector against the state, although later, with successful economic stabilization, privatization became more accepted. That large question has disappeared.

Judicial decisions have finally begun to catch up with the escalating backlog of cases within the federal and state court systems. This is an impressive number. Table 2-1 indicates the recent distribution of cases among components of the judicial system. An improving ability to cope emerges, and carryover has been progressively reduced. Complaints will continue, as they should. Yet these should not divert attention from the advance over time.

Constitutional Amendment 45, altering the initial array of judicial responsibilities, went into effect at the end of 2004. This measure had two principal objectives. The first was to reorient the total independence of the judiciary granted by the constitution. The judiciary itself largely opposed change; they did not want to give up the right to manage their budget and were unwilling to accept a National Judicial Council with oversight responsibilities. Such concern—reflected in studies of the views of lower-level judges—proved excessive. There has been no reduced independence of the judiciary as a consequence. On the other hand, there has been social gain, as reflected in the elimination of nepotism within the court system and imposition of limits on wage increases.[21]

The second objective was forward looking: an explicit grant of *súmula vinculante* to the supreme court, enabling two-thirds of its members, or eight justices, to make their decision binding on subordinate courts. Such cases have now reached double digits, and more will accumulate over time. The intent is clear: to eliminate a confusing and conflicting multitude of lower court opinions that contribute to uncertainty. Sample studies have shown that lower court judges value their ability to reach decisions without legal precedent. Now the Brazilian juridical process has structure, although some doubt that precedent will avoid repetitive cases.[22]

Final passage of Amendment 45, under discussion for well over a decade, became possible as a result of gradual acceptance of increased judicial authority. Ten major reforms of the Cardoso period came before the supreme court for decision. Seven of these were altered or delayed by the court.[23] Substantive reforms, nonetheless, did move ahead, even if sometimes changed significantly. Perhaps the best example is the 1998 amendment altering social security payments and benefits. While the

TABLE 2-1. Court Cases, 2008

Units as indicated

Category	Millions of cases		
	State	*Federal*	*Federal labor courts*
District courts			
New cases	12.3	0.6	3.2
Judged	9.3	0.5	3.2
Pending	33.1	1.5	2.8
Appeals courts			
New cases	1.9	0.5	0.9[a]
Judged	1.9	0.5	0.9
Pending	1.2	0.7	0.4
Small claims courts[b]			
New cases	4.5	1.6	...
Judged	4.4	1.6	...
Pending	4.1	1.2	...

	Thousands of cases
Superior Court	
New cases[c]	271
Judged	274
Pending	175
Supreme Court	
New cases	101
Judged	131

Sources: Conselho Nacional de Justiça, *Justiça em Números* (Brasília, 2008); Superior Tribunal de Justiça, *Relatório Estatístico* (Brasília, 2008); Supremo Tribunal Federal, "Movimento Processual" (www.stf.jus.br/portal/cms/verTexto.asp?pagina=movimentoProcessual&servico=estatistica).

a. Combines Labor Courts of Appeal and Superior Court.

b. Combines Juizado Especial and Turma Recursal (Special Appeal Courts).

c. Excludes Embargos de Declaração and Agravos Regimentais (Clarifications and Appeals).

initial level of taxes imposed upon public sector employees was held to be unconstitutional, a lesser sum was acceptable. Court judgment was respected even when it ran counter to preferred policy.

During the Lula government, there were fewer large issues before the court. Privatization had already occurred and would neither be extended nor reversed. Further amendment was necessary to cope with public sector pensions, but key components had already been discussed within the National Congress. This freed the administration to press for successful passage of Constitutional Amendment 45.

Judicial Extension

Extension of judicial power appears over time in three areas: an enhanced role for the Supreme Electoral Court, new legislation dealing with bankruptcy, and expanded responsibilities for the Public Ministry.

The Supreme Electoral Court has become more important in enforcing electoral standards. There are elections every two years, and a sharply increasing number of cases have come to its attention. Introduction of electronic voting machines in the 1990s was a first step; it was a great success. Final electoral results are announced hours after the polls close, and no one challenges the count. Those powers have increased to recent review of seven elections for governors. Some incumbents have been stripped of their office for violation of campaign rules, and others have been absolved.

Most recently, in June 2010, came a rapid supreme court decision allowing the new Ficha Limpa (Clean Record) law to apply in the 2010 elections rather than postponing application to the future. That matter has hardly run its course; many related cases will come to the supreme court for appeal. Yet the episode reveals the extent of judicial engagement in the electoral process.

Rules for party affiliation within states during presidential elections are a constant issue. In 2002 parties supporting a presidential candidate at the national level had to sustain that alignment for other offices within all states. The rule survived in 2006 but is no longer valid. In 2010 there was reversion to state-by-state independence. These decisions, within the multiparty structure characteristic of Brazil, have considerable political consequence. But they are accepted.

Criticism of delays inherent in reaching a final decision has been common. The cases of the governors went on for years, starting in April 2007, before verdicts became final. There is a similar lack of immediate outcome for the much greater number of cases dealing with the municipal electoral process. Several hundred mayors have been removed from office over the years; those cases have similarly lingered. Yet the final results have been sufficient to merit praise by *The Economist*: "Brazil already sets a good example to other developing countries in running relatively clean and orderly elections. If its courts continue to raise standards, the benefits could be felt beyond its own borders."[24]

A new bankruptcy law, replacing that of 1946, passed in June 2005.[25] Its operation affords additional insights into Brazilian judicial practice. The legislation provided an efficient way for failing firms to reformulate their activities, with active participation of creditors. Chapter 11 of United States law was a model. The average time required to complete the previous process of Concordata (creditor agreement) was something like ten years; the new law reduced this to four years. That still remained above the Latin American average of 2.6 years.

This law altered the priority order of claims, moving creditors up. The average sum recouped increased from 0.2 cents on the dollar to 12.1 cents. While still far less than achieved within countries of the Organization for Economic Cooperation and Development, where recompense amounts to 72 cents, this amount approaches the Latin American average of 26 cents. Just as important, with the reestablishment of an operating facility, previous liabilities to labor, government, and others were no longer absorbed by the new unit. There was a statistically significant reduction in credit costs immediately after the law came into force, suggesting that banks took notice. Brazil, after more than a decade since the law was first discussed, has moved forward.

The experience of Varig, once the principal airline in the country, offers an unfortunate counterexample. Mere days after Law 11.101/05 took effect, Varig invoked bankruptcy to reconstruct its impaired balance sheet. For years the firm had used increasing debt to survive; there were also large legal claims against the government for freezing ticket prices in various failed counterinflationary episodes. Because of Varig's long history—dating back to 1927—pension obligations regularly took the form of expanded equity granted to unions.

Nine executives presided between 2000 and 2005, as its financial position worsened. Operating costs were much higher than those of the new airlines, TAM and Gol, which had newer aircraft and no accumulated retirement liabilities. Varig retained only 12 percent of domestic traffic by May 2006 but still garnered 66 percent of international flights.

This prominent test case failed to highlight positively the properties of the new bankruptcy law. Instead, a very complicated history followed, including a story of favoritism involving a member of the National Civil Aviation Agency (ANAC) directorate governing aviation. That tale extended to supposed intervention by Dilma Rousseff and even the presidency. The case went from one court to another, even up to the supreme court at various times, as conflicting interests contended.

Varig was finally sold off in 2006 to VarigLog, a component of the company dealing with logistics, without retaining its past fiscal and pension obligations. In turn, the year after, Gol purchased the operations and the name persists. Involved at the center of this arrangement was an American equity firm, Matlin Patterson.

Labor interests failed to purchase in 2008 what was left. But the enterprise persisted. Flex, the remaining entity, had only a single operative plane. In August 2010 the First Business Court of Rio initiated its liquidation, but appeal to the supreme court in September halted the process once more. Aerus, the remaining pension fund, survives as a name but without resources for retirement benefits for former employees.

There is evidence of a better outcome elsewhere. As *Gazeta Mercantil* put it, "Parmalat is proof that the Bankruptcy Law works."[26] Parmalat's crisis began in Italy with accusations of accounting fraud and failure to pay taxes. The Brazilian branch of the company encountered difficulty and sought protection under the new statute. Recuperation occurred with a new investment group, and a significant market share, 12 percent, was retained. Indeed, the firm was able to acquire the interests of the French firm Danone, thereby solidifying its market position. Parmalat continues to operate.

Overall, the record is demonstrably positive. Between January 2006 and May 2006, in São Paulo alone, 137 actions were taken, and 76 additional cases were deferred. Many lawyers argue in behalf of needed adjustments. Bankruptcy law is a complicated business. One of the first requirements—on which both creditors and jurists concur—is a greater number of specialized bankruptcy courts. That will surely come.

Finally, the Public Ministry has been extending judicial intervention. This agency, not subordinate to the formal judicial structure, defends the public interest. The institution has progressively elaborated its constitutional assignment to be the "governmental defender of society's collective rights."[27]

The number of prosecutors, both state and federal, has more than doubled between 1988 and the present. There are now more than 12,000, mostly engaged within the states; only about 10 percent of prosecutors are employed at the national level. Qualification is exacting: many young lawyers eagerly seek entrance, but only a few, sometimes less than one percent of applicants, gain admission after a difficult and multiple examination process extending over almost a year. The reward for success is significant, placing the Public Ministry at the apex of civil employment and in the first decile of the income distribution as a whole.

Over time, legal specialization increased not only in depth but equally in extent. Civil and criminal functions were separated, with the former becoming dominant. Within the civil area, the constitutionally assigned focus on the environment, minors, and consumers has grown into a broader agenda encompassing virtually all areas. Sometimes, with the federal police serving as agents, there is seemingly no subject bereft of interest. Lack of a defined agenda and the strong degree of individual autonomy has converted the organization into a "key element in the process of conversion of formal rights into actual ones."[28]

The Public Ministry has joined with nongovernmental organizations and civil society in this effort. For example, its presence has grown in the areas of public health—with the decentralization of the Sistema Único de Saúde (Unified Health System)—and the environment. In other areas, like agrarian reform, there has been little involvement. Where civil society has utilized the Public Ministry as a chosen instrument, the combination has challenged the executive and legislature, and sometimes the judiciary itself.

Formally, there are eight areas that fall within the sphere of the Public Ministry, ranging from citizens' rights to international judicial cooperation. Not everyone is comfortable with this enhanced role. Political actors can resent its independence and control, the more so when they are forced to comply with unshared priorities. The former head of the supreme court has asserted the need for a judicial check upon the Public Ministry's broad authority, extending, as it does, to supervision of the federal police. Supreme Court Judge Gilmar Mendes suggested abuse of power when the Public Ministry acted in the investigation of Correa Camargo about contributions to political parties and officials.[29] This is hardly the first time such an accusation has been made.

Brazil has developed a native grown institution of considerable power. Not only is the judiciary able to counter the inclinations of the executive and the legislature but so is the Public Ministry. It remains subject, as with the other branches, to horizontal contestation, with ultimate authority subject to the supreme court. Some suggest that its qualities merit replication elsewhere within the developing world: "The prosecutorial mode of enforcement is a culturally and politically sensitive candidate for legal transplant."[30] Others are less certain:

In sum, despite its strong independence and the high caliber of its prosecutors, the MPF is poorly equipped for oversight. At the same time, however, it has little control over the application of sanctions on wrong-doers at the other end of the accountability process, and has not always upheld prosecution as its first priority. . . . While much of the blame . . . falls on court delays, the MPF's incentive structure itself also plays a role.[31]

The ultimate verdict will only emerge over time. For the foreseeable future, the Public Ministry plays an important role in Brazilian political life and "is singular because it combines elements—autonomy, instruments of action, discretion and full array of attributes—that are not common in institutions with few characteristics of *accountability*."[32] This structure has become an integral part of the institutions undergirding an evolving democracy.

Decentralization and Federalism

When the Constitution of 1988 was formulated, there was a virtual consensus in favor of decentralization. Reconstruction of Brazilian federalism emphasized municipalities; they were explicitly mentioned within the constitution, a circumstance not found in most other federal states. the constitution distributed resources but without assigning well-defined responsibilities to the recipient units. Instead, in article 23 there was recognition of the need for a later complementary law to define the rules for cooperation among the federal, state, and municipal levels, "having in mind the equilibrium of development and welfare." Such a complementary law has never been passed.[33]

Transfers to state and local governments were made automatic. The principal mechanisms were the State Participation Fund and the Municipal Participation Fund. These were scheduled to expand gradually from 14 percent and 16 percent of federal income tax plus industrial products tax revenues in 1985 to 21.5 percent and 22.5 percent in 1993, respectively.[34] A vast majority of the resources—85 percent—went to the states of the north, northeast, and center-west, being allocated by population size and inversely to per capita income.

Table 2-2 shows the receipts and transfers for all three levels of government for several years through 1994. By then the government had managed to secure a constitutional amendment giving the federal government the power to withhold some part of those transfers to the other levels. Even so, both federal collections and expenditures remain dramatically different than had been the case in 1980, when both had been relatively larger.

TABLE 2-2. **Government Revenues and Expenditures, 1980–94**

Percent

Year	Tax burden/ GDP	Revenue collection			Expenditures		
		Federal	State	Municipal	Federal	State	Municipal
1980	24.6	75.3	21.8	2.9	69.4	22	8.6
1985	23.8	72.8	24.8	2.7	64.2	25.1	10.7
1988	23.6	67.4	29.8	2.7	59.8	28	12.1
1990	30	67	29.6	3.4	56.7	28.5	14.9
1991	26	63.4	31.1	5.4	53.5	29.5	17.1
1992	25.9	66.2	29.3	4.5	57	28.1	14.9
1993	26.4	68.6	26.6	4.7	57.8	26.4	15.8
1994	28.6	67.9	27.4	4.7	59.4	25.4	15.2

Source: Centro de Estudos de Políticas Públicas,USP-Campinas, as reproduced in Maria Hermínia Tavares de Almeida, "Decentralization and Centralization in a Federal System: The Case of Democratic Brazil," p. 6 (http://socialsciences.scielo. org/pdf/s_rsocp/v1nse/scs_a02.pdf).

The clear beneficiaries, as can be seen, were the municipalities. They benefited from required transfers of a quarter of state value added taxes. In response, there was a rush to create units eligible to benefit from these resources. The number of municipalities went up by about a fifth between 1988 and 1994, and then grew more slowly until the Cardoso administration succeeded in ending expansion after 1997. In poorer states, like Piaui, the number of municipalities grew more than threefold. There was a political logic: each of the new units required a mayor, a vice mayor, and members of the city council. Starting from such a modest base, a potential path to future advancement lay open to the most skilled initiates.

There was a parallel economic logic: revenues of almost half of municipalities, those with fewer than 10,000 inhabitants in 1992, principally derived from transfers from the federal and state governments. These came to 95 percent of their total funds. For the largest cities, with populations above 50,000, taxes and other sources amounted to more than a third of their receipts; transfers from receipts of the state value added tax exceeded federal funds by a factor of almost three.[35]

States were not without their own capabilities in this pre–Real Plan period. They could, and did, greatly expand their own indebtedness. That was largely financed by the development banks found in almost all states; these, in turn, could appeal to the Bank of Brazil for loans, thereby ultimately increasing the money stock. On two separate occasions, 1989 and 1993, state debts were directly transferred to the federal government, thereby reducing state interest obligations.

There was no real budget constraint operating; it was, at best, a very "soft" limitation. In the words of Janos Kornai, a Hungarian economist focusing on Eastern Europe (who stressed its applicability there), "The 'softening' of the budget constraint appears when the strict relationship between expenditure and earnings has been relaxed, because excess expenditures will be paid by some other institution."[36] That truth was equally relevant in Brazil.

The "Citizen's Constitution," as it was termed, restored local participation within government. "Democracy *plus* decentralization was a dominant political idea and as such had a power of its own."[37] Economics was put off to the side, although stabilization was equally vital. Elsewhere, successful economic reform preceded decentralization, but in Brazil, to some extent, such circumstances were reversed. Kurt Weyland goes beyond this assessment, arguing that "democratization . . . reduced the autonomy of the Brazilian state from interest groups and clientelistic politicians, undermined its internal unity, and diminished its capacity to attain its goals."[38]

Brazilian federalism depended upon political circumstance. Ending inflation imposed inescapable financial burdens upon the federal government, leading to pressures for centralization. A turning point in the stabilization exercise in 1994 occurred with passage of a constitutional amendment reducing the outflow of funds from the federal government to the states and municipalities. Thereafter, this issue has remained contentious.

That amendment has been renewed every four years, thereby changing the contours of the resource flow specified in 1988. This was accompanied by a large increase in federal taxes that boosted government receipts from 24 percent of gross domestic product in 1995 to 37 percent in 2008. Most of this change occurred during the Cardoso period. Additional revenues came from levies not distributed to the lesser units of government, such as the tax on financial transactions, the excise tax, and hikes in contributions to help finance social security and in the levy upon profits. Income taxes also rose. The focus was upon "contributions," thereby avoiding the constitutional change required if new "taxes" were established. The worst part has been extensive use of taxes that cumulate, where payments are not netted out, as in the value added tax; that leads to demonstrable productivity losses, especially for smaller enterprises.

Over time, the fiscal structure has not much changed. In 2003, for example, duplication in social security taxes was corrected, although little else was done. In 2006 came an easier tax system for small enterprises, Super Simplex. A full tax reform, continuously promised, still awaits. What impedes reform is not difficult to guess: the pressure for more federal resources, or at least maintaining them, dominates concern over efficiency.

Individual states have different tax rates, and rules, for the ICMS (a value added tax).[39] They have competed by offering special advantages and tax exemptions for new investments. This was particularly prevalent during the expansion of the automobile sector in the latter 1990s, when São Paulo lost out to Rio Grande do Sul, Minas Gerais, and Parana in establishment of modern factories. Bahia gained a Ford facility, not least because the PFL was allied to the PSDB of Cardoso. This "war," characteristic of other federal nations, was eventually brought to a halt, but only after important prizes had been gained. Conflict again seems to be resurgent. The large states prefer taxing production, whereas others gain by taxing consumption.

There is an unspoken conflict in federalism: the interests of the national unit and its component parts do not coincide. Within a Brazilian congress where the political party of the presidential winner is far from a majority, states and municipalities sometimes can assert independent interests. Nor is the composition of coalitions firm. As explained earlier, congressional representation, both in the Câmara and Federal Senate, is biased in favor of the smaller states of the north and northeast. These are the poorer states, which gain from the distribution of federal tax receipts and benefit from the presence of small municipalities eligible for rebates.

To meet the increased primary surplus imposed after the devaluation of 1999, states and municipalities have had to contribute. Previously, they had been in deficit; now they are obligated to finance primary and secondary schools and extension of the health care system. During Cardoso's first term, when politics could be guided by the principle of inclusion and the economy did not impose severe constraints, federalism came at a lesser cost.

Even before that definitive shift, there were already signs of change. Through the Program for Reducing the Presence of the State Public Sector in Banking Activity, established at the end of 1996, the federal government privatized state (and municipal) development banks. Those institutions could no longer survive in a noninflationary world; their raison d'être had been monetization of state deficits. They benefited from the constitutional provision permitting senate approval of new state debt. Political favors kept the banks alive, at least until São Paulo's Banespa ran into difficulty in 1997. Thereafter, the federal government stepped in to issue federal debt replacing state and municipal bonds. States and the very large municipalities were obligated to the federal government on favorable terms: a thirty-year redemption period at a real interest rate of 8 percent. The federal government limited future issues, gaining implicit control over future expenditures.

Soon after this constrained federalism took shape in 1999, it was formalized by the Law of Fiscal Responsibility passed in May 2000. This legislation, a complementary law requiring a majority of the number of seats within congress rather than only of attendees, became a guideline for fiscal policy. Its passage permitted the government "to attack one of the central problems of federalism, that is, the tendency of states and municipalities to transfer the costs of their activities to the Union. This happens when states and municipalities spend more than they collect, they rely on debt, and then seek the help of the federal government."[40]

Two features of this law, applicable to all governmental levels, were central. One required detailed specification of outlays, sufficient to eliminate many of the congressional efforts to direct expenditures for local advantage or "pork." A second ruled out federal assistance to the subnational units, thereby requiring their fiscal integrity; this much diminished, if not eliminated, appeals by governors and mayors from the ruling political parties for special help. The law also restricted contracting of new employees during the last six months of mandates. Not all of these limitations worked perfectly, but they have had an effect.

The need to ensure a reliable governmental primary surplus inspired the process. Success is measured by the quarterly results: during periods both of slower and faster growth, the surplus has been regularly achieved. Federal tax collections increased as a percentage of income in the years after 1999. The previous pattern of unrestricted allocation of resources at the local level ended, replaced by required matching of outlays and closer supervision of past expenditures. A regular accounting by the Federal Court of Accounts (TCU) now occurs, with a number of municipalities cited for inability to satisfy the rules. Some states still have difficulty keeping wage expenditures under 60 percent, as required, as well as complying with matching requirements for health and education outlays.

Federalism is not an immutable matter but an ongoing political question. The debate over allocation of the future surplus deriving from subsalt oil is one illustration. Another is the request of the newly elected governor of São Paulo for another look at federal charges for absorption of state debts. José Antonio Cheibub puts it nicely: "One cannot say that federalism in Brazil introduces a bias toward the status quo that cannot be overcome by the national government."[41] The contest is a continuing one.

Regulatory Authority

The Cardoso government introduced independent regulatory authority into Brazil. Extensive privatization in the sectors of electric energy, communication, and oil and natural gas exploration and production during his first term required new rules governing the subsequent behavior of these enterprises. A series of other agencies was established, extending from sanitation to the cinema.

There is justification for such regulation: monopoly in supply requires public oversight to ensure that consumer interests are not violated by pursuit of private profit. What is apparently simple becomes more complicated in the process of application, especially when underlying technology is rapidly changing. Differentiated purchasers and economies of scale must be taken into account, not to mention ensuring access for potential suppliers. That this process is lengthy—capital investment is substantial and durable—further complicates matters.

In the Brazilian case, prior efforts at regulation had been eroded by inflationary pressures. Prices were not adjusted for producers, and that was why private infrastructure investment ceased. Similar limitations hindered successor public enterprises. Regulation lost out to other objectives: the same ministry had to cope with trying to expand services while regulating their use. There was precious little time to deal with the latter.

In many ways the process was starting from scratch in 1995. Congressional competence in these areas was very limited. Relatively few members had the technical sophistication and experience required to draft legislation. Models from the United States and Great Britain could be informative, but their implicit Anglo-Saxon legal traditions were not directly transferable. There was interest in practices adopted by the European Union. One cannot help but be impressed by the magnitude of the undertaking and the permanence of the result.[42]

Energy, communications, and petroleum and natural gas were central concerns. That was inevitable owing to the importance of privatization revenues in sustaining stabilization. Success in securing approval for the

National Electricity Regulatory Agency (ANEEL), National Telecommunications Agency (ANATEL), and National Petroleum, Natural Gas, and Biofuels Agency (ANP) led to the establishment of regulatory entities for other sectors. Many of the states quickly became adherents. Almost everywhere the basic form was the same: an *autarquia*—legally granted independence—with specified sources of finance that ensured continuity.

Essential to the regulatory function was agency credibility. That was no easy task when privatization inevitably aroused opposition. Moreover, consumers, always vastly outnumbering producers, were also voters. Although they would benefit from increased services, they also were victims of higher prices imposed by private firms in search of profitability. That helps to explain why early surveys in Brazil regularly found these agencies rated negatively. Contributing to this problem was an inherent contradiction confronted by the government: it could maximize revenues from the sale of its assets by conferring monopoly privileges, or it could impose more control over the enterprises and accept a lesser price.

Brazil, for the most part, chose the former. That was explicit when congress was considering the law governing communications: "The third objective would be maximizing the sales value of telecommunication enterprises, without prejudice to the former objectives [privatization, regulation, investment, and technical change] and with adequate planning of the privatization process."[43] That did not alter the inherent need for autonomy, transparency, and permanence for the agencies to perform their functions adequately. Those were characteristics required to achieve credibility. Higher sale prices made them even more necessary.

The operations of ANEEL, ANATEL, and ANP were different in important ways. Both in the provision of electricity services as well as petroleum and natural gas production, the government exercised a prominent role. Distribution facilities were the major area privatized, whereas the great bulk of energy generation and some transmission and distribution remained in the hands of the states and the federal government.

Petrobras dominates within the energy area, both as a producer as well as distributor, and it will gain with its new legal authority to deal with subsalt oil deposits. The government has extended its share of capital and retains control, although private equity constitutes a slightly greater share. Petrobras will have to borrow large sums to finance planned future exploration.

Communications were entirely redesigned. Both land lines and cell phone licenses, within defined regions, were sold off to international and national interests. These have continued to consolidate. Concentration is much greater than at the start, more than a decade ago.

Determination of prices charged to consumers, a major component of regulatory activity, also differed. ANEEL and ANATEL directly determined prices to be charged, and both have been regularly criticized by consumers as a consequence. Regulatory independence from the government turned out to have political advantage; the steady relative increase of utility prices could be criticized by the PT but without further consequence. By contrast, ANP has not set gasoline prices since 2002, leaving their levels to the market. Since Petrobras is the largest retailer, it implicitly determines domestic prices. However, that decision really emanates from the Ministry of Mines and Energy, as has been seen over the last years, and political considerations do enter into the calculation.

ANATEL more closely parallels regulatory agencies operating internationally. The cell phone revolution and resultant lesser growth in regular telephone lines helped. Increases in fixed rates otherwise would have generated greater controversy and complaint. ANEEL was a victim of the energy shortage afflicting Brazil in 2000–01 owing to decreased rainfall and a dysfunctional wholesale market. Management shifted back to the Casa Civil and executive decisionmaking. ANP's role, both because of Petrobras and increased production of ethanol, biodiesel, petroleum, and natural gas, has taken a somewhat different turn. The agency has become less independent and more committed to facilitating production than exerting regulatory oversight.

The election of Lula in 2002 was a decisive moment. Many hoped for reversion to former practices. But even if nationalization was ruled out, a governmental role in important decisionmaking about infrastructure might substitute. Initially, that expectation was confirmed.

> Armed with a number of complaints about the agencies' poor performance, Lula accused them of moving beyond their proper jurisdiction and meddling in issues that were legally in the province of the president and his cabinet. This included things such as the development of sectoral policies, which were part of national development policy and never meant to be part of the agencies' jurisdiction, as well as not maintaining neutral rules for investors.[44]

After election, Lula authorized studies to revamp the regulatory framework dealing with energy. These led to measures altering the wholesale energy market. Purchases and sales of energy through auctions were conducted within a greater pool. Sales from new power plants were contracted differently from those already established. In light of the previous rate increases, the focus was on keeping electricity tariffs low. That was not fully doable: rates were 35 percent higher in the 2006 auctions. Private investment has taken place but not enough to meet anticipated demands.[45] That, of course, is one of the reasons for the government's Programa de Aceleração do Crescimento (Growth Acceleration Program), which features greater energy investment and emphasizes new hydropower sources.

In the case of telecommunications, the PT opposed use of the general price index, rather than the consumer price index, to readjust fixed-line telephone rates. With rapid devaluation the former—in which wholesale prices have a weight of 60 percent—rose more than the latter. ANATEL's June 2003 decision favoring an increase of 29 percent instead of 17 percent set off a tempest. Lula accused the regulatory agencies of outsourcing (*tercerização*) the ministries and government. There was a consequent rash of legal cases across the country, with active engagement of the Public Ministry and a lower court decision favorable to consumers. There was a daily fine imposed upon the companies for noncompliance.

Eventually, in January 2004, the issue found its way to the Superior Tribunal of Justice, where a Solomonic judgment emerged. Since the currency had appreciated in the interim, the wholesale price index was now more favorable to consumers. As a consequence, the earlier finding was overturned in favor of the original law—without companies having access to reimbursement for the erroneous initial judgment.[46]

By this time, the tide had also begun to turn. The draft law drawn up in the fall of 2003 to eliminate the agencies' right to authorize concessions and to integrate them into the relevant ministries was altered. As introduced into the congress in April 2004, but never subsequently passed, the proposed changes were modest. Significantly, they failed to secure unanimous support within the Lula administration. Finance Minister Palocci, fearing a negative reaction from foreign investors who had worried about modification of rules, clearly won the day over José Dirceu, the head of the Casa Civil.

The agencies thus remained substantially intact. Legislation did pass in 2007 restructuring the rules for sanitation enterprises. Autonomous authorities, with representation from civil society, are established at the municipal level, giving them and their states access to federal funds for expanded investment. While the act satisfies PT insistence on broader public participation, this authority retains an independence characteristic of federal agencies in their operation.

This regulatory effort within Brazil recognizes that private decisions do not ensure a social optimum. Negotiation of specific rules and controls over private activity is an essential ingredient of modern democracy. Institutions are not immutable, as one easily ascertains by observing the variety of amendments to current financial practices being introduced within the United States, Europe, and elsewhere. There are also limits. They are imposed by the need to reconcile satisfactorily the variety of interests engaged: consumers and producers, domestic and foreign investors, developed and less developed regions, suppliers of inputs and outputs, and so on. What one sees in the recent Brazilian experience is an impressive learning process. Continuity and change are reconcilable.

A Final Word

Political evolution in Brazil over the last twenty-five years has hardly been linear. The New Republic was sorely tested by a presidential death at its very beginning and a presidential impeachment a few years later. The results of the Constitution of 1988 were not entirely foreseen. Presidentialism took root with stronger powers than had been anticipated because of the medida provisória. Congress became a more passive instrument than intended. The courts were hampered by an excess of cases, and liminares soon became a mechanism for imposing delays. State and local governments increased in authority and resources.

Since 1995 these processes have begun to reverse. The presidency, while still powerful, has been partially checked by an expansive congress. The judiciary has settled into a less independent but more powerful role. Federal taxes have grown but so have cooperative relationships with states and municipalities. Federal regulatory authority has increased. A combination of centripetal and centrifugal tendencies prevails.

Political leadership during this period remained in the hands of those who resisted and overturned military rule. But now a new generation of leaders is imminent, and their interests are oriented to the future. Contested issues will arise. But, as in other substantive areas, political divergence has narrowed as institutions adapt but do not disappear. Compatible solutions are now easier to attain and sustain.

3

Economic Growth Is the Priority

Over the last twenty-five years, the Brazilian economy dramatically changed. In 1985 inflation and debt owed to the outside world were the main subjects of interest. Today, a fast-growing Brazil is a respected and active participant within the Group of Twenty. That transformation is the subject of this chapter, which is organized around six topics.

The first subject, not surprisingly, is inflation. Its mounting level, until successful stabilization in 1994, prevented progress. In 1999, with devaluation of the *real,* and once again in 2003, with Lula's election, doubts emerged about continuity of stability.

A second part deals with a revamped public sector. The focus here is twofold: privatization of state enterprises that continued until 2002, and reform of the financial sector. Both contributed to the fiscal reform undertaken in the 1990s and sustained thereafter.

A third section examines Brazil's movement outward. Tariffs declined dramatically in the early 1990s, and exports became a source of dynamism. As increased Brazilian exposure to international competition became the norm, complaints from the industrial sector arose and have intensified in parallel with appreciation of the exchange rate.

Fourth is discussion of Lula's two administrations, starting with retrenchment in 2003 and economic advance in 2004 and beyond. In his second term, the Program of Accelerated Growth highlighted efforts to grow more rapidly by imposing greater central control. Macroeconomic principles did not change and, consistently applied, yielded positive results.

Return to an active industrial policy was another Lula initiative. The fifth topic treats efforts to integrate such policies within a range of competing ministries and interests. Early attempts have given way to new formulations.

Last is Brazil's rapid recovery from the Great Recession of 2008 and its economic growth of over 7 percent in 2010. Monetary easing and a larger fiscal deficit greatly helped in the midst of declines around the world. That success raised hopes for resumption of high growth levels into the future. Discovery of impressive oil reserves off the coast, deep beneath a salt layer, helped to spur expectations. But renewed global commodity inflation and approaching domestic full capacity ensure monetary and fiscal tightening over the course of 2011. The central bank has begun to increase the interest rate, and cuts in federal expenditures have been announced. Will these be enough?

Stopping Inflation

Brazil reverted to civilian control in 1985. Income continued its recovery begun the year before. What also did not stop was inflation. With the death of president-elect Tancredo Neves, hopes for a social pact as a solution disappeared. Following the rules of the International Monetary Fund (IMF) since 1982 had not worked. The rise of prices at a rate of more than 200 percent during 1985 required a response: in only four years, inflation had quadrupled. Some novel attempt to stabilize was required.

Sarney's Cruzado Plan

The principal economic task confronting the administration of Neves' successor, President José Sarney, was ending inflation. Figure 3-1 records monthly price increases during his administration. They are not encouraging. Apparent success in 1986 soon gave way to resurgent inflation that reached 80 percent a month by the beginning of 1990.

Increasingly, by the mid-1980s, analysis of inflation had become more sophisticated, shifting away from IMF monetary models to more heterodox alternatives.[1] There were good reasons. Conventional wisdom did not work very well with a highly indexed economy: Brazil went through seven amended versions of IMF plans after 1982 without success. Inflation doubled while economic growth failed to recover. The first civilian

FIGURE 3-1. **Change in IPCA, Sarney Administration, 1985–90ª**

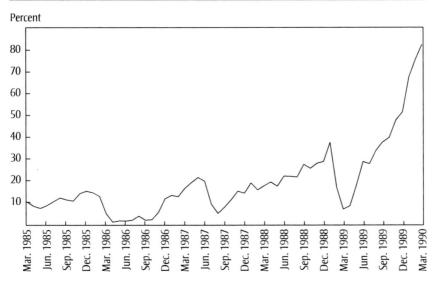

Percent

Source: Ipeadata (www.ipea.gov.br).
a. IPCA, Broad National Consumer Price Index; used as an indicator of inflation.

government in more than twenty years wanted something else. That alternative was heterodox, versions of which had been implemented in Argentina in June 1985 and in Israel at the beginning of July.

Such heterodoxy was based upon prior application of fiscal and monetary measures to eliminate excess demand.[2] Relative prices then would have adjusted, and accumulated foreign reserves would have canceled any constraint upon imports. All inflation experienced would be a result of indexation: "Prices rise today because they went up yesterday, in accordance with the perverse ricochet mechanism of an indexed economy."[3] Under such circumstances, there could be an instantaneous fall of inflation and conversion to price stability. To suppress society's memory, a new currency with fewer zeroes would be helpful.

There were two ways to proceed. Pérsio Arida and André Lara Resende offered one, the "Larida" proposal. They advocated a temporary dual currency, with a varying exchange rate between new money and the old. A daily exchange rate would be calculated between the two. The new currency, however, would be fixed in dollar terms, ensuring its preference. Rising money balances would grant the government access to seignorage. Prices and salaries would adjust to market forces over a period of time; administered public sector prices would likewise be permitted to rise. Future financial contracts also would be specified in the new currency. Under these conditions,' old money would soon disappear.

As the Sarney government implemented its Cruzado Plan, it chose instead the approach used by Argentina and Israel, which emphasized sudden shock rather than the market adjustment of the Larida proposal. Such immediacy could breed popular enthusiasm, but implementation could become problematic. According to Lara Resende, writing before the Cruzado Plan:

> With respect to disindexation with price controls—the so-called heterodox shock—the monetary reform program proposed here has the advantage of not being compulsory, not depending upon administrative controls, and of keeping the market working. . . . One has to take care in the conversion formula for salaries and administered prices to be readjusted at greater intervals. It is absolutely necessary that such a conversion is allowed only for the real average price operative in the period between [inflationary] adjustments.[4]

The Cruzado Plan was introduced on February 28, 1986, converting the *cruzeiro* to the *cruzado,* and eliminating three zeros.[5] There was an immediate price and exchange rate freeze. New real wages were implemented based on the average level of the last six months, but a substantial increase was added to ensure acceptance. Minimum wages went up by 16 percent, and other wages, by 8 percent. Wage bargaining was converted to an annual exercise, as had been in effect in 1979, before becoming more frequent as inflation accelerated. Furthermore, there was provision for an automatic wage increase to be granted if accumulated inflation exceeded 20 percent.

The intent was distributional neutrality. Loans contracted under the old currency were converted to the new one through formulas published on a daily basis; this avoided favoritism for creditors or debtors. Rents had their own rules, following the same logic. Administered prices were retained with the exception of electric energy prices for industry. Indexation was abolished. A new end-of-month date was established for price indexes to purge the inflationary carryover from the previous midmonth basis.

Euphoria soon reigned, and Sarney's sagging popularity soared. Inflation had come to an end. Low rates of interest prevailed. Real money held by households and businesses doubled over the first three months of the plan, providing sufficient seignorage revenue to the government to offset its operational deficit. Three external factors also favored the plan. First, a decline in international interest rates reduced payments on outstanding external debt. Second, there was a substantial decline in petroleum prices, relevant because oil imports were 45 percent of the import bill. Finally, dollar devaluation had just begun, after the 1985 Plaza Accord, allowing Brazilian exporters—who were on a dollar standard—a more competitive position.

Consumption virtually exploded and so did imports. Industrial production grew by 12 percent in the first half of the year. Real wages rose by more than 10 percent, and unemployment dropped. Government expenditure likewise expanded, but anticipated revenues did not keep pace. Instead, broader reliance upon price controls substituted. Already, by June some were counseling limits to demand. With prices fixed but wages higher, firms became progressively less interested in production. Instead, after allowing inventories initially to expand, firms depleted those stocks as demand continued to grow.

Shortages of various goods appeared. Real estate prices went up, as did those of durables. The public's response could be ingenious. For example, second-hand automobiles, whose prices were not fixed, sold for more than new ones; a quick drive round the block was sufficient to augment value. Black markets arose: the margin on the parallel dollar exchange rate increased from 26.4 percent in March to 103 percent in November. Compensatory fiscal policy was limited to a small increase in indirect taxes in July. To limit recorded inflation, official price indexes were redefined—as was done earlier in 1973—guaranteeing low rates of increase.

In retrospect, the government relied excessively on seignorage for its finance; the monetary base doubled between March and June. In its stead, greater, although admittedly more expensive, use of internal debt would have been preferable. Higher interest rates—despite their negative effects on government outlays—might have diminished consumption demand. By December 1985, fiscal adjustment was already coming unraveled. Tax collection was not increasing as rapidly as had been anticipated. Reduction in the percentage of income withheld reinforced the surge in demand for consumer goods. An increase in taxes on financial assets proved irrelevant because such assets no longer were much in demand as an offset to ongoing inflation.

Finally, there was the significant rise in real wages during 1986, adding to the gains achieved the year before. This increase occurred at the expense of producers, reducing their willingness to save and invest to expand capacity. Concession of large wage increases at the start of the plan ensured enhanced demand. In the cases both of Argentina and Israel, where union pressure was greater, real wage gains granted were deliberately negative to restrain such increased consumption.

Fixed prices and wages, despite mounting criticism, did translate into a smashing victory for the PMDB in the November 1986 elections. For the only time in the New Republic, there was a single majority party in the National Congress: the PMDB of Sarney. Thereafter, the inevitable denouement came to pass. Immediately after the election, the government sought to raise indirect taxes by something like 4 percent of GDP There was resistance. Indexation began to reappear. Exchange rates were allowed to vary on a daily basis; interest rates paid on internal debt became set by market forces. In February 1987, the wage trigger initiated a salary increase; full financial indexation returned. Inflation had quickly reemerged—now with even greater force.

Another problem soon became evident. The government could no longer meet its obligations to private creditors. Official reserves had been exhausted in a vain and belated effort to obtain imports to counteract rising demand. Questions arose about the accuracy of the published trade data. Brazil now was insolvent and would remain so for years. Despite initial apparent success, the Cruzado Plan had failed. Soon after, Finance Minister Dilson Funaro resigned, replaced by Luiz Carlos Bresser-Pereira.

Thereafter, the Sarney government never came to grips with inflation. Efforts were made, and a variety of different plans were formulated, but all lacked needed credibility once the Cruzado Plan had failed. The Bresser Plan in June 1987 was unable to gain traction within a society now suspicious of official price freezes. As generalized inflation returned, relative claims of government, labor unions, and producers for shares of income were no longer compatible. All parts of society felt that they had lost.

Bresser was succeeded by Mailson de Nobrega. He started by seeking to reduce the accumulating governmental deficit. Public expenditures, administered prices of public utilities, and public salaries were the focus during this "Rice and Beans Plan." That managed to stabilize inflation— but at a rate amounting to almost 20 percent a month. Despite a return to negotiations about the external debt in June 1988, no additional net foreign resources were made available. The need to adjust lagging administered prices initiated a new acceleration in inflation; prices rose by 24 percent in September and 27 percent in October 1988.

Another price and wage freeze was just a matter of time and, not surprisingly, well anticipated, thereby limiting its effect. The Summer Plan, announced on January 14, 1989, was to be the last of the Sarney years: another new currency, eliminating three zeros, the *cruzado novo;* another end to indexation, including wages, which had increased every three months since 1987; and a tight monetary and fiscal policy with high real interest rates. Exchange rates were also frozen. Discussions about a possible social pact were initiated again. It was too late.

This failed effort carried the administration to its end. By the March 15, 1990, inauguration date of the new president, Fernando Collor, price increases soared to 80 percent a month. On March 13, a three-day bank holiday was declared. Everyone was eager to see what Collor's plan would contain and whether the steady Brazilian march toward hyperinflation would cease.

The Collor Plan

The Collor Plan had historic roots in the Erhard Plan of post–World War II Germany.[6] There the Allied governments significantly reduced the quantity of money in circulation, substituting a new currency and monitoring its subsequent supply. Price controls could then be lifted. This was the essential component of the plan announced on March 16, a "silver bullet" directed against an inflationary tiger impeding modernization of Brazil. Figure 3-2 sets out the quantitative record of that misfiring.

There were four components to the plan.[7] The quantity of extant deposits and financial assets was immediately reduced by some 80 percent in the form of a compulsory loan to the government, to be repaid in later installments after eighteen months; only very small deposit holders escaped. A fiscal reform sought to increase governmental revenues substantially, including cancellation of part of the internal debt and imposition of a tax on financial transactions. Prices were frozen, as were wages, but the exchange rate was permitted to fluctuate. And there was, of course, a new currency in circulation, the *cruzeiro* instead of the *cruzado novo.*

Collor's team managed to get the first part of the program right. Government revenues substantially increased. For the first time, Brazil generated a large fiscal primary surplus, amounting to almost 5 percent of GDP. Expropriation of financial assets, and failure to compensate fully for past inflation, helped. Increased prices for nationalized public utilities

FIGURE 3-2. Change in IPCA, Collor Administration, 1990–92

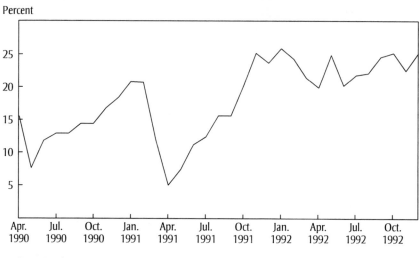

Percent

Source: Ipeadata.

likewise assisted. For the year as a whole, total taxes amounted to more than 29 percent of gross domestic product, an extraordinary gain over the preceding years. Such a level would not be matched until well into the Cardoso period.

On the monetary side, however, there was virtual chaos. Firms found themselves short of working capital and loudly complained. They reacted by decreasing production; unemployment expanded. Then, a whole array of special arrangements emerged allowing for greater exchanges of the old currency for the new. Business interests were attended to, however inconsistent such treatment was with the original plan. These responses led to a doubling in aggregate money supply within the first months. Indeed, this monetary increase—and the attendant rise in prices—was sufficient to require the central bank in June to increase the real rate of interest back to the heights of the Summer Plan of 1989.

Inflation survived and flourished, despite Collor's silver bullet. Prices soared during the last months of the year at double-digit, and accelerating, monthly rates. Collor's fault was not passivity; he pursued help wherever it might be found. In the second half of 1990, there were meetings with business and trade unions in search of a social pact. Those yielded nothing. Business wanted reduction of the high interest rate while labor sought to restore indexation to ensure against real wage loss. Neither, understandably, was acceptable to a government searching for new solutions. National product declined by 4.3 percent for the year.

In February 1991, a standard price-wage freeze, Collor II, had only temporary effects, as could have and should have been foreseen. By the end of the first week in May, the entire economic team resigned. The appointment of Marcílio Marques Moreira as finance minister and recruitment of a series of new ministers throughout the cabinet marked another tack. Hardly surprising was Moreira's promise that economic policy henceforth would avoid novelty, committing to monetary and fiscal discipline; no further shocks were to be expected. More unusual, perhaps, was that he kept his word. But that effort to restrain inflation was likewise doomed to failure. Given the need to repay the bank deposits frozen by the Collor Plan, the best that could be achieved was high, but stable, inflation.

Bresser-Pereira argues that the Collor failure emanates from a distributive imbalance: "The Brazilian inflation is inertial and was very high—in truth, hyperinflation was nearing—when the stabilization plan was implemented. The neo-structural explanation gives emphasis to relative price disequilibrium on the date of the freeze and to the corresponding distributive conflict."[8] That judgment seems incorrect. After all, hyperinflation resolves relative price disequilibrium. Then a fixed exchange rate, adequate international reserves, and elimination of the fiscal deficit can work their magic. That is what the successful Bolivian and Argentine experiences affirm.

Rather, the Collor failure shows that shock treatment, even with a major fiscal effort, is insufficient to produce an end to inflation when it is accompanied by erratic monetary policy, a fluctuating exchange rate, and a labor market in disequilibrium. There was no anchor to guarantee price stability. Both heterodox and orthodox approaches need to convince the public of likely success. Initial confidence otherwise rapidly erodes.

Cardoso's Plano Real

In October 1992, there was a new leader, Itamar Franco, the vice president, serving in place of Collor, whose trial for impeachment had been voted by the Câmara. Itamar's views did not coincide with those of his predecessor. Immediate return to higher growth was his administration's principal objective. But inflation was continuing without pause despite, or perhaps because of, a succession of finance ministers. There was no coherent policy. But, as figure 3-3 makes clear, success was imminent.

FIGURE 3-3. **Change in IPCA, Itamar Administration, 1993–94**

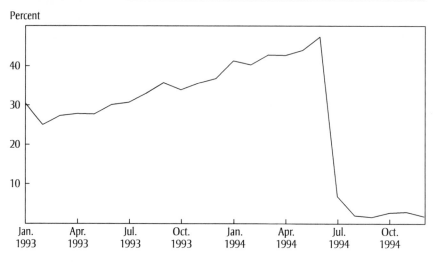

Percent

Source: Ipeadata.

Fernando Henrique Cardoso, already serving as foreign minister since October, was appointed Itamar's fourth minister of finance in May 1993; the average term of his predecessors was less than two months. In the midst of political turmoil, Cardoso assumed economic leadership, assembling around him a group from the Pontifícia Universidade Católica do Rio de Janeiro (PUC-Rio) that had been prominent in the earlier Cruzado Plan.[9] These included Pérsio Arida, Edmar Bacha, and André Lara Resende, as well as two new individuals, Gustavo Franco and Pedro Malan. Most were identified as *tucanos,* members of the PSDB.

Cardoso describes his initial months in office, and the complicated evolution of the modified Larida proposal, in his *A arte da política.*[10] By June 1993, the Programa de Ação Imediata was prepared, emphasizing reduction of the government deficit through increase in revenues and cuts in outlays. A key contribution was recognition that inflation had historically operated to reduce the real primary deficit by increasing revenues—indirect taxes were price adjusted—while reducing deflated outlays, because they were fixed in nominal terms. The primary surplus in 1992 had amounted to 2.3 percent, and 1993 was already a little better at 2.7 percent. With reduced interest payments abroad, the operational surplus had even turned positive in 1993.

Thus fortified, in December Cardoso announced a definitive stabilization process that was to continue over the following months. In a first phase, during January and February 1994, his efforts were directed to congressional approval of measures required to ensure a large primary surplus during 1994. Cardoso took advantage of the delayed constitutional revision process to pass an amendment creating the Fundo Social de Emergência, permitting the federal government for two years fully to retain, rather than redistribute, 20 percent of revenues directly collected.[11] This transferred to the federal government approximately 0.5 percent of GDP in 1994 and 1995, thus modestly altering the decentralization inherent in the 1988 Constitution.[12] Additionally, a final agreement was reached with the foreign commercial banks ending the default in place since 1987. Those terms canceled a third of the balance owed to the private banks while making the country more attractive to external investors.

At the beginning of March, a new phase of voluntary adjustment of prices began, utilizing a second virtual currency, the Unidade Real de Valor (URV), alongside the regular one. The URV approximated the dollar, thereby appreciating vis-à-vis the existing *cruzado real*. Firms could adjust prices as they wished; wages were determined by the average real salaries of the previous four months. Indexation, however, was eliminated for all contracts of less than a year. Originally, this phase was to continue for a full year, but only three months later, its imminent end was announced; the departure of Cardoso from the Finance Ministry in April to contend for the presidency had something to do with that. Inflation, measured in the old currency, continued at a high rate but one that was stabilizing, as the URV was changing little on a daily basis.

As Bacha points out, the delicate problem now was absence of an anchor to the inflation rate, since the growth rate of money was entirely responsive to demand. Expectations became critical. "On the one hand, perfecting the indexation system was necessary to free the economy from price and wage inertia. . . . On the other hand, the better was the indexation, the more susceptible the economy became to enter a hyperinflation."[13] Lags were therefore introduced into the adjustment process: the URV moved in response to past inflation, financial contracts were only slowly and progressively converted to URVs, the prices of goods and services for immediate payment were required to be in *cruzeiros reais,* and public sector prices were converted in stages.

The new currency, the *real,* was introduced on July 1, 1994. This Real Plan applied the strategy put forward by Arida and Lara Resende in the early 1980s. This time there was no initial price and wage freeze, nor would public sector prices have to be held constant, as was the case during the Cruzado Plan. This time there was no automatic inflation trigger built in to guarantee a real wage level. Indexation was not yet eliminated, but at least there was a full year of grace. This time there was a considerable primary surplus rather than the earlier reliance upon seignorage revenue emanating from enhanced money balances. This time monetary policy could become an active policy tool at the very beginning and was employed, along with high real rates of interest, to check excess demand.

This time, with lower tariffs and larger international reserves, actual imports and the threat of yet more could limit domestic price increases. Very favorable terms of trade—which had gone up by more than 20 percent between 1993 and 1995—allowed income growth to exceed product expansion. This time, there was access to external credit; in addition, debt service requirements declined. Agricultural income grew rapidly during 1994, allowing food prices to trail the general price index. And perhaps above all, there was a genuine anchor provided by a stable exchange rate.

All of these mattered. Future expectations of inflation counted as well. An initially hesitant public gradually came to believe in the stability of the *real* as time passed.

Cardoso I: The Dollar as Anchor

Cardoso was elected president and took office on January 1, 1995. At the start of his administration, it was agreed that monetary policy would have to be restrictive and the real interest rate high. No one wanted repetition of surging domestic demand characterizing the Cruzado Plan failure. Initial conditions were favorable: Brazil entered stabilization in 1994 with a positive balance of trade and excess foreign exchange reserves.

There, however, agreement ended. One position, espoused by Pérsio Arida, president of the central bank, argued for an early move to a floating exchange rate and a reduced interest rate. An active monetary policy would defend against resurgent inflation. Gustavo Franco, at the other extreme, wished to keep an almost fixed exchange rate as anchor. Continued strength of the *real*—it had appreciated in value to $1.20—facilitated competitive imports and foreign capital inflows. An intermediate position was espoused by Francisco Lopes; he wanted faster devaluation, avoiding an overvalued exchange rate, and lower interest rates.[14]

The die was cast in favor of Franco, who soon succeeded to the central bank presidency. As figure 3-4 illustrates, nominal interest rates remained

FIGURE 3-4. Nominal Interest Rates, 1995–2002

Percent change

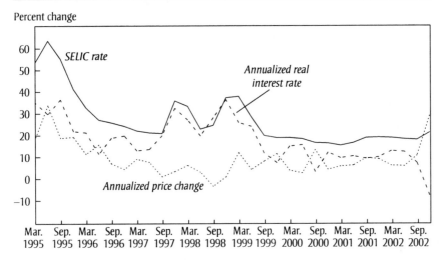

Source: Economist Intelligence Unit and Instituto Brasileiro de Geografia e Estatistica (IBGE).

high, although declining, until the fall of 1997, when a speculative attack occurred. Real interest rates became the highest in the world, as inflation rates declined. Foreign inflows of capital responded to this incentive. Not all entry was speculative or short term: a tax imposed on short-term funds discouraged entry. Direct foreign investment accelerated in response to privatization sales.

One crucial policy component was lacking: reform of public finance.[15] Between 1994 and 1998, federal taxes declined from 18.9 to 18.7 percent of gross national product; at the same time, expenditures rose from 16.5 to 18.0 percent. The primary surplus ensuring the success of the Real Plan had disappeared. Between 1994 and 1997, this surplus fell by more than 6 percent of GDP, most of it concentrated in 1995. Increase in minimum wages, with attendant rise in pension payments, was a prime cause; interest payments on public debt also went up. At the federal level, receipts from privatization were accounted below the line and used to cancel debts. Something in excess of 90 percent of sale receipts was used for amortization. Only in the instance of Telebrás in 1998 was some part—40 percent—of the total registered as a one-time tax item. These inflows from asset sales kept the net debt level from rising more.

This first Cardoso term is the only one after 1985 that recorded a primary deficit all four years. Earlier presidents benefited from high inflation's reduction of real expenditure; Cardoso did not. There was much legislation requiring support. Members of congress reaped gains for their support, not always for themselves, but for their electoral bases. There was never a serious debate about the fiscal problem as a whole. Discussions were instead focused on particular reforms—social security, health, education, public employment, and privatization. As long as financing was available, even at high interest rates, the conventional budget constraint disappeared. It is doubtful that the "main sources of pressure on the public sector accounts could have been controlled but were not fully allowed during discussions of the reforms."[16] These deficits, including interest payments, came to an annual operational shortfall of 6 to 7 percent of GDP.

The effects were considerable. Inflation rates were low, but public debt rose. Elimination of hidden "skeletons" in the government accounts contributed. Limited economic growth restrained rising imports. In 1997 recession in Asia began, and in the fall of that year, a speculative attack on the *real* led to soaring domestic interest rates and diminishing capital inflow. That turned into sizable outflow after the Russian collapse in August 1998. Even an agreement with the IMF in November 1997 for a very large support package of $41.6 billion failed to stabilize matters. Soon after Cardoso's second inauguration in 1999, Brazil had to let the exchange rate devalue considerably.

Could an earlier move away from the exchange rate anchor have helped? A flexible exchange rate, and a rigorous fiscal constraint, in the brief window available at the end of 1996 and beginning of 1997, would have been the alternative. Lower interest rates resulting from a looser monetary policy might have stimulated domestic activity. Smaller inflows of foreign capital would have been welcome. Primary surpluses certainly would have had to start sooner and might have avoided the later political trauma.

The IMF, in a subsequent report, criticizes its mistake. "In retrospect, the IMF should have encouraged an earlier exit from the crawling peg regime at an opportune moment. . . . Indeed there were windows of opportunity to exit from a position of strength in late 1996 or early 1997, and again in the first half of 1998."[17] Such a policy shift was widely discussed. Rudiger Dornbusch was critical of overvaluation in 1997, without anticipating the international pressures to come. The worst he saw was continued slow growth, large capital inflows, and high interest rates: "If Brazil fails to make dramatic improvements, it is very unlikely that it will experience a Mexican-style collapse or a pervasive loss of confidence."[18] That article came after an earlier market flurry surged in the summer of 1996, when he was sounding the alarm—akin to his correct prediction of Mexican difficulties in 1994. By November 1998, he saw imminent disaster, anticipating overvaluation of the *real* by 35 percent or even more.

Cardoso II: A New Macroeconomic Basis

When the crisis came in early 1999, Brazil finally responded. A shift to a floating currency preserved diminishing reserves, as Brazil negated IMF proposals, and Argentine hopes, for a fixed exchange rate as a bulwark against market speculation. Despite those early tremors, the situation soon righted. Brazil's exchange rate steadied, a second agreement was signed with the IMF, and a different set of macroeconomic principles appeared.

This macroeconomic trinity included inflation targeting, a floating exchange rate, and openness to foreign capital inflow. It became the set of principles undergirding subsequent economic policy.

Income did not decline in 1999, and domestic inflation, as measured by consumer prices, did not go to double digits, contrary to dire predictions from the press. Economists' predictions did not fare much better. The IMF expected a fall in income of 3.5–4 percent and a price increase of 10 percent in the first half of the year, quickly declining thereafter. Those estimates were modest compared to market expectations of an income fall of 5–6 percent and inflation of 30 percent. As late as 2000, the Brazilian public remained uncertain; only a minority expressed confidence in the *real*.[19]

Brazil's economy expanded in 2000 at a rate of 4.3 percent. The current account deficit narrowed to 4.2 percent of GDP, from 4.7 percent the previous year. Inflation retreated to less than 7 percent. Interest rates declined, and by December the real SELIC rate (the central bank's benchmark overnight rate) was less than 10 percent. No wonder the estimates for growth at the beginning of 2001 signaled prospects of unhampered advance. The Brazilian economy was expected to expand at a rate of 4.5 percent. In the age of the "new economy" within the United States, there was reason to believe.

Increased taxes and expenditure restraint ensured a primary surplus. This time, congressional support did materialize. Annual targets were set and fulfilled. Social policy, the intended objective of the second presidential term, had to yield. The Ministry of Finance became the villain, enforcing restrictions on all others; the Ministry of Planning and Budget was an ally, putting into place transparent guidelines not easily ignored.

The Law of Fiscal Responsibility was crucial. Promised to the IMF in the first agreement, this legislation passed in May 2000. It transformed Brazil by eliminating public sector deficits and restricting access to future indebtedness. Congressional procedures were imposed to ensure budgetary discipline. A longer-term plan of four years extended into the first year of a successor administration, the Multiyear Plan (PPA); there was a rolling three-year plan, the Budget Guidelines Law (LDO); and, of course, an annual budget.

It was easier to increase receipts than reduce expenditures. In these years, between 1997 and 2002, tax collection steadily rose from 27.4 to 32.8 percent of gross national product. That was impressive. New levies helped, but increased rates for the tax on financial transactions (CPMF) and the social security contribution (COFINS), and greater income tax collection made the largest contribution. To achieve the primary surplus, state enterprises, and Petrobras in particular, contributed, along with states and municipalities. In 2002, despite mediocre economic growth, the surplus reached the target 3.5 percent of GDP.[20]

The public debt was also a focus. Deficit and debt are intimately linked: what is not obtained by taxes must be financed by issue of bonds. As debt rises, so will interest payments, thereby increasing future indebtedness. That pushes up interest rates, debilitating economic activity. This disequilibrium scenario threatened as a consequence of the substantial devaluation in 1999. Indebtedness rose by 11 percentage points of gross national product due to revaluation of external liabilities—only about 20 percent of total debt—and a growing portion of domestic debt tied to the exchange rate. There was, as well, a shift in preferences of domestic bond holders to shorter-term securities. Annual amortization payments went up.

Everything revolved around the public debt. How would the economy react to the burden of interest payments already amounting to close to 8 percent of product? Table 3-1 provides two alternative scenarios comparable to the many being produced as 2002 concluded. The calculation is easy. One can generate a future sequence of debt relative to income with growth of product, domestic inflation rates, domestic interest rates, presumed devaluation, and share of domestic debt held in dollar-adjustable form.[21]

TABLE 3-1. Projected Debt-Income Ratios, 2002–10

Percent, unless otherwise indicated

Pattern	Debt-income ratio	Primary surplus	Growth rate	Inflation rate	Real devaluation	Real interest rate
Stabilizing						
2002	0.562	3.25	2.7	12	25	6
2004	0.556	4.5	5.7	8	0	13
2006	0.515	4.5	3.7	6	−20	12
2008	0.486	4	4.5	4	2	8
2010	0.424	3.5	5	4	0	5
Destabilizing						
2002	0.564	3.25	2.7	12	25	6
2004	0.563	2	5.7	12	0	10
2006	0.635	1	3.9	12	15	6
2008	0.693	0	4.5	14	15	3
2010	0.792	0	3	14	15	4

Source: Author's calculations. See text.

The two options diverge sharply after 2004. That is when policy shifts. One pattern presumes a continuing primary surplus and a rapidly declining share of debt indexed to the dollar, as was actually the case. The other goes for immediate growth, lower real interest rates, higher inflation, and greater devaluation. In the first case, the debt-income ratio declines; in the other, it increases. One should not exaggerate the significance of such exercises. In the absence of a full structural model of the economy, these results are illustrative rather than conclusive.[22]

In early 2001, the United States, after a record forty consecutive quarters of expansion, entered into recession. In September 2001 came a surprise al Qaeda attack on the New York World Trade Center that rattled international markets. Within Brazil lower rainfall led by midyear to compulsory rationing of 20 percent of previous energy consumption. Petroleum prices began to rise, aggravating the situation.

In 2001 as well, Argentina was careening toward an economic crisis. The elected government, a leftist successor after Carlos Menem's two terms, recalled Domingo Cavallo as minister of finance in March. He failed in his efforts to counter inflation. By December he was gone, and President Fernando de la Rua lasted just a few days longer. By this time,

Argentina was Brazil's third-largest export market, after the United States and the European Community, and Brazil's participation in Mercosul had become a source of weakness rather than a guarantee of strength.

As the election approached, Lula seemed unbeatable. Markets reacted adversely. Substantial devaluation of the *real* occurred in the months following April. Foreign inflows became shorter term, and some were not renewed. An additional IMF credit was arranged, after approval by the presidential candidates. That did not prevent an increase of 300 points in the SELIC rate right after the first election round. By then the political race was all but over. Everyone now waited to see what the Lula administration really intended. Some did not believe Lula's earlier campaign pledges about continuity.

Revamping the Public Sector

There was hope that the Cardoso policy of selling off state-owned facilities could be reversed. These activities extended widely, encompassing a variety of productive sectors. At the same time, the financial sector was opened to foreign banks.

Privatization

Brazil emerged from two decades of military government with a large public sector.[23] This went beyond the normal range of public utilities such as production and distribution of electric power, and communication and transportation facilities. Important industrial areas such as steel, petrochemicals, chemicals, fertilizer, aircraft production, and computers were state owned and operated. Petrobras and CVRD were the leading producers within the petroleum and mining sectors.

A growing tide of nations reconsidered state participation in the 1980s, and Brazil was among them. The reasons, according to *The Economist*, were twofold: "One is to shrink the state, in pursuit of greater economic efficiency; the other is to raise cash. These hopes are often in conflict. . . . Often the success of a government's privatization programme turns on the way this dilemma is resolved."[24] Higher sales prices can be obtained by the grant of special privileges and hence immunity from competition that could yield gains in economic social efficiency. Lower sales prices mean less immediate revenues and less reduction in public debt.

The fiscal benefits of privatization can be illusory. There is only a one-time benefit. The long-term public sector deficit may be affected adversely if the enterprise had been profitable; that source of surplus permanently disappears. If the firm has an annual deficit, that cost is ended; but any sum received is likely to be small.

Typically, as the Brazilian experience over this period shows, privatization proceeds were used to retire extant debt. Then there is a reduction in both assets and liabilities of the government, with no financial consequence. Privatization involves a single transfer of cash, not an ongoing increase in governmental receipts with continuing positive effects on the annual fiscal deficit.[25]

Before the return to civil government in 1985, twenty state enterprises were sold for receipts of almost $200 million, amounting to less than 0.1 percent of the level of gross national product. Most of them were transacted on a competitive basis, although the largest, Riocell (dealing in wood pulp), responsible for 40 percent of total proceeds, was sold directly.[26] Most enterprises were simply returned to the private sector where they had originated; they had been nationalized by dint of their earlier failure.

The Sarney government favored privatization—but only modestly. In November 1985, a presidential decree (91,991) established an Interministerial Council of Privatization and specified some firms under consideration. There was still another decree in March, 1988 (95,886) that recognized reduction in the public deficit and deregulation as objectives, in addition to the possible use of external debt as a means of payment. A new title was conferred: the Federal Program of Privatization. Yet little was accomplished.

Pressure for privatization emerged from the state-owned development bank, Banco Nacional de Desenvolvimento Econômico e Social (BNDES). As a principal source of finance for state enterprises, the bank had invested in the steel, fertilizer, and other strategic sectors. A subsidiary, BNDES Participações (BNDESPAR), controlled such activities, and was experiencing regular shortfalls over the period 1982–87. That limited the capacity of the bank to finance new investments.

This decision to privatize was eminently practical rather than a firm commitment to displace the state by favoring the private sector. The BNDES had no formal role, as it was later to acquire. The advantage of delegating responsibility to the bank soon became apparent. Apart from its own sales, it became an agent for the federal steel holding company Siderbrás in the sale of two subsidiaries, Cofavi and Usiba. Rules for dealing with the individual cases soon developed, including financial restructuring where required. Additionally, the BNDES's internal privatization committee consulted with the new Federal Council of Privatization regarding activities other than those of BNDESPAR.

During the presidential election campaign in 1989, privatization emerged as one of the issues emphasized by then governor Collor. This marked a new phase. Until that time, the issue had not gotten abundant press coverage. An overwhelming majority within Brazil believed that economic development and the state were inseparably linked. Privatization and foreign presence were both viewed with hesitancy. Congress reacted after the decree of March 1988, requiring the government to ensure that privatization of Petrobras was out of the question.

Once elected, Collor sought to promote privatization. While he failed badly in his attempts to deliver price stability, he set in motion a process that has altered Brazil. The policy, embodied in the Programa Nacional de Desestatização (PND), was approved by the National Congress on April 12, 1990, as Law 8031, less than a month after its initial appearance as *medida provisória* 155. Its principal goal was "to reorder the strategic position of the State in the economy, transferring to the private sector assets inappropriately managed by the public sector."[27] Unlike the previous Sarney decree, this time the resources emanating from sales were never intended to reduce the public sector deficit but rather to decrease outstanding debt.

There was allowance for outstanding public sector obligations to be used for payment. This was intended to increase bidder interest as well as to focus on debt reduction. Various forms of payment were allowed. These included the frozen *cruzados novos* as well as privatization certificates, newly acquired assets held by financial intermediaries whose only use was for purchase of state-operated enterprises. Potential sources also incorporated the unpaid debts of these enterprises, certified by the Brazilian National Treasury.

Opponents of privatization emphasized the worthlessness of these *"moedas podres"* (rotten money). External debt, at 75 percent of its face value, was also accepted. Internal debt proved to be far the largest potential source of payment, amounting to more than 60 percent of the eligible forms. Foreign investment was permitted to the extent of only 40 percent of voting shares, a limitation imposed by the congress. In fact, foreign participation turned out to be minimal during this first phase of privatization.

In all, sixty-four firms were specified for privatization, as shown in table 3-2. These encompassed three major areas: steel, petrochemicals, and fertilizer production. In half the cases, federal participation was controlling; in the other half, there was only minority participation. These enterprises extended to the railway and internal shipping sectors as well as two electricity distributors and a bank. As a share of the fifty-six largest federally operated enterprises, they came to a little more than a quarter of 1990 sales; the proportion of net worth and of net fixed assets was higher.[28]

All this elaborate preparation yielded surprisingly little, as measured by actual sales receipts. During the two and a half years that Collor was in charge, total sales receipts were around $4 billion, almost all emanating from the sale of steel and petrochemical firms. Debt of $1.4 billion was transferred from the state to the newly privatized firms. Something more than a quarter of these payments went to the benefit of Petrobras, owner of the petrochemical companies being sold. No great gains in governmental receipts occurred, especially since these values were exaggerated by the use of domestic instruments selling at much less than par value.

On the microeconomic side, however, as measured by efficiency and renewed investment within the privatized units, the picture that emerges is more favorable. Armando Castelar Pinheiro emphasizes this point: sales per employee doubled while labor productivity went up almost as much. Profitability improved while debt diminished and investment expanded greatly.[29] The steel sector evolved as a growing participant in international trade.

Itamar, when he assumed office, delayed the privatization program. He, like many others in the congress, had not been a supporter of the directions economic policy had taken. But the die had been cast. There was no way to reverse, or even to cease, the sale of public enterprises. Accordingly, Itamar, however reluctantly, resumed course, with few changes. CSN, the Brazilian steel firm created by the Vargas-U.S. agreement in 1941, was sold off during the spring of 1993 as planned sales resumed. The most important change was a higher proportion of cash payments. During 1994, of the total receipts of $2 billion, 72 percent were in cash; 89 percent of all cash receipts received by the PND in 1991–94 were received in that single year.[30]

When Cardoso became minister of finance in May 1993, he sought to remedy the fiscal imbalance, as a prelude to the Real Plan. While there was apparent interest in privatizing other state-dominated sectors, and a new decree centralized the program in the Ministry of Finance, this idea was never realized.[31] The process moved ahead, but slowly. Although

TABLE 3-2. State-Owned Enterprises in the Privatization Program, 1990

Units as indicated

Enterprise by sector	Net revenue (U.S.$ million)	Net worth (U.S.$ million)	Net assets (U.S.$ million)	Employees	Government share in common stock (percent)
Steelmaking	4,722	6,833 (6,864)[a]	11,409	76,190	...
1. CST (31)[b]	454	2,178 (2,163)	2,375	9,320	74
2. USIMINAS (12)	930	464 (508)	881	13,547	85
3. COSINOR	18	4	20	693	100
4. AÇOS PIRATINI	74	−24	36	2,500	97
5. ACESITA (28)	339	170 (172)	258	8,693	92
6. AÇOMINAS (30)	429	1,129	1,370	5,849	100
7. COSIPA	1,054	2,368	3,888	15,285	100
8. CSN	1,424	544	2,581	20,303	100
Petrochemicals	4,136	3,822 (3,830)	3,111	17,288	...
9. COPESUL (21)	482	557 (561)	544	1,449	98
10. PPH	110	33	90	592	20
11. PETROQUIMICA TRIUNFO	127	75	43	394	45
12. POLISUL	116	31	45	570	33
13. PETROQ. UNIÃO (27)	321	427 (430)	449	1,375	68
14. PTROFLEX (40)	248	114 (115)	110	1,759	100
15. NITRIFLEX	94	25	32	799	40
16. COPENE	736	1,122	966	1,903	36
17. ACRINOR	66	41	20	345	18
18. CIA. BRAS. POLI-URETANOS	11	15	20	14	24
19. CIQUENE (58)	130	136	95	802	31
20. CIA. PETROQ. CAMAÇARI	137	41	66	n.a.	28
21. DETEN	123	71	56	378	34
22. EDN	169	90	72	732	27
23. METANOR	16	17	7	107	30
24. NTROCARBONO	93	53	42	434	20
25. NOTROCOLOR	24	36	56	460	22
26. POLIADEN	96	95	36	475	14
27. POLIPROPILENO	11	74	0	6	34
28. POLITENO	130	130	49	455	25
29. PRONOR	146	117	35	837	35
30. CINAL	16	54	n.a.	270	16
31. COPERBO	130	63	54	´688	23
32. CIA. BRAS. ESTIRENO	84	13	13	280	23
33. OXITENO (71)	66	150	40	587	25
34. POLIBRASIL	203	62	33	780	26
35. POLIDERIVADOS	n.a.	25	23	20	48
36. POLIOLEFINAS	251	155	115	777	31

Enterprise by sector	Net revenue (U.S.$ million)	Net worth (U.S.$ million)	Net assets (U.S.$ million)	Employees	Government share in common stock (percent)
Transporatation	1,065	3,060	5,429	61,500	. . .
37. FRANAVE	6	2	1	445	100
38. ENASA	13	7	12	340	100
39. SNBP	9	4	n.a.	235	100
40. LLOYD	136	−368	160	1,797	100
41. RFFSA (18)	901	3,415	5,256	58,683	90
Fertilizers	528	408 (411)	449	8,673	. . .
42. GOIASFERTIL	23	24	26	716	100
43. ICC	22	2	24	458	100
44. FOSFERTIL	125	143 (144)	153	2,190	100
45. ULTRAFERTIL (44)	142	129 (130)	105	2,303	100
46. NITROFERTIL	116	61 (62)	95	1,398	100
47. ARAFERTIL (70)	81	34	31	804	33
48. INDAG	19	15	15	804	35
Chemicals	458	436 (437)	505	3,220	. . .
49. ALCALIS (61)	80	70 (71)	88	1,791	100
50. COR	27	42	59	223	37
51. SALGEMA	233	167	257	774	45
52. ALCLOR	4	18	22	240	24
53. FCC	57	9	46	42	40
54. PETROCOQUE	57	30	33	150	35
Miscellaneous	4,484	3,307	1,073	34,159	. . .
55. MAFERSA (transportation equipment)	86	−27	13	1,910	100
56. CELMA (machinery)	60	27	8	1,681	87
57. CARAIBA (mining)	22	11	313	1,000	100
58. EMBRAER (aircraft)	417	−281	258	9,007	93
59. COBRA (computers)	102	6	13	2,214	98
60. AGEF (warehouses)	17	6	6	920	100
61. VALEC (engineering)	n.a.	184	174	200	100
62. LIGHT (electricity) (15)	1,160	3,074	109	14,237	82
63. ESCELSA (electricity) (43)	215	140	179	2,990	73
64. MERIDIONAL (banking)	2,405	167	n.a.	n.a.	82
Total	15,393	17,866 (17,909)	21,976	201,030	. . .

Source: Armando Castelar Pinheiro and Fabio Giambiagi, "As empresas estatais e o programa de privatizações do governo Collor," Discussion Paper 261 (Brasília: IPEA, 1992), p. 38.

a. Values in parentheses represent slight differences from alternative data sources as reported in Pinheiro and Giambiagi.

b. The figure in parentheses, to the right of the name, gives the rank of the firm among the 500 largest Brazilian companies according to sales.

TABLE 3-3. Brazilian Privatization, 1985–94

Billions of U.S. dollars

Period and sector	Direct receipts from sales	Debt transferred	Total	Total estimated cash value[a]
Sarney, 1985–89	0.5	0.6	1.1	n.a.
Collor, 1990–92[b]	4.0	1.4	5.4	1.8
Steel	2.4	1.1	3.5	...
Petrochemicals	1.3	32.0	1.5	...
Fertilizers	0.2	0.1	0.3	...
Other	0.1	0.0	0.1	...
Itamar, 1992–94	4.6	1.8	6.4	3.1
Steel	3.2	1.5	4.7	...
Petrochemicals	0.6	0.0	0.6	...
Fertilizers	0.2	0.0	0.2	...
Other	0.6	0.3	0.9	...
Total	9.1	3.8	12.9	4.9

Sources: For Sarney, see Licinio Velasco Jr., "Privatization: Myths and False Perceptions," p. 2. For Collor and Franco, see BNDES, "A nova fase da privatização" (www.planalto.gov.br), in conjuction with the timing of sales reported in Francesco Anuatti-Neto and others, "Cash and Benefits of Privatization: Evidence from Brazil," Research Network Working Paper R-455 (Washington: Inter-American Development Bank, 2003), appendix 1.

a. Estimated cash value in the Collor period from Pinheiro and Giambiagi, "Brazil Privatization in the 1990s," p. 746, for the ratio of cash value to direct receipts. For the Itamar period, cash values are obtained from the BNDES report cited above, and a value of 0.5 is applied to other assets utilized. This may slightly understate cash values.

b. Sales of the firms scheduled for sale in October–December 1992 are credited to the Collor period although Franco was already serving as acting president. The sales had been planned before Franco took office.

both Light and Escelsa in the electricity sector had been on the initial list of sixty-four firms approved for sale in the PND, there was no movement there. Nor was any of the railroad sector sold off. Privatizations during the Itamar period rendered $4.6 billion, a modestly increased sum relative to the Collor years. Additionally, $1.8 billion of debt was transferred to the private sector.[32]

Table 3-3 provides details of the sales from 1985 through 1994. Not only is sectoral composition specified, but there is subdivision by period. From the Cosipa sale in August 1993, when stabilization became the central policy issue, until the end of 1994, only $1.9 billion including debt transfer, or less than a third of total receipts, was recorded. The Real Plan had no effect.

Tables 3-4 through 3-6 provide, respectively, a statement of resources utilized, a list of principal investors in the larger privatizations, and a

T A B L E 3 - 4 . Funds Used in Purchase of State Enterprises, 1990–94

Billions of U.S. dollars

Data source	Cash	Privatization certificates	Domestic debt	Total
BNDES	1.6	1.3	5.7	8.6
Instituto de Pesquisa Econômica Aplicada (IPEA)	1.2	1.3	5.5	8.0

Sources: For the BNDES, see Pinheiro and de Oliveira Filho, "Privatização no Brasil." For the IPEA, see Armando Castelar Pinheiro, "Structural Adjustment and Privatization in Brazil," Discussion Paper 356 (Rio de Janeiro: IPEA, November 1994), pp. 28–29, to which has been added the sale of Embraer in December 1994.

T A B L E 3 - 5 . Principal Investors in Largest Privatizations, 1991–94[a]

Units as indicated

Date	Company	Sector	Auction result (U.S.$ million)	Purchasers
October 1991	Usiminas	Steel	2,310	Nippon Steel, CVRD, Previ, employees
February 1992	Piratini	Steel	109	Gerdaw
April 1992	Petroflex	Petrochemicals	255	Suzano, employees
May 1992	Copesul	Petrochemicals	871	Odebrecht, Suzano, Petrobras
July 1992	CS Tubarão	Steel	837	Bozano Simonsen, Unibanco, CVRD
August 1992	Fosfértil	Fertilizer	226	Consórcio Fertifós
September 1992	Polesul	Petrochemicals	188	Iperanza, Hoescht
October 1992	Aceseta	Steel	697	PREVI, SISTEL, Banco Safra
April 1993	CSN	Steel	2,028	Employees, Docenane, Vicunha, ESN pension fund
June 1993	Ultrafértil	Fertilizer	226	Fosfértil, employees
August 1993	COSIPA	Steel	1,470	UNIMINAS, employees
September 1993	Açominas	Steel	721	Grupo Medespar, employees
January 1994	PQU	Petrochemicals	328	Consórcio Poloinvest, Polibrasil, employees
December 1994	Embraer	Aeronautics	455	Bozano Simonsen, SISTEL, PREVI, employees

Sources: Anuatti-Neto and others,"Costs and Benefits of Privatization," p. 43; Andrea Goldstein, "Brazilian Privatization in International Perspective," *Industrial and Corporate Change* 8, no. 4 (1999): 710; BNDES, as replicated in Aloysio Biondi, *O Brasil privatizado* (São Paulo: Editora Fundação Perseu Abramo, 1999), pp 42 ff.

a. All privatizations in excess of $100 million in period 1990–94.

TABLE 3-6. Privatization Purchases, by Type of Investors, 1990–94
Units as indicated

Type of investor	Proceeds (U.S.$ million)	Percent of purchases
National enterprises	3,116	36
Financial institutions	2,200	25
Individuals	1,707	20
Pension funds	1,193	14
Foreign investors	398	5
Total	8,608	100

Source: Pinheiro and de Oliveira Filho, "Privatização no Brasil," p. 12.

specification by investor type: national or foreign, financial institutions, and so on. Is the result a modest start toward increased productivity—or a distribution of valuable state assets to privileged private recipients, as critics from the Left have asserted?[33]

The negative view criticizes *moedas podres* as a form of payment. Firms were sold too cheaply, the argument goes, using debts acquired at less than par by purchasers. Table 3-3 includes an estimate of this overstatement of sales proceeds. This indicates the actual value received as slightly less than half of what was reported by the BNDES in the Collor period; the exaggeration declines subsequently as greater cash was required.

Still, a contrary conclusion does not automatically follow. If sales were open to competitive bids—none of the larger companies was sold as a single unit—winners were unlikely to achieve great hidden profits.[34] The variety of successful bidders, as shown in table 3-5, also speaks against that point, as does the explicit subsidy conceded to employees purchasing participation at a discount.

Moreover, in recommending a minimum bid price, consulting firms had to take the discounted securities into account; this raised the nominal asking price. In the case of a fertilizer firm whose value was criticized for being too low, valuation by a third consultant did not increase. Setting a lower value could be advantageous: the realized auction premiums garnered wider public support for the program. There is nonetheless a valid point: some exaggeration is inherent in conventional totals.

The Left was unhappy with privatization, and there were many attempts to halt the process. In the case of Usiminas, the first sale by the Collor government, there were thirty-seven lawsuits requiring response by the government.[35] Subsequent privatizations elicited the same response. Unions and political parties joined in this effort. But the policy of incorporating employees for 10 percent of the shares at a discount price began to pay off. Workers at Usiminas, who favored privatization by a margin of 55 to 45 percent in 1991, split with the Central Única dos Trabalhadores (the principal trade union federation). In June 1995, *Veja* estimated that more than 100,000 workers had participated in the purchases and had managed a capital gain of more than three times the initial cost.[36] Tables 3-5 and 3-6 provide evidence of their participation. The formal presence of state employee pension funds as leading bidders further divided the opposition.

Subsequent privatization, in Cardoso's first term, is set out in table 3-7 for the period 1995–1998. A total of $73.4 billion was received, or a little more than 2 percent of gross national product. Resources were concentrated in 1997 and 1998, constituting approximately 4 percent of total GNP, a significant inflow indeed. The expansion of state government participation in 1997 indicates the states' need for resources to conclude debt restructuring agreements with the federal government. States sold off fourteen electricity distributors in 1997. The BNDES allowed states to borrow in the short term against future revenues to be received from privatization.[37]

The sale of the federal telecommunication system, Telebrás, in July 1998 was a major operation. Holdings were divided into twelve individual components. Three consisted of fixed-line communications in different regions; eight were for cellular communication via the A band; and one was Embratel, the long-distance service provider. Bidding was intense, involving foreign firms from Spain, Italy, and Portugal, sometimes, but not always, in alliance with domestic interests. Private pension funds and financial firms were represented. Sale prices were highly profitable for the government, as a comparison with later declining stock values of the private firms reveals.

Unlike previous privatizations, where partial payment could be made in depreciated debt, purchases after 1994 were paid in cash. The bidding process was competitive and uniform. One carryover was the number of court injunctions invoked to bar the process, as well as attempts to gather popular opposition. Their effect was delay. As before, employees were frequently participants, weakening union opposition. Foreign enterprises

T A B L E   3 - 7 .   Privatization Proceeds, 1995–98

Units as indicated

Sector	(U.S.$ million)				(U.S.$ billion)		
	1995	1996	1997	1998	Proceeds	Debt trans- ferred	Total
Federal[a]	1,004	4,080	8,999	23,478	37.6	7.7	45.3
Industry							
Mining	0	0	3,299	0	3.3	3.6	6.9
Infrastructure							
Railroads	0	1,447	15	205	1.7	0	1.7
Ports	0	0	251	149	0	0	0
Electricity	400	2,358	270	880	3.9	1.7	5.6
Telecom	0	0	4,734	21,823	26.6	2.1	28.7
Financial	0	0	240	0	0	0	0
States[a]	0	1,406	13,617	7,497	22.5	5.5	28.0
Infrastructure							
Railroads	0	25	0	240	0.3	0	0.3
Electricity	0	587	9,945	5,166	15.7	4.7	20.4
Telecom	0	0	0	1,018	1.0	0.8	1.8
Financial	0	0	401	0	0.4	0	0.4
Total[a]	1,004	5,486	22,616	30,975	60.1	13.3	73.4
Number of state-owned enterprises							
Federal	8	16	21	7	...	...	...
State	0	2	15	11	...	...	...

Source: Armando Castelar Pinheiro, " The Brazilian Privatization Experience: What's Next?" Discussion Paper 87 (Rio de Janeiro: BNDES, November 2000), p. 17.

a. Totals include minority stakeholder sales as well as other sectors not specified.

became players, and their investments represented a majority of purchases. National firms were half as important. Domestic financial firms, pension funds, and individuals shared equally in the residual, typically participating as a minority in groups organized to bid competitively in the auctions.

There has been no movement backward, notwithstanding the election of Lula and a rising PT. Indeed, over time, through an attempted industrial policy, the search has been for greater joint public-private participation, not less.

Financial Reform

A weakened financial sector and failing banks complicated stabilization policy after the Real Plan. State governments afflicted by indebtedness also required assistance. The consequence was an increase of more than 23 percentage points in the ratio of gross debt to GDP between January 1995 and January 1999. Net public debt went up by less, only 11 percentage points.

Assistance to the banking sector had not been fully foreseen. As activity surged in later 1994 and early 1995, liabilities in arrears and bankruptcies mounted. In 1995 the overdue debt of the private sector more than doubled, from 7.5 to 15.4 percent of assets. This was in addition to the loss stemming from inflation's end: banks had been a principal beneficiary of the inflation tax, offering only partial interest compensation to overnight depositors.

A minicrisis began in August 1995 with the failure of Banco Econômico, the seventh-largest banking institution in the country, and fourteenth in Latin America. Banco Econômico was a fixture in Bahia. Its precarious situation occasioned a complicated set of political and economic responses. Cardoso provides an account, describing the opposing role of Antônio Carlos Maghalães. The episode, worthy of a brief *telenovela,* nearly resulted in a mass resignation by directors of the central bank. The final decision was not to save Banco Econômico, hardly an easy choice since Banespa of São Paulo, Credireal of Minas Gerais, and BANERJ of Rio had all been nationalized months earlier to avoid failure.[38]

The Program to Support the Restructuring and Strengthening of the National Financial System (PROER) followed thereafter, as did insurance of R$20,000 to guarantee individual bank deposits. The scheme involved sales of good assets of problematic banks to purchasers, offering subsidized interest rates on the PROER loans needed to increase assets to equality with deposits. PROER financed the acquisition of federal debt, at a large discount, by the bad bank sufficient to cover 120 percent of the PROER loan. PROER loans thus had a dual structure: the assets provided to the good bank and the liabilities of the bad bank. One expected repayment of the former, while the latter would represent the real cost of intervention. There was no increase in current expenditures or in net public debt.[39]

Four big banks, including Econômico, were involved in the operations of PROER. The others were Nacional, Bamerindus—both quite large— and Noroeste. Four smaller banks, involving less than a tenth of the asset size of the larger ones, were also included. The three largest Brazilian private banks, Bradesco, Itaú, and Unibanco, benefited. The first two acquired smaller units in difficulty, while Unibanco doubled in size by incorporating Nacional. These firms expanded their national presence as the number of private banks declined by a quarter.

Foreign banks from Europe also entered; the constitutional prohibition adopted in 1988 was ruled not to apply. In 1997 HSBC purchased Bamerindus, and Santander acquired Noroeste. In 1998 BBVA bought Excel-Econômico, and ABN, AMRO Real. Brazilian banking was transformed. For the first time, large foreign banks were a factor. By the end of 1998, they accounted for more than twice the 8.4 percent of Brazilian assets they had held at the beginning of 1995.

The Program of Incentives for Reduction of State Participation in Banking Activities (PROES) followed in August 1996. This was a larger undertaking, directed at institutions that had been created, like the BNDES nationally, to finance development projects within states. They had received public deposits and contributed to inflationary excess by expanding loans and underwriting state deficits. They were still important, accounting for more than 18 percent of national banking assets. Now, after emergency intervention of the central bank in three institutions—Banespa, BANERJ, and Credireal—allowing them to continue operation, there was a major federal effort to eliminate the rest. At the end of this process, only 3 percent of banking assets remained in the hands of state governments.

The willingness of São Paulo to allow federal acquisition of Banespa was vital. This was the third-largest bank within the country, trailing only the Bank of Brazil and Caixa Econômica. It exceeded in size, by a very large multiple, all other state banks. Banespa alone accounted for more than half the entire cost of PROES.[40] That decision came in the fall of 1996, before BANERJ and Credireal had been bought by Itaú and Bradesco in 1997. Cardoso's closeness to Governor Mário Covas helped conclude the agreement. The program ended in 2009 with the sale of the last two banks in Santa Catarina and Piaui to the Bank of Brazil; Nossa Caixa had been acquired from São Paulo only a bit earlier.

A final component was resolution of state debt.[41] Demands grew in the Federal Senate for help in 1996 as the Banespa case was under discussion. All the poorer states wanted assistance. That happened in September 1997 with Law 9496. Three times within a decade—always on occasion of national plans to combat inflation—the federal government intervened in behalf of indebted states and municipalities. There was a reason. The wage bill increased from 52 to 70 percent of state expenditures with the end of inflation and minimum wage gains. States also were paying high short-term real interest rates demanded by the market because the grace period on their earlier 1989 renegotiation had ended.

This was intended as a last intervention. States assumed a real interest burden of 6 percent with a thirty-year maturity period. That applied to 80 percent of their debt; 20 percent was to be amortized before the end of 1998. Any further indebtedness, and the ratio of debt service to total expenditures, was restricted. Since the federal government was paying higher real interest rates on its own debt, this arrangement transferred resources to individual states. It is no wonder the process proceeded rapidly, with the last contract signed in June 1998. State interest payments were guaranteed; the federal government had initial access to revenues passed to the states under prevailing constitutional rules.[42]

Over time, federal intervention to reduce state interest payments had become more substantial. In 1989, 1.4 percent of state income was involved; in 1993, 7.2 percent; and in 1998, 11.7 percent. According to a study from the Inter-American Development Bank, four states accounted for almost 90 percent of the total debt exchanged: São Paulo, Minas Gerais, Rio de Janeiro, and Rio Grande do Sul. Of these, São Paulo alone accounted for more than half. Income and population work as explanations for federal assistance. Political factors do not count in the regressions, although they did enter into this extended process of negotiation.[43]

All this resolution of problems of the banking system and of state finance added up to a sizable bill. Much remained hidden. In the instance of PROER, the net public debt was unaffected owing to the balance between increased assets and liabilities. In the case of PROES, matters were similarly treated: one can see it as a simple debt swap between the federal government and state banks. The federal government was now owed large sums by the individual states—more than 10 percent of gross national product—and issued new bonds to compensate. Differences in interest rates paid did not affect the nominal valuation.

Table 3-8 provides an estimate of the costs of these policies. They were neither as small as the 3 percent of national income cited by Cardoso nor as large as the 12.4 percent of income—excluding the refinance of state debts—claimed by the political opposition in the 1999 Parliamentary

TABLE 3-8. Net Cost of Financial Interventions, 1994–98

Units as indicated

	Net cost (1998 R$ billions)	Percentage of income
PROER	8.5	0.9
PROES	54	5.5
Excluding Banespa and BANERJ	18	1.8
Bank of Brazil	8	0.8
State indebtedness	68	6.9
Immediate subsidy	18	1.8
Interest rate differential	35	3.6
Possible failure to pay	15	1.5
Total I[a]	102	10.4
Total II[b]	87	8.9

Sources: See notes 45–47.
a. Includes PROER, PROES less Banespa and BANERJ, and state indebtedness.
b. Includes all above, less cost of failure to pay.

Inquiry Commission (Comissão Parlamentar de Inquérito [CPI]) on Banking.[44] The expense is much less than the loss from doing nothing. In other countries, saving the financial system had cost a great deal more. The recent Great Recession provides examples.

For PROER outlays were around R$27.7 billion: R$13.1 billion in loans to the acquiring banks and R$14.6 billion in credits to the residual bad banks. Since the former would be paid back, albeit at a lesser interest rate, as would a small part of the latter, the central bank assessment of a net loss of R$8.5 billion for the program provides the right value. A later CPI on PROER in 2001–02 saw arguments by the opposition for much larger sums than this.[45]

For PROES, assessments are more uniform. There was an outlay of something like R$40 billion by the end of 1997; by August 1999, that had gone up above R$54 billion. The sale of Banespa in 2000 produced receipts of R$7 billion, reducing the balance. A final accounting, based on the time most of the transactions occurred, yields a total of R$54 billion in 1998 values. Goldfyn offers a comparable figure, expressed as a percentage of income, of 5.7 percent.[46] In table 3-8, an additional cost of R$8 billion is included for recapitalization of the country's largest bank, the publicly owned Bank of Brazil. This was not the last time it, or the Caixa Econômica, received such assistance. In the state restructuring program, about 78 percent of state indebtedness was converted into federal obligations. All sums are measured in constant *reais* of 1998.[47]

None of this exercise involved an increase in net federal debt, but gross federal debt went up. Total public debt was unaffected: state debt declined in 1997 and 1998, and the federal debt increased. Yet there was a real cost in this process, defined by two factors. One was the subsidy from charging states 6 percent in real interest when federal costs were higher. The other was possible future state inability, or willingness, to pay. This was plausible; after all, federal restructuring had happened twice before within a decade.

The immediate subsidy from lower interest rates comes to R$18 billion. The rest depends upon a projected thirty-year future for federal interest rates. An earlier estimate, made by Rigolon and Giambiagi, is between R$8 billion and R$20 billion; my calculation yields a higher subsidy of R$35 billion.[48] The probability of state default, and its extent, is difficult to assess. Bevilacqua and others calculate a cost of 1.5 percent of gross domestic product for a simulated distribution of varying outcomes with a mean payment of 4 percent, instead of the 6 percent specified in the contracts.[49]

The total bill for PROER and PROES comes to 10.4 percent of gross national product. A small part involved transfers from taxpayers to bankers. But by far the largest part, involved in refinancing the states, went back to citizens of São Paulo and other large states.

Trade Liberalization

In 1985 the General Agreement on Tariffs and Trade talks preliminary to the Uruguay Round were under way. There were also mounting differences with the United States about specific cases. Brazilian export subsidies were a matter of dispute. Additionally, there were accusations of illicit protection for domestic computer manufactures and software, and complaints by the U.S. Pharmaceutical Manufacturers Association about neglect of patent rights. That led to a successful U.S. lawsuit in 1987–88, based on the "Super 301" clause of the 1988 Omnibus Trade Act; actual penalties were averted only by Brazilian willingness to negotiate.

Modest Brazilian efforts at tariff reform began in 1988. The intent was to increase fiscal revenue by enforcing, rather than exempting, provisions of the tariff code. In 1985 two-thirds of all imports occurred under special regimes granting favored access. With a rising fiscal deficit, any source of revenue was welcome. Liberalization was already entering the scene internationally. The World Bank emphasized the virtue of greater trade as a source of better economic performance.[50]

In Brazil, the Commissão de Política Aduaneira proposed, at the end of 1987, a reform, the first since 1967, consisting of three parts: reduction of tariffs to eliminate redundant protection where the domestic price was less than the sum of the international price and the nominal tariff; elimination of the forty-two special import regimes, with the exception of those linked to international agreements, regional development, exports, and the Manaus Free Trade Zone; and elimination of all the additional taxes levied upon imports, such as the tax on exchange operations, the tax for port improvement, and an additional charge on freight revenues for improvement of the Brazilian merchant marine fleet.[51]

This reform, undertaken as the constitution neared completion, was scaled back as influential domestic sectors defended their interests. In June 1988, tariffs were cut to a lesser extent, and some taxes and a small number of the special import regimes were eliminated. Less than a fifth of imports were involved. Simultaneously, the government sought to encourage exports by exempting them from the sales tax.

Another reduction of tariffs occurred in 1989, as well as administrative consolidation. One of the reasons these changes were possible is a positive trade balance: in 1988 there was a surplus of more than $19 billion and even, for the first time, a large current account surplus. Imports as a percentage of gross national product had fallen to around 5 percent in 1988; there could not be great complaint.

What remained after these modest reforms were extensive nontariff barriers to trade. Appendix C, established by the Department of Foreign Trade of the Bank of Brazil (CACEX) and specifying goods unable to be imported, was reduced by half, to 1,200 items. Actual tariff revenues, because of exemptions, remained only a third of those implied by the structure in force in 1989.

Liberalization was part of Collor's commitment to modernization. A program to open the economy was announced at the start of his administration. That ended the list of prohibited imports and terminated many import duty exemptions granted to state enterprises and firms within special investment programs. Tariffs—by no means low—were imposed to replace quantitative restrictions, and issuance of import licenses became automatic. A revised tariff schedule was announced at the beginning of 1991. That entailed a continuing decline until 1994, when the average tariff, which had been 43 percent in 1988, would be reduced to 14 percent as a result of annual reductions.

Tariff categories were simplified. One, with zero protection, applied to products with high transport cost, goods not produced domestically, and commodities with low value added. A second, at a rate of 5 percent, included those products already at that level in 1990. A third rate of 10 percent would apply to agricultural products and their derivatives. Rates of 10, 15, and 20 percent were established for goods using zero-tariff products as their main inputs; this was done to reduce their rate of effective protection. Additional, and higher, rates of 30, 35, and 40 percent applied to fine chemicals, automobiles, and imports in competition with the domestic computer sector.

Tariff reduction imposed larger initial declines for intermediate and capital goods, with the reverse to follow in the next phases. Domestic producers were less apt to complain under these circumstances, while, through lower costs, investment might be stimulated. In February 1992, under Finance Minister Marcílio Moreira, scheduled dates for tariff reductions were accelerated in hopes of mitigating inflation. A further range of tariff reductions occurred in 1994 to limit price increases when domestic demand exceeded supply. Imports rose dramatically in 1994, contributing to the success of the Real Plan.

Table 3-9 shows the sequence of tariff reduction. From an initial, and somewhat exaggerated, level of more than 50 percent in 1987, the nominal tariff declines to 10 percent in 1994. Accompanying that trend is a dramatic fall in tariff variability, as measured by the mean deviation. Effective protection, the impact on value added of the combination of output and input tariffs, moves in parallel fashion. Note the decline in the standard deviation of tariffs across sectors: some industries lost special privileges. This global tariff liberalization was accompanied by a parallel movement toward regional integration through Mercosul.

All these changes added up to a bold commitment to liberalization. This conversion managed to survive the political imbroglio of the period. One reason the process worked was the offsetting movement of the real exchange rate. Continuing devaluation of the Brazilian currency is registered between the beginning of 1990 and the middle of 1992. As a result, domestic producers did not suffer from gradual tariff reduction. Afterward, as the Real Plan surfaced, this effect reversed; then, the circumstance of greater demand growth, fed by imports of foreign capital, satisfied most domestic interests.

TABLE 3-9.   Nominal and Effective Tariff Rates, 1987–94

Percent

Tariff	1987	1988	1989	1990	1991	1992	1993	1994
Nominal	54.9	37.7	29.4	27.2	20.9	14.1	12.5	10.2
SD[a]	21.3	14.6	15.8	14.9	12.7	8.2	6.7	5.9
Effective	67.8	46.8	38.8	37.0	28.6	17.1	15.2	12.3
SD[a]	53.8	36.6	44.5	60.6	36.5	17.2	13.5	8.4

Source: Honório Kume, Gunda Prani, and Carlos Frederico Bráz de Souza, "A política brasileira de importação no período 1987–1998," in *A abertura comercial brasileira no anos 1990: Impactos sobre emprego e salário*, edited by Carlos Corseiul and Honório Kume (Rio de Janeiro: IPEA, 2003), chap. 1.

a. Weighted by value added.

A second reason was the pattern of sectoral tariff reduction. Table 3-10 indicates the level of effective protection for industrial categories for 1987, 1990, and 1994. Care was taken to avoid adverse effects upon production of capital goods as a consequence of liberalization. Net protection for capital goods declines but remains greater than for consumer goods. Intermediate sectors fall to the lowest rates.[52] This Brazilian pattern is quite different from the Argentine one, where capital goods have lower rates in 1994: 7.4 percent versus 13.9 percent for intermediate goods and 18 percent for consumption goods. Comparable Brazilian values are 18.6 percent versus 7.3 and 14.6 percent, respectively.[53] Even in the midst of dramatic tariff reduction, the government did not ignore the special features of Brazilian industrialization.

Despite this liberalization, imports did not immediately react. They were limited by real devaluation and meager income growth. Not until the first months of 1993 did these determinants move in the other direction and provide positive incentives for import growth. What is evident is a sudden boom in entries from abroad in the twenty-one months from the second quarter of 1993 to the end of 1994. Over the last six months of 1994, the quantity of imports grew at an annual rate of some 50 percent!

The most important factor—reflected by increases in specific tariffs introduced to satisfy domestic protest—was growth in domestic demand. An abundant stock of international reserves and an increasing inflow of foreign resources paid for these imports. Short-term credits became available. Thus in 1994, 23.1 percent of imports were paid at terms of more than 180 days; only a year earlier, that proportion had been 18.5 percent.[54]

TABLE 3-10. **Levels of Effective Protection, by Import Type, 1987, 1990, and 1994**

Tariff in percent unless otherwise indicated

Category	1987	1990	1994
Consumer goods			
Apparel	117.2	67.0	24.5
Footwear	96.9	28.8	15.9
Pharmaceuticals and perfumes	91.7	35.8	3.0
Intermediate goods			
Steel products	30.9	15.8	8.8
Chemical products	12.3	29.4	9.2
Vehicle parts and components	73.3	44.6	21.8
Capital goods			
Machinery and tractors	47.5	41.5	22.4
Electrical equipment	88.5	62.5	25.8
Automobiles, trucks, and buses	308.1	351.1	27.0
Summary statistics			
Average weighted by value added	67.8	37.0	12.3
SD	53.8	60.6	8.4

Source: See table 3-9.

I measure the contribution of these two variables—price and income—to the outcome. A simple quarterly logarithmic regression relating the aggregate quantity of imports, LnM, to a lagged measure of their price, including the annual tariff declines, $LXR(-1)$, and to the level of national product, LY, over the period 1987–94 yields sensible results; there is also a correction, $AR1$, for autocorrelation of the residuals:

$$LnM = -4.58 - 0.69LXR(-1) + 2.46LY + 0.50AR1.$$
$$(0.72) \quad (3.17) \quad \quad (1.81) \quad \quad (2.37)$$

The elasticity of import response to price is 0.69, less than unity but significant; the income elasticity of imports is more than 2, reflective of increased demand for capital goods in the midst of domestic expansion.[55]

Import response helped successful stabilization, but it also set in motion adverse domestic reaction. Protection increased, particularly involving the imports of automobiles and other consumer durables. The adjustment did not go much beyond. Brazil, through membership in Mercosul and ratification of the Uruguay Round agreement, never returned to past protectionism. Liberalization became a constant with which Brazilian industry would have to cope.

An annual increase in Brazilian total factor productivity began to register. Was this a consequence of the strides taken toward liberalization? Donald Hay offers evidence in favor, putting his case as follows:

> Of the 50 percent growth in total factor productivity [1990–94], at most 5 percentage points can be accounted for by the cyclical effects, leaving some 45 percentage points to be explained. . . . Of these . . . perhaps 22 were due to the abandonment of non-tariff barriers in 1990 and 10 were due to the progressive reduction of effective tariffs over the period; the remaining 13 points may be attributable to the general liberalization of the economy, including privatization/deregulation in some sectors, e.g., the steel industry.[56]

This gives the elimination of nontariff barriers too large a role. When this occurred, so did compensating increases in protection. Frequently, they were redundant.[57] The meager increase in imports corroborates a limited effect. Too much importance is given to privatization as well. That had minor consequences. Only 5 percent of the manufacturing sector's labor force was affected, as the totals shown in table 3-2 confirm.

Too little credit is given to the progressive reduction of effective protection over the period. Liberalization was structured to stay, and entrepreneurs had to respond. Productivity change is procyclical, and in Brazil at that time even more so. Tariff reductions were seen as permanent. Firms adjusted by shedding workers and modernizing. There was a focus on introducing new technology, as occurred in the automobile sector. Many smaller firms, unable to cope, went out of business. Inflow of foreign direct investment increased in 1993 and especially in 1994. Domestic capital formation gave a greater weight to purchase of machinery than construction. Such an opening, so quickly after tariff reduction, would later be checked but not reversed.

Another version of this story is told by Mauricio Moreira and Paulo Correa.[58] They find a significant decline in sectorwide markups over costs between 1990 and 1995, except for nontraded goods. In some of the sectors, such as electronic equipment, automobiles, petrochemicals, electric machinery, and appliances, the decline in price that could be charged was dramatic. Industry groups were less powerful then, in the midst of successful stabilization and increases in domestic demand.

Eventually, compensating changes would occur. As trade progressively increased in importance, playing the leading role in Brazilian growth early in the Lula period, tariff reduction converted to tariff stability. A notable commercial surplus developed, and while it decreased progressively as growth accelerated, it still remains. Agricultural and mineral exports, aided by favorable prices, expanded as a share of earnings. More recently the problem has shifted as competitive Chinese imports have become an increasing challenge to domestic industry.

Changes under the Lula Administrations

With Lula's election in 2002 came a decisive moment. Would the new administration reverse the many changes in economic policy put in place, as markets feared? Or would continuity emerge?

Lula I: Plan A

President Lula began his term on January 1, 2003. He emphasized commitment to a new Brazil, more equal and more just. "Change" was the key word in his inaugural address. To emphasize his personal support for a social program to end hunger, he followed up with a cabinet meeting in the northeast: that was where the poverty problem was most severe and also was the place of Lula's birth.

By April a World Socialist website headline concluded: "Lula's first 100 days—austerity for the poor, tax cuts for the rich."[59] That response was not unique. Others on the Left were equally disturbed. Instead of promised change, all they could see was economic continuity. No default on external debt had happened, no break with the IMF and the World Bank had occurred, and no renationalizations were planned. The central bank maintained its quasi-independence and raised the SELIC rate twice in succession in January and February. The target primary surplus increased from 3.75 to 4.25 percent.

In that same month, state governors were called to Brasília to support a constitutional amendment to reduce the mounting social security deficit, this time by limiting claims of public workers. They did, but there was no agreement, then or later, on reform of the federal tax structure. This was not an administration planning an overhaul of economic policy but one apparently committed to perfecting the previous policies. That would earn Lula the title of traitor from those who had hoped for a social revolution.

TABLE 3-11. **Contributions to Growth of Gross National Product, 2002–06ª**

Percent per year

Component	2002	2003	2004	2005	2006
Family consumption	1.1	–0.4	2.3	2.6	3.1
Government consumption	0.9	0.2	0.8	0.4	0.5
Investment	–2	-0.3	1.9	–0.4	1.7
Exports	0.9	1.5	2.3	1.5	0.8
Imports	1.6	0.2	–1.6	–1.1	–2.1
Income	2.7	1.2	5.7	3.2	4

Source: Ipeadata (www.ipeadata.gov.br).

a. Calculated as previous year GDP weight times current growth rate. A positive entry for imports signifies reduction during the year. Actual growth is recorded in the last line.

Economic growth was limited in 2003. A large positive contribution of foreign trade was notable. With domestic demand restrained, sales abroad were encouraged. This external orientation averted a performance that could have been worse: personal consumption, by far the largest source of expenditure, declined during the year. In 2004 higher real export growth again was the feature. Much of the gain followed from a rising participation of primary products like soy, meat, and others; but real exports of manufactures were up even more. This experience was different. It had been many years indeed since exports had served as a leading sector.

Table 3-11 measures the contribution of different components of national product to annual growth from 2002 until 2006. In 2002 expansion of exports and reduced imports explain the economic growth achieved. In 2003 these two elements again are responsible for the small gain. An accelerating role for exports continues through the middle of 2005. Thereafter, their effect diminishes but remains significant. Offsetting imports are large when the economy accelerates, as in 2004 and 2006. Inputs to the industrial sector, through imports of intermediate and capital goods, especially rose.

Increases in export prices and improvement in the terms of trade added to the foreign trade surplus. Not until rising petroleum prices at the end of 2004 canceled the effects of primary product price increases did terms of trade turn downward. For the first time since 1992, surpluses in the commercial account exceeded return flows of interest and profits, and service items. A current account surplus appeared in the second half of

2002, rising to almost 2 percent of product in 2003; that surplus continued through 2007, when higher rates of product growth and consequent
larger imports led to its disappearance.

Accompanying export advance was extension to new markets and
inclusion of new goods. China entered as an important destination
for primary products. Other countries within Asia, growing in world
trade, also absorbed more. Manufactured products primarily flowed to
the United States and Latin America. A measure of concentration, the
Hirschman-Herfindahl index, is smaller over this period, reflecting the
reversal of the earlier focus upon Argentina and Mercosul. Diversification served Brazil's broader international objectives.

Foreign investment also recovered. In 2003 plans were put on hold,
awaiting better definition of what the Lula accession portended. As it
became clear the new administration welcomed entry of technology and
capital, and as recovery began, larger inflows occurred. In 2003 foreign
direct investment reached about $10 billion. In 2004 this total doubled,
and sustained an upward trajectory. Brazil, second only to China, was
eagerly sought out. Such foreign participation contributed to increased
domestic productivity.

The balance of payments accounts registered a new entry. Brazilian
commitments abroad began to increase. Between 2003 and 2006, accumulated Brazilian foreign capital expanded from $11 billion to $43 billion. In 2006 Brazil invested more abroad than entered the country. Brazilian multinational enterprises moved to the developed world; this went
beyond entry into Argentina and other Latin American countries.[60]

A large number of firms and countries were involved. Entries included
a range of sectors: manufacturing, mining, petroleum, and construction,
among others. Brazilian foreign assets ranked high, beginning to compete with Asian leaders like China, Singapore, and Taiwan. These were
primarily market-seeking or resource-seeking ventures, and were acquisitions rather than new enterprises. Ambev, the major Brazilian beer company, bought Belgian Interbrew. Petrobras was active in nine countries,
Gerdau in eleven. Odebrecht, Camargo Corrêa, and Grupo Votorantim
were others among a long list. Vale was the largest in terms of the foreign
assets acquired as of 2006, almost matched by Embraer. This was a very
different Brazil than just a decade ago.

As Brazil emerged from its 2003 minirecession with increased credit-
worthiness and greater domestic confidence, a decisive moment arrived.
In September 2004, the central bank announced an increase in the SELIC

rate to 16.25 percent; at almost the same time, the primary surplus, which had been running above 4.25 percent, was scheduled to rise to 4.5 percent. Contrary to the hopes of loyal party advocates, who had favored a smaller surplus and greater public investment, Brazil was now being guided to *slower* economic growth.

Public response was predictable. This decision to raise the SELIC rate led business groups—the Federation of Industries of São Paulo and the Brazilian National Confederation of Industry—to join with labor's Unified Workers' Central in opposition. Their argument was direct: why should Brazil face such high real rates of interest when all other countries in the world had lower costs? For the Far Left, the answer was straightforward: Marxist exploitation by the financial sector. Even for the less doctrinaire, high bank profits were troubling. The SELIC rate was but the tip of the iceberg. Interest costs for enterprises, especially the smaller ones, were always greater.

Many neo-Keynesians argued in favor of a Reaganomics-like policy. Less government primary surplus but more public investment would yield larger output, thereby preventing inflationary pressure. Moreover, tax collection would increase with consequent growth, and there would be funds to finance greater capital formation. Tight monetary and fiscal policy translated into low levels of expansion and dependence upon foreign investment. This logic was no more applicable to Brazil than it had been in the United States two decades before: there is a time gap before any increased capacity appears, and in that interim, increased demand can be satisfied only by imports, financed by increasing external debt.

These SELIC rates ascended until May 2005. A total rise of 375 basis points occurred, paralleling increases in United States. The differential rate did not change much, and there was little effect on foreign resource flow. There was no feared mass exit. Economic growth began to recede, investment expansion ceased, capacity utilization measures fell, and, most important, price inflation began to ebb.

Such success occurred at a cost. With the interest rate much greater than the growth rate, the debt ratio could not decline, despite a higher primary surplus. The burden of interest payments continued. Needless to say, with Argentina thriving after its debt default, that revived the issue of Brazil doing the same. There was hardly a lack of supporters for that option. Yet Minister of Finance Antonio Palocci and central bank head Henrique Meirelles did not waver in their commitment to inflation targeting and central bank independence.

Improvements occurred with final approval of new legislation that dealt with bankruptcy as well as lower-cost credit advances—*crédito con-signado*—to a rising lower middle class. Brazilian banks, like many of their Latin American counterparts, had a limited portfolio of loans. Public debt, entirely secure, and paying high real rates were preferable. Between 2003 and 2005, the share of voluntary bank commitments, as opposed to preallocated ones, rose steadily from 16 to 21 percent of GDP; total loans went from 26.2 to 31.2 percent. This increase has subsequently continued.

Having survived lower popularity ratings after the mensalão bribery scandal, and the resignation of Finance Minister Palocci, Lula sought reelection in 2006 against Governor Geraldo Alckmin of São Paulo. In the second round, Lula won more than 60 percent of the valid ballots.

Lula II: Accelerating Economic Growth

The Program for Accelerated Growth (Programa de Aceleração do Cresci-mento, or PAC), was announced by Lula soon after his second inauguration in 2007. This plan foresaw sustainable economic growth of 4.5 percent in 2007, and 5 percent in each of the years 2008–10. Beyond accelerating expansion and increasing employment, there was also explicit commitment to economic fundamentals: limited inflation, fiscal primary surpluses, and continued exports. The PAC covered all bases.

Heading up the entire effort was the minister of the Casa Civil (Civil Affairs), Dilma Rousseff, joined by the ministers of finance and planning, Guido Mantega and Paulo Bernardo. Their personnel would handle the administrative tasks. Transparency and regular six-month reports were pledged and subsequently fulfilled. Congressional passage of some legislation was required but would not be too difficult to secure since greater expenditure was involved.

The PAC specified five principal lines of activity. Of these, the one gaining most attention was the commitment to increased infrastructure investment of R$503.9 billion—around $235 billion—but involving few resources from the federal government. Most of the funds would come from public companies, like Petrobras, or from the private sector, with expansion of public-private cooperative projects. Federal resources would derive from reducing the primary surplus by 0.45 percent of GDP. Even so, the federal component of R$67.8 billion came to only 10 percent of the package.

This investment was divided into three parts. A first section was dedicated to logistics; this incorporated projects such as road reconstruction, airport facilities, and ports. The sum of R$58.3 billion was assigned to this objective, with federal participation at R$38 billion. A second section was related to energy; Petrobras was to be the principal source, involving new exploration as well as investment in existing facilities. There was also provision for expansion of ethanol production by building sugar refineries as well as biodiesel plants. Their contribution was to be R$274.8 billion, or almost 60 percent of the program, and direct federal contribution was nil. The third area was a social and urban component, designed to respond to needs for housing, sewerage, public lighting, and the like. This amounted to R$170.8 billion, with federal participation at R$34.8 billion.

Other parts of the PAC incorporated economic policies. One involved stimulus to the financial market. There was an expected decline in the SELIC rate controlled by the central bank; that was scheduled to fall to 5 percent in real terms by 2010, a nominal rate of 9.5 percent with inflation of 4.5 percent. And the investment rate would rise somewhat.

There was passing attention to fiscal reform and another meeting with governors. As before, that went nowhere. Regional differences persist on the basic issue: collection of value added taxes based upon production or consumption. The exporting states of the south stand against the importing states of the northeast. Within the National Congress, the latter have greater weight.

Another part of the program was intended to remove regulatory barriers to investment in infrastructure. Implicit was a curb to the efforts of Environmental Minister Marina Silva to prevent incursion into the Amazon and her insistence upon strict application of standards before permitting projects to commence. There was an early, negative response of environmental groups to this provision of the PAC. That opposition was heightened by Lula's clear bias in favor of investment, even when environmental harm might occur. The large Belo Monte hydropower project was, and remains, a particular bone of contention. Minister Silva resigned in 2008 and subsequently ran for president as a candidate of the Green Party.[61]

Commitments were made to reduce federal expenditures for personnel from a projected 5.3 percent of GDP in 2007 to 4.7 percent in 2010; that was to happen by limiting real increases in wages for all civil servants to 1.5 percent a year. Private sector social security benefits were projected to remain constant.[62]

Federal personnel outlays, however, did not diminish as a percentage of income but rather increased. The initial base was a much lower 4.4

percent. Such details were forgotten in the midst of rapidly rising income in 2010 and the proximity of national elections. Fiscal manipulation was overt in official calculation of the primary surplus for 2010, where the federal contribution for the BNDES was transformed into increased debt rather than actual expenditure.

The program of PAC infrastructure expenditures has also lagged. Despite their slower advance, TCU evaluations were sometimes unfavorable. These assessments blocked outlays in the next year due to irregularities. Relationships with the executive branch deteriorated: criticisms, and rebuttals, emanated from political parties, frequently during congressional committee meetings. That is hardly surprising. The PAC was a powerful instrument of Dilma's campaign for the presidency, and she traveled extensively, in the company of Lula, on its behalf. The title "mãe do PAC" (mother of the PAC) was bestowed on her, and she took advantage to emphasize her central role in increasing public investment. A repeated theme was criticism of the neoliberal Cardoso administration for eliminating all capacity to plan.[63]

There has been, almost inevitably, more promise than accomplishment in the PAC. Infrastructure projects require a long time for completion. Only about three-fifths of PAC resources had been spent by the end of 2009. Lula nonetheless launched a larger PAC II of R$1.4 trillion, or $886 billion, in March 2010, to extend well past 2014. This time, 70 percent is concentrated in the energy sector, with Petrobras and subsalt oil field investment benefiting. There are other pillars, as before, emphasizing housing construction, transportation, urban infrastructure, and sanitation. This commitment figured as a popular PT campaign promise.

Veja featured a critical account of the PAC in mid-2009.[64] Its argument is made on two grounds. First, the projects put together have little coherence. They encompass diverse and long advocated activities where political gains are as important as economic returns. The extension of the North-South Railroad, initially launched by President Sarney in 1987, is an example. Another is transposition of the Rio São Francisco to permit construction of two canals to the north and northeast.

A large part of the PAC was housing investment, much already under way in response to improving economic conditions and an area where Brazil has long lagged. In energy, where no federal investment is presumed, the activities of Petrobras dominate. This firm alone made up more than a third of total planned outlays. Petroleum and natural gas investments are the bulk of the program. These had been long planned, and their inclusion within the PAC does little to accelerate them. These also constitute the largest component of completed undertakings by a considerable margin.

Second, federal expenditures were not as large as planned. The government has regularly pointed to large increases in its realized investments over recent years, from 0.64 percent of GDP in 2006 to 3.3 percent in 2010. But only a small part of those outlays has shown up in PAC projects. Federal government participation was supposed to reach 14 percent, but after four full years, it only amounted to about 10 percent of expenditures.[65]

PAC II points to higher average growth rates, lower real interest rates, and even an overall fiscal surplus by 2013. In the midst of rising inflation, increasing central bank SELIC rates, and promises of tighter fiscal policy, achieving these goals becomes increasingly unlikely. Planning is not quite as easy as Dilma suggested during her campaign.

Industrial Policy

As macroeconomic policy continued unchanged, the Lula administration, not surprisingly, sought to innovate elsewhere. The introduction of a comprehensive industrial policy—touted as the first since the Kubitschek years—served that purpose. An initial document was circulated in November 2003, and on March 31, 2004, the Program for Industry, Technology, and Foreign Trade (PITCE) was officially launched.

The PITCE's logic depended on two principles. One was a balance of payments constraint and inadequate access to essential imports; the other was the ability to preselect winners: sectors chosen to receive support because of their dynamic effects upon industrial growth as a whole. In the 1970s, intermediate goods had been singled out; now capital goods could claim special help, along with software, electronic components, and pharmaceuticals. Biotechnology and nanotechnology were mentioned for the future, and biomass and other renewable energies were later added, reflecting the interests of Petrobras and ethanol producers.

The PITCE was a collaborative initiative, launched by the Ministry of Development, Industry, and Commerce but engaging other ministries, in addition to the BNDES, the Institute for Applied Economic Research (IPEA), and other agencies. The policy was intended to deal with regional differences and to even the distribution of income. There were eleven programs and fifty-seven specific measures. These involved reduction of taxes and tariffs for capital goods for which no comparable domestic version could be found, as well as access to credits on a privileged basis. Congressional action added implementing legislation.

Matters moved slowly within the bureaucracy. Moreover, exports had risen as a driving force. Fabio Erber credits the latter for diminished interest: "The evolution of international demand for raw materials and for semi-manufactured goods eliminated the foreign exchange constraint and dampened the enthusiasm for technology-intensive sector policies. . . . The role of PITCE as a vector of change of the productive structure has been reduced. . . . The emphasis has shifted from a developmental neo-Schumpeterian approach to an endogenous-cum-natural-comparative-advantage growth."[66]

A different and more modern perception of industrial policy also competed. For Glauco Arbix, among others, industrial policy was a strategy of dynamic comparative advantage for the medium and long term. This meant attention to individual firms and their strategy for attaining technological and productivity advances. This was the style of research around the world; now Brazil would join in the undertaking. International competitiveness, rather than domestic tariff protection and governmental subsidies, was the key to success. To attain that objective required large increases in expenditures for research and development, and continuing investment in better quality education.[67]

Despite renewed economic growth, industrial policy did not flourish. Accordingly, Lula announced yet another program formulated by BNDES president Luciano Coutinho in May 2008. This went beyond the earlier PITCE. More resources and greater direction were incorporated in the Política de Desenvolvimento Produtivo (Productive Development Policy).

The PAC and the Productive Development Policy were intended as policy complements. Infrastructure and energy were central to the former; industrial development was the focus of the latter. The BNDES was to nearly double its annual lending over the next three years. Resources were to increase. The Inter-American Development Bank provided some support. Total Brazilian investment was scheduled to rise from less than 18 percent of GDP to 21 percent, with the BNDES playing a central part. That would permit sustainable development at an annual rate of 5 percent.

The emphasis was on innovation and increased productivity. This was partially a return to the policy in the 1970s when industrial sectors received considerable government support. This time, however, exports, particularly of small and medium-size enterprises, were emphasized.

Competitiveness was central. The private sector would increase its research and development outlays in parallel. A number of sectoral executive committees were created.

This effort barely got beyond a first meeting, under Dilma Rousseff, in October 2008. The reason was clear: global economic recession had struck. While the BNDES would greatly increase its loans in 2009 and 2010, the emphasis had shifted to stimulating demand rather than innovative breakthroughs on the side of supply. In 2011 a limit to federal outlays is again being enforced, and the BNDES will experience slower growth. Industrial policy, like the PAC, may have to wait longer before it is fully launched, although it remains one of Dilma's special interests.

Expansion, the Great Recession, and Rapid Recovery

Accelerating economic growth in 2007 satisfied domestic interests. Brazilian performance exceeded forecasts of the IMF and international banks. Table 3-12 records this expansion on a quarterly basis. Expenditures rose, and for the first time since the early years of the Real Plan, imports rose as fixed investment increased. Expanding consumption, however, was the real secret: its contribution to total growth steadily rose between the last quarter of 2006 and the first quarter of 2008, from 2.7 to 6.2 percent a year. This meant a return to an increasing current account deficit. Total demand began progressively to exceed supply.

Employment opportunities surged, as 2 million formal sector jobs were created. Measured unemployment fell to its lowest level since 2002. The automobile sector expanded, selling 30 percent more cars and trucks than during 2006. Other consumer durable purchases grew. Holiday sales at the end of 2007 were higher than they had been in a decade. Lula, in his year-ending address, noted the conjunction of economic growth with social inclusion under his leadership. That combination was difficult to surpass; memories of the mensalão scandal totally faded.

Brazil accomplished two somewhat contradictory objectives simultaneously. SELIC interest rates continued to decline regularly beginning in October 2005, falling from 19.75 percent to a record low 11.25 percent two years later; that brought the real rate down from over 13 percent to less than 6. International reserves, attracted by the higher returns available in Brazil, began a steep ascent. By the beginning of 2008, they had doubled and stood at a record $190 billion. Not surprisingly, the exchange rate appreciated.

TABLE 3-12. Quarterly GDP, 2006–10ᵃ

Percent

Year and quarter	Relative to same quarter, previous year	Relative to previous quarter
2006		
Q1	4.3	1.8
Q2	1.9	0.3
Q3	4.7	1.6
Q4	4.8	1.2
2007		
Q1	5.1	2.0
Q2	6.4	1.6
Q3	6.1	1.1
Q4	6.7	1.8
2008		
Q1	6.4	1.7
Q2	6.5	1.8
Q3	7.1	1.6
Q4	0.8	−4.2
2009		
Q1	−3.0	−1.9
Q2	−2.8	1.9
Q3	−1.8	2.6
Q4	5.0	2.5
2010		
Q1	9.3	2.2
Q2	9.2	1.6
Q3	6.7	0.4
Q4	5.0	0.7

Source: Brazilian Institute of Geography and Statistics, Contas Nacionais Trimestrais, April 2011.
a. Seasonally adjusted.

Some saw this central bank policy as total folly. Those reserves obtained small interest returns invested abroad, while the counterpart debt paid a higher rate. This was good reason for foreign investors to exchange dollars for *reais* and to benefit from an appreciating currency. The declining interest rate, as a consequence, had not led to depreciation helpful to the domestic industrial sector. For these critics, domestic interest rates could, and should, fall sharply, thereby eliminating the entry of foreign capital and encouraging some departure. At the end of 2007, a modest sovereign wealth fund was created to help accomplish this purpose.

This debate returned to past vociferous levels when the central bank ceased interest rate reductions in October 2007 and began to increase the SELIC rate in April 2008. By then, the international economy was under increasing pressure. Bear Stearns had failed within the United States, and U.S. Federal Reserve interest rates had fallen close to zero. Europe and Japan were in parallel difficulty. The European Union faced excess housing construction in Great Britain, Ireland, and Spain, among others, and mounting problems surged in the financial sector. Japan was faltering with lagging exports and inadequate domestic demand.

A new view gained Brazilian adherents: this business cycle was different. While the advanced economies were admittedly awash with problems, the developing countries, for the first time, could remain exempt. South-South trade was expanding, and outward capital flows from China, Brazil, and other surplus countries were evidence of their importance. Rapid increases in petroleum and commodity prices during 2007 and the beginning of 2008 ensured access to imports, permitting domestic income to exceed production. There was a clear decoupling within global economic growth. Independent policies were not only possible but necessary.

Brazil's central bank did not concur and, fearful of rising inflation, moved to restrain expansion by elevating the SELIC rate from 11.25 to 13.75 percent by September 2008. Paulo Gala, writing in April, signaled the division within the government: "Currently in Brazil heterodox economists form the majority in President Lula's government. . . . The Central Bank is the bunker of orthodox economists in Brazil today."[68] As SELIC rates were going up, the Ministry of Finance raised the tax on capital inflows to discourage them. As interest rates declined elsewhere, Brazil's real level increased. The exchange rate appreciated to levels not experienced in a decade.

Soon the international financial market was in total disarray. Brazilian attention was focused on the immediate term. Lehman Brothers had failed within the United States, followed by AIG and others. The U.S. government massively intervened. Banks refused to lend to other banks, even overnight. Many around the world were predicting another Great Depression—there was impressive statistical similarity to the descent in 1929–30.

Suddenly, global economic growth everywhere was in doubt, including within the South. Financial coordination among world central banks occurred: credits were extended everywhere to impede an intertwined failure of international banks. Mergers saved weaker institutions; in some countries, outright nationalization occurred. Stock markets plunged. Exchange rates altered, as dollar holdings were deemed preferable to others. Direct foreign investment ceased. The advance of petroleum and commodity prices came to an end and began to reverse.

In this difficult moment, the Brazilian central bank emerged as a strength. With its impressive international reserves, the bank could intervene without fear of running short. To backstop that freedom, the U.S. Federal Reserve announced a sum of $30 billion of swaps available to Brazil. Domestic financial mergers occurred: Unibanco was purchased by Itaú; Nossa Caixa was acquired by the Bank of Brazil, as was Banco Votorantim. There were central bank credits for export finance. Enterprises like Aracruz and others that had hedged expecting a stronger *real* received support. Reserve requirements were reduced.

The Brazilian financial system was spared. This did not impede a sizable decline in domestic activity. In the fourth quarter of 2008, the economy moved sharply downward, as shown in table 3-12. The fall was at an annual rate of more than 14 percent, but other countries performed worse. Most Asian economies contracted, Japan and South Korea especially, as international trade plummeted. Investment fell off sharply in Brazil, as it continued to do at the beginning of 2009.

Projections forward for Brazil in 2009 varied. Morgan Stanley foresaw an annual decline of more than 4 percent; most other analysts were less extreme, but virtually all, except for a few Brazilian optimists, made negative projections. With large declines anticipated for the developed world, and international trade in ruins, such estimates appeared reasonable. Only China and India, relying on large-scale government intervention, were deemed able to advance at positive, but lesser, rates.

Brazil, along with most countries in the world, opted for larger public expenditures and reductions in taxes to encourage consumption, particularly of durable goods. A smaller primary surplus and a larger fiscal deficit did not evoke criticism: countercyclical response was clearly correct when activity, particularly within industry, had fallen so. Monetary policy eased dramatically. The SELIC rate fell 500 basis points until July 2009, reducing the real rate to its lowest level ever. Inflation fell after acceleration during 2008. Although first quarter 2009 growth was again negative, the rate had fallen to an annualized 4 percent.

Global news gradually became more positive. Financial disaster had been avoided, if only barely. There was strong recovery in stock markets beginning in March. With inflation minimal, developed country interest rates continued at virtually zero nominal levels and negative real levels. Private credit markets remained slow to react, and unemployment stayed higher than expected. The London meeting of the Group of Twenty in April 2009 did not push for actions to ensure economic revival but took satisfaction from the generalized response.

Brazilian recovery was apparent by that point. Based on two consecutive negative quarters, a recession had technically occurred, but a strong upturn continued thereafter. In table 3-12, one can see this accelerating growth beginning in April. Expectations altered and production, with domestic consumption leading the process, responded.

Government countercyclical intervention worked. The Bank of Brazil, Caixa Econômica, and the BNDES all lent more, and the private sector retracted. Total credit increased. This change went along with larger public expenditure. The BNDES benefited from long-term treasury loans, increasing the gross public debt but not the net. Annual lending doubled over 2008, at subsidized TJLP real rates close to zero. Some went to public enterprises in the electricity sector, but most went to large private firms. An implicit industrial policy—of larger magnitude than conceived—has thus occurred. The full consequences will play out in the future.[69]

For 2010 growth has registered 7.5 percent. Favorable gains in the terms of trade enabled domestic income to rise even faster. Domestic inflation has picked up. At the beginning of 2011, the central bank increased interest rates; market expectations indicate they will pause by midyear. The government is also seeking to impose a tighter fiscal policy to help restrain demand. Many analysts are doubtful of success: among other factors, a much higher minimum wage, averted in 2011, will go into effect at the beginning of 2012. Dilma's first year in office is beginning to fray. Expected growth has been lowered by the central bank to 4 percent.

Significant petroleum finds will contribute only in the medium term. These were first reported at the end of 2007. The Tupi oil field, a deep, subsalt layer discovered far offshore, was estimated to contain, minimally, some 5–8 billion barrels. Later exploration and new fields have added to this total. Petrobras has been cautious in its estimates, suggesting an increase to something like 30–35 billion barrels. Politicians have shown less restraint. In the last year, they have scaled up the projection first to 50, then to 80, and, most recently, to 100 billion barrels, as the National Congress debated division of the resultant profits.

New rules governing future development of these subsalt discoveries have been formalized. All unassigned areas for future exploration, something like 71 percent, will revert to a small national unit, Petrosal. In turn, Petrobras will become sole operator in these fields. That is the reason it needs massive future resources. Much of the resultant investment, in ships, oil rigs, and the like, will be directed to domestic firms.

Foreign oil companies can bid for licenses to participate in joint ventures with Petrobras, which will retain a minimum 30 percent stake. They will no longer have an ownership claim. Future contracts will permit a rate of return for their investment but one much lower than historically earned. The justification is the proven resource; there is no longer a need to compensate for uncertainty. Production sharing agreements will be valid for a period of up to thirty-five years.

The government has granted rights for exploration for 5 billion barrels to Petrobras. In return, it received equity. Petrobras raised a record $70 billion in new shares at the end of September 2010. Of that sum, $43 billion was the increased share in equity held federally in return for concession of drilling rights. The Brazilian share of Petrobras, including pension funds and other units, went up from 40 to 49 percent, with control of almost two-thirds of voting shares.[70]

Net resources from petroleum sales will be set aside in a social fund, modeled on Norway's. Expenditures will accelerate Brazilian social and educational progress, with special attention to investment in science and technology and combating poverty. Final allocations are to be determined. Such a fund is intended to avert appreciation of the exchange rate—"Dutch disease"—that has afflicted other oil producers. Brazil will rank among the ten largest oil exporters in 2014 and needs balanced economic progress.

A question remains: how large will oil profits be? That depends on the yet uncertain costs of drilling for oil at a depth of more than seven kilometers through sand, rock, and a layer of salt. After the BP disaster in the Gulf of Mexico, those are likely to rise as environmental concerns intrude. Petrobras, with all its skills, will require technological help as it seeks to develop this resource. Early estimates suggested expenses as high as $60 a barrel. With oil prices soaring to $150 a barrel in the summer of 2008, cost disappeared as a worry. With prices currently above $100 (as of this writing), great profit appears inevitable. But some have projected a future price retreat as alternative sources come online and cheaper natural gas begins to compete.

In 2010 Guilherme Estrela, head of exploration and production at Petrobras, put forth a more favorable assessment that reduced by half previous cost estimates. As he saw the situation, "The challenge of the pre-salt is not technology." Instead, given all the component parts of the exercise, including floating production units, "it [just] requires a new way of looking at things."[71] That positive assessment remains to be fully tested.

Concluding Observations

Over the last twenty-five years, the Brazilian economy has successfully modernized. This is a new Brazil.

Inflation has ended as a way of life; primary surpluses recur year after year. International trade has grown and diversified. Foreign investment has become positive; indeed, Brazil, in the last decade, has even emerged as a source and not just a destination. Agriculture, mining, and petroleum have all increased as sources of international supply. Industry and much infrastructure are now in the hands of private entrepreneurs. The industrial sector has revived and gained in productivity rather than disappearing.

Cardoso and Lula, despite their different political perspectives and priorities, have presided over a coherent evolution. That is true not only in macroeconomics but also at the microeconomic level. Bank credit has increased, bankruptcy legislation has changed, and regulations govern mergers and acquisitions and other activity. The ideological divide of the past has become narrower, and policies are more stable.

Even the Great Recession has not deterred this advance. Brazil now will have to follow through. High rates of future economic progress will require larger domestic savings and investment capable of competing with a rising China and India. Further advances in productivity will need a better-educated labor force and application of modern technology, acquired internationally as well as locally. The public sector will have to control consumption expenditure and convert to more productive outlay: transportation, schools, public health, and housing add up to massive needs. At the same time, Brazil will have to commit to the global economy and opportunities in the North as well as the South.

Positive development does not automatically repeat. Continuity is not ensured. That is a clear lesson from Brazilian economic experience in the 1980s and early 1990s. Good economic policy makes a big difference.

4

Sustaining Social Progress

The New Republic faced an inherited social debt. Prior Brazilian economic growth led to only marginal gains in education, health, and old age security. Advances occurred, but almost always, they were skewed in favor of the well situated. As a single indicator, the high degree of Brazilian inequality stands out. Earlier policy had not compensated for the sometimes harsh outcomes of the marketplace.

The Constitution of 1988, as promulgated, was unequivocal in its commitment to social progress. Implementation was another matter. Only after economic issues began to be resolved after 1994 could progress be made. Expenditures for education and health mounted, but quality of services has remained a problem. Old age pensions have expanded but not in an equalizing manner. On a happier note, Bolsa Família has had success in attacking poverty, and movement toward greater equality has become regular.

These advances date to the administrations of Cardoso and Lula. They happened despite differences between those preferring outright intervention and those favoring greater efficiency. In the recent electoral campaign, one could note evolving substantive convergence. Stabilizing social progress has begun to occur.

Successive sections in this chapter treat education, health, social security pensions, and poverty and inequality.

Education

Brazil confronts a need to move toward quality universal elementary and secondary education. Not only is it necessary to ensure continuing gains in productivity in the years ahead, but such an extension will alleviate the high degree of inequality and begin to eliminate poverty. Few countries have successfully transformed without educational advance.

Primary Schooling

In the two decades subsequent to 1980, close to 15 million additional students were enrolled in primary schools; up to the end of 1994, more than 9 million gained entry, an increase of 40 percent over previous levels. Higher rates of enrollment, not prior demographic changes, explain more than three quarters of this increase. Table 4-1 illustrates this change over time. By the turn of the century, Brazil received a UNESCO award for achieving full attendance for those aged 7–14.

Primary school enrollment increased faster after 1985 than before. Increased state and municipal expenditure was responsible for almost all that gain. The federal connection came through ancillary programs such as provision of supplementary meals within schools, distribution of textbooks and materials, and, most important, direct transfer of resources. The Calmon Amendment specified an allocation of 13 percent of federal tax receipts to states and municipalities; these units were to spend a quarter of the funds for education. In the Constitution of 1988, the federal contribution rose to 18 percent. Those obligations entered into place gradually, and they were not entirely satisfied; intended transfers occasionally were diverted to other ends.

Brazil confronted two principal problems in achieving universal primary education. One was regional differences; the other was grade repetition. The first of these factors led to a low national attendance rate when dissimilar results in the northeast and the south were combined. That was good reason for increasing federal transfers since they were predominantly allocated to the northeast.[1] Grade repetition, the second factor, yielded high gross enrollment rates, even exceeding 100 percent, when the total number of primary school students was divided by the relevant group aged seven through fourteen; however, relatively few students, typically from better-off families, advanced in a continuous progression and concluded their education.

Figure 4-1 shows, for a series of years, how these two features affected attendance in the entry-level grades. Net enrollment (including only those of the relevant age for the grade) in the south and southeast in 1981 is above 80 percent, while age-grade distortion in the fourth year is about 30 percent.[2] For the northeast, the record is far inferior, beginning with a net enrollment of less than 60 percent, with an age-grade distortion of similar magnitude. Note the regional evolution over the period: the northeast shows large increases in net enrollment while the degree of grade repetition hardly changes. The same comparative conclusion is valid for grades 5–8.

Costs were considerable: effective charges per year of education attained were 40 percent greater than the nominal levels due to average repetition rates of a third and more reported in table 4-1. Students completing four years of education in the early 1990s typically spent more than six years in school, and those completing eight years, a much smaller group, spent more than eleven years doing so. Many older students dropped out rather than remain in classes with younger ones.

Increasing primary school enrollments incorporated children from poorer families. Only those not dependent on income contributions from working children sent them to school. Enrollment from this group was limited: in the 1992 National Household Sample Survey (PNAD), participation of lower-income families was 22 percentage points below that of the middle class and above. Experimentation later began in Campinas and the Federal District with the Bolsa Escola, a program of income transfers to encourage students to stay in school. As will be shown, this effort has been quite successful and has progressively narrowed this differential.

Extension of primary education to all awaited the Cardoso government and Constitutional Amendment 14 in 1996. A law in the same year, the Lei de Diretizes e Bases da Educação Nacional (Guidelines and Basis for National Education) implemented the changes. Responsibilities for all three units of the federation were specified. Simply put, an integrated structure took form: municipalities would focus on primary education; states, on the secondary level; and the federal government, on universities. The federal government, through an active education ministry, would promote regional uniformity by imposing minimal expenditures per pupil. Some resources would come from the center to ensure those minimums, but the major responsibility for outlays devolved to state and municipal governments.

T A B L E 4 - 1 .   Primary Education, Various Years, 1980–95

Units as indicated

Year	Total number (millions)	Source of funding (percent)			
		Federal	State	Municipal	Private
Total enrollment					
1980	22.6	0.7	52.8	33.6	12.8
1985	24.8	0.5	57.3	30.2	12.1
1991	29.2	0.3	57.2	30	12.4
1994	31.9	0.1	56.5	31.8	11.6

	Total number (thousands)	Distribution (percent)		Student-teacher ratio
		Urban	Rural	
Teachers				
1980	884	76.6	23.4	25.6
1985	1,016	76.4	23.6	23.8
1991	1,296	78.4	21.6	22.5
1994	1,378	79.6	20.4	21.9

	Percent		
	4–6 years	7–14 years	15–17 years
Participation by age group			
1980	19.1	81.1	56.3
1985	28.6	81.8	59.2
1992	35.8	86.6	59.7
1995	53.5	90.2	66.6

	Percent	
	Grades 1–4	Grades 5–8
Net enrollment rates		
1981	74	31
1985	83	34
1990	86	40
1995	92	50

	Percent		
	Completion	Repetition	Drop-out
Student flow rates			
1985	58	36	6
1990	60	34	6
1995	65	31	4

	Percent	
	Grade 1	Grade 4
Age-grade distortion[a]		
1981	28	40
1985	20	34
1990	18	32
1995	15	32

Sources: Ministry of Education (MEC)/National Institute of Educational Studies and Research (INEP)/Statistical Office of Education and Culture (SEEC). See also the World Bank and National Household Sample Survey (PNAD) sources referred to in text.

a. Two years or more above expected age.

F I G U R E   4 - 1 .   Net Enrollment, First through Fourth Grade, and Age-Grade Distortion by Region, 1981–93[a]

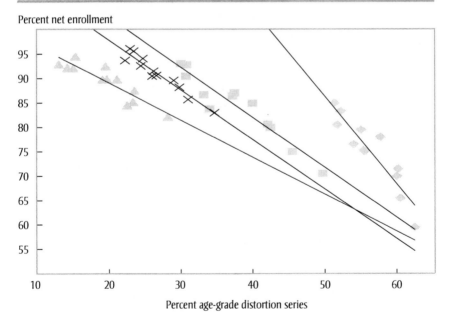

Percent net enrollment

Percent age-grade distortion series

Source: Estimated from Sergio Soares, "Aprendizado e seleção: Uma análise da evolução educacional brasileira," Discussion Paper 1185 (Brasília: IPEA, 2006), p. 24.

a. Geographical distribution of net enrollment as follows: *diamonds*, northeast; *squares*, central-west; *triangles*, south; *Xs*, southeast.

The National Fund for Primary Education Development and Improvement of the Teaching Profession (FUNDEF) was created in 1998 to finance the program. It received 15 percent of a considerable sum: state value added taxes plus mandated federal transfers to states and municipalities plus compensation for export taxes. The federal government further complemented these funds to ensure a minimum level. In practice, this meant federal allocations to poorer municipalities of states in the north and northeast.

At least 60 percent of the funds went for teachers' salaries; federal standards for their training and education now applied. Average wages for teachers in municipal schools in the northeast in 1997 were less than a third of those paid in the southeast for grades 1–4; they were only slightly better for grades 5–8. One could hardly hope for qualitative improvement under such circumstances.

The goal of full attendance was accomplished, along with reduction of regional differences. For Brazil the proportion of those aged seven to fourteen in school rose from 90.2 to 97 percent between 1995 and 2002; all of the regions showed increases. Empirical studies show statistical significance for the effect of federal transfers in augmenting enrollment in the states and municipalities.[3] Over these same years, the share of primary enrollments funded by municipalities increased as state responsibility for basic education declined. At the beginning, almost two-thirds of expenses were financed by the states; currently, that proportion is reversed.

Teacher qualifications also demonstrate progress; the number of teachers without university training has decreased, notably within the northeast. In that region in 1995, only about 20 percent of the teachers had gone beyond secondary school; by 2005 the number had grown to almost half. The reason was dual: better recruitment for the lower grades and more teachers, better educated, in the higher grades. Special programs to encourage training had an effect.

Table 4-2 catalogs the later distortion rate. By 2005 circumstances had changed for the better; the major improvement was halving the rate in grades 1–4. Within the southeast and the south, the gains were such that students were close to normal progress. But the northeast in 2005 remained far behind. In grades 5–8, progress within the northeast again was less. This regional distinction remains and continues to argue for federal help.

High repetition rates persist. Almost 45 percent of students in elementary school experienced delay in 1995; a decade later, the proportion fell

TABLE 4-2. Distortion Rates, Primary Education, Various Regions, 1996–2005

Percent

Year and type	Brazil			Northeast			Southeast			South		
	Primary	Grades 1–4	Grades 5–8	Primary	Grades 1–4	Grades 5–8	Primary	Grades 1–4	Grades 5–8	Primary	Grades 1–4	Grades 5–8
1996												
Total	47.0	43.8	53.1	65.7	63.9	70.6	34.8	27.3	45.7	27.2	20.5	37.2
Public	50.7	47.0	57.7	70.9	68.5	77.8	38.0	29.8	50.1	29.3	22.0	40.2
Private	17.0	14.3	21.0	29.4	25.7	35.7	9.1	6.1	13.1	4.9	3.4	7.0
1998												
Total	47.2	43.4	52.6	65.1	62.7	70.2	34.4	24.7	48.8	26.5	9.0	34.7
Public	50.8	46.5	57.1	69.4	66.3	76.4	37.7	27.2	49.2	28.5	20.4	37.5
Private	12.6	9.8	15.6	21.6	18.0	26.0	8.5	5.6	11.5	3.9	2.6	5.2
2000												
Total	41.7	36.2	48.9	59.8	54.4	69.0	27.0	17.9	36.3	23.5	16.1	31.6
Public	44.9	38.8	53.0	63.6	57.4	74.2	29.7	19.6	40.0	25.2	17.2	34.0
Private	9.9	6.8	11.2	15.0	12.1	18.5	6.4	4.4	8.4	3.6	2.7	4.5
2002												
Total	36.6	29.8	45.0	53.6	45.1	65.5	22.3	15.0	30.2	20.3	13.3	27.8
Public	39.6	32.1	48.9	57.2	48.0	70.1	24.7	16.5	33.6	21.8	14.2	30.0
Private	7.3	5.8	9.1	11.9	9.6	14.8	5.4	3.9	7.0	3.0	2.2	3.7
2004												
Total	31.5	24.9	39.5	45.6	36.9	57.4	19.6	13.4	26.5	18.3	11.9	25.2
Public	34.2	27.0	43.1	49.0	39.6	61.6	21.7	14.8	29.5	19.6	12.7	27.1
Private	6.4	5.0	7.9	9.8	7.9	12.3	4.9	3.6	6.2	2.8	2.2	3.4
2005												
Total	30.0	24.2	37.1	43.9	36.1	54.2	18.2	12.7	24.5	17.9	12.0	24.2
Public	32.7	26.3	40.5	47.3	38.9	58.4	20.2	14.0	27.3	19.2	12.8	26.0
Private	6.1	4.9	7.5	9.2	7.6	11.5	4.9	3.8	6.1	2.8	2.0	3.5

Source: MEC/INEP, Censo Escolar, for various years (http://sitio.educacenso.inep.gov.br/index.asp).

to 25 percent. More than a third of children enrolled in the eighth grade were older than fifteen years. Despite movement toward automatic promotion, an average student requires ten years to complete the eight-year curriculum. That is better than before; in 1991 it was 11.7 years with a completion rate of only 38 percent. The national average is two additional years for completion, but it is only one year in the south compared to three in the northeast.[4]

These efforts to universalize education underwent objective evaluation. Every two years, the Sistema de Avaliação de Educação Básica (SAEB), established in 1988 with a grant from the United Nations Development Program (UNDP) and applied, but little utilized, in 1991 and 1993, was given to a sample of students in the fourth and eighth grades, and at the end of secondary school.[5] Every two years from 1995 on, SAEB provided data to evaluate progress. Student achievement in Portuguese and mathematics was measured. There was additional information from questionnaires distributed to students and school personnel, along with records of school characteristics.

Student socioeconomic background and school environment influenced outcomes exactly as one would anticipate. Children of mothers with higher levels of formal education performed better. Superior physical and human capital within the schools had positive effects. Specific findings vary among the studies and depend upon the sample selected and the statistical technique applied to the data, but this broad conclusion holds.[6]

These SAEB results, regularly published after 1995, were not encouraging. Table 4-3 provides a temporal sequence for the two primary levels, the fourth and eighth years. The tabulation starts at a low level and declines until the last results for 2007 show a slight improvement. Half the students fall below a critical level; less than a tenth scored well. Of those performing well, most come from private schools where the scores are, on average, 25 percent higher than in public schools.

There may be a positive side to this pattern. Because increased enrollment involved those previously excluded, overall improvement was unlikely. P. R. Souza, in his evaluation, gets it right: "That does not signify that the system has worsened in quality with entry of students from less well educated families. From the start, new entries into the system are much better off than they were before they began schooling, for they are learning. Their initial performance, however, is inferior to that of other students who already were in school and come from better educated families."[7]

TABLE 4-3. SAEB Scores, 1995–2007; IDEB Scores, 2005–07[a]

| Year | IDEB | | SAEB | | | |
| | 4th year | 8th year | Portuguese | | Mathematics | |
			4th year	8th year	4th year	8th year
1995	...	...	188	256	191	253
1997	...	...	186	250	191	250
1999	...	...	171	233	181	246
2001	...	...	165	235	176	243
2003	...	...	169	232	177	245
2005	3.8	3.5	172	232	182	240
2007	4.2	3.8	176	234	193	247

Source: MEC/INEP.
a. IDEB, Index of Basic Education Progress.

Elementary education has not disappeared as a concern, despite universal enrollment. Large numbers of students, most from poor families, still lag behind. Their functional literacy is limited and as a consequence, so is their capacity to compete for better jobs with attendant higher income. Many, moreover, do not finish the minimum years of schooling required by law. In 2004 less than 40 percent of students in the northeast were expected to complete eight years compared to almost 70 percent in the southeast. For Brazil the overall average increased to 54 percent.[8]

The consequence weighs upon the public fisc. One estimate cites the cost of primary grade repetition at R$12.6 billion in 2006, or a quarter of public expenditure that year on basic education.[9] More important, there are the longer-term inadequacies of a future labor force competing with the rising powers of China and India.

Secondary Schools

Before 1985 participation in secondary school was an exception. Secondary attendance first began to expand in the early 1990s (see tables 4-4 and 4-5). Many public secondary school students enrolled in night classes taken after the work day. Approximately 60 percent of all secondary students attended evening classes in 1994; the proportion was higher in the northeast. Almost a third of students were older than predicted by a sequence of regular promotion.

A high, although declining, proportion of secondary attendees enrolled in private schools. In 1985 that fraction reached almost a third, falling

T A B L E   4 - 4 .   Secondary Education, Various Years, 1980–95

Units as indicated

Year	Total (millions)	Source of funding (percent)				Faculty (thousands)
		Federal	State	Municipal	Private	
Secondary initial enrollment						
1980	2.8	3.1	47	3.5	33.3	198
1985	3	3.3	59	4.4	30.4	206
1991	3.8	2.7	65.6	4.7	27	259
1994	5.1	2.1	71.8	5.3	20.8	320

	Enrollment total (millions)	Type (percent)	
		Evening	Private
Secondary attendance			
1989	3.5	58	46.3
1994	5.1	59.4	33.4

	Percent		
	Promotion	Repetition	Drop-out
Secondary student flow rates			
1981	67	25	8
1985	60	31	9
1990	60	32	8
1995	65	27	8

	Total (thousands)	Private (thousands)	Percent part time
Secondary graduates			
1980	541	302	55.8
1984	585	271	46.3
1990	659	253	38.4
1993	851	232	27.3

Source: MEC/INEP, Censo da Educação Superior, various years (www.inep.gov.br/web/guest/superior-censosuperior) .

off to a fifth in 1994. Secondary school graduates were still more concentrated: fully 46 percent came from private schools in 1984, declining
to 27 percent in 1993 as attendance at public secondary schools rose.
That was not the end of the story. Private school graduates had a higher
probability of passing the *vestibular,* or entrance examination, required

TABLE 4-5. Secondary Education, 1995–2007

Thousands of students

Year	Total enrollments	Private school enrollments	Afternoon and evening school	Graduates		Net enroll-ment rate, 15–17 years
				Public	*Private*	
1995	5,375	1,164	3,156	707	253	22.1
1997	6,405	1,267	3,581	992	338	26.6
1999	7,769	1,224	4,236	1,420	367	32.7
2001	8,398	1,114	4,305	1,855	362	36.9
2003	9,073	1,128	4,259	1,852	316	43.1
2005	9,031	1,090	3,985	1,559	300	45.3
2007	8,369	897	4,705	1,749		48

Source: MEC/INEP, EdudataBrasil: Sistema de Estatisticas Educacionais (www.edudatabrasil.inep.gov.br), for all except net enrollment, which comes from PNAD tabulations.

for tuition-free national or state universities. Only about a quarter of the applicants succeeded, as shown in table 4-4. Those emerging from public schools over this decade were at a disadvantage, and that made the educational system prejudicial to reduction of income inequality. Those able to afford the fees for private secondary school went on to a free university education, earning much higher incomes thereafter.

Secondary school advancement remains an issue. In quantitative terms, as can be seen in table 4-5, increasing attendance occurred at 5 percent a year between 1995 and 2007. The net enrollment rate more than doubles. Poorer regions exhibit the greatest gain, but this is a consequence of low beginning values. In the northeast in 2007, the enrollment rate is only 34.5 percent. In São Paulo, by contrast, the level is twice as great, at 66.3 percent. Over time, as more students have entered, the percentage of graduates has declined.

Private schools account for a higher proportion of students at the secondary versus primary level. Most private students go to day schools. Much of the increased public secondary attendance has been at night schools where older adolescents, working during the day, can attend. That is where half of enrollees can be found. Their instruction is not always satisfactory, and the physical characteristics of the schools are deficient. There are ongoing differences in the quality of private and public education.

**FIGURE 4-2.   Proportion of Nineteen-Year-Olds Completing
Secondary Education, 1987–2007**

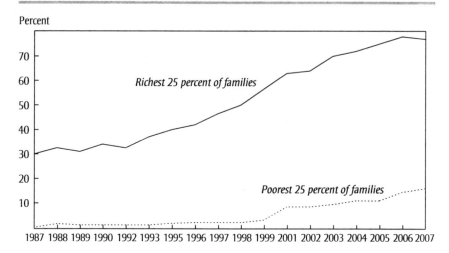

Source: Ministry of Education.

At the high school level, the relationship between attendance and household income is manifest. The net enrollment rate for children aged fifteen to seventeen years is 74 percent for those from the richest quintile of households; for those from the poorest quintile, the rate is 19 percent. Within regions the same pattern prevails: in the northeast, the net enrollment rates are 51 and 11 percent, respectively; in the southeast, they are 80 and 32 percent, respectively.[10]

Figure 4-2 illustrates secondary school completion rates over time of those age nineteen, contrasting the highest income group with the lowest. After 1995 the rate for the highest income group rises steadily from 40 percent to almost 80 percent; for the lowest, the rate rises, but from a tiny base, reaching 15 percent by 2007. More than 60 percent of the students in private schools come from families with income in the top quintile whereas only 2 percent come from the bottom quintile. Public school students are more equally distributed, with 15 percent from the highest group and 13 percent from the lowest. Public school attendees who repeat years or drop out come predominantly from lower-income families.

All this adds up to an obvious conclusion. While this is now changing somewhat, those competing for university admission come from the top of the income distribution. The educational system reproduces past levels of inequality and explains why change within a single generation, à la Korea, is difficult to attain within Brazil. In 1982 half of secondary school graduates age thirty or less did not continue onward. In 2006, with a larger number of graduates, the proportion terminating climbed to 62 percent.

Rising secondary school attendance has brought attention to curriculum inadequacies. Secondary education serves a varied clientele. For some it is preliminary to university attendance; for others it is terminal and offers access to a better job. A uniform curriculum cannot easily reconcile these objectives. That is why many European countries and Japan separated academic and vocational schools The United States did not, combining both within a single institution, but with different curricula.

Brazil has opted in favor of a third model for public secondary education: a single school with little differentiation. All students are similarly taught. Vocational training is limited to less than 10 percent of students. As Claudio de Moura Castro has pointed out, this solution makes little sense: "Sooner or later, courage will be needed to resolve the impasse of a single system, which, in theory, offers the same school for all, and in practice, offers nothing, not even a good education. Furthermore, it discriminates against the poorest."[11]

Resolution is not a trivial matter. The goal is universal secondary education within a decade. Entrants will remain heterogeneous. Differences are plain to see in results of the international Program for International Student Achievement examinations, where Brazil has been near the bottom of the scale three times since 2000. The best-performing Brazilian participants are a small percentage of the national sample.[12]

University Education

As seen in table 4-6, between 1985 and 1995, higher-education enrollment in Brazil showed little increase. Globally, university attendance was expanding everywhere. The higher-education gross enrollment rate in Argentina was 29 percent, France attained 49 percent, and in the United States it reached 79 percent; Brazil's gross enrollment rate was 12 percent—both public and private—in the mid-1990s.[13] As a result, Brazil also fell behind in the percentage of the labor force with advanced training: 12 percent, compared to 24 percent for France and 37 percent for the United States. The country's failure to expand supply translated into a high rate of return for university training, one that exceeded gains for primary school.[14]

TABLE 4-6. University Education, Various Years, 1980–95

Thousands

			Enrollment						
Year	Total	Federal	State and munici- pal	Private	Faculty	Gradu- ates	Places offered	Compe- titors	Entrants
1980	1,377	317	176	885	110	226	405	1,803	357
1985	1,368	327	230	811	114	234	430	1,737	346
1990	1,540	309	270	961	132	230	503	1,906	451
1996	1,869	374	252	1,133	164	254	634	2,548	514

Source: MEC/INEP, Censo da Educação Superior, various years (www.inep.gov.br/web/guest/superior-censosuperior).

Figure 4-3 plots the percentages of students enrolled in the three education levels by quintiles of per capita family income. In the latter 1990s, close to 80 percent of students enrolled in higher education came from families in the top fifth of the distribution. By contrast, more than 40 percent of the students in primary schools came from the bottom two quintiles, partially reflecting higher birth rates within poorer families.

Swelling secondary education enrollment in the early 1990s—up by more than 10 percent a year—led to changes. Initially there was major expansion of private universities, followed after 2003 by growth of public facilities. The federal Ministry of Education spent most of its annual budget on higher education. Transfers granting assistance to lower-level students via the Fundação da Assistência ao Estudante, transfers to the states to support basic education, and direct transfers to schools added up to half again as much.

Approximately half of secondary school graduates now go on to universities. Table 4-7 gives information on applications, attendance, and university graduates. Private facilities offered twice as many openings in 1995; by 2005 that ratio expanded to seven. Public universities filled 90 percent of their vacancies; among private institutions that proportion declined from 80 percent to 50 percent. The probability of success in application remained a low 14 percent in 2005 for public universities but expanded to almost 80 percent for private institutions. Graduates of public universities were three-fifths those of private facilities in 1995, declining to two-fifths by 2005.

Expansion of private facilities occurred as the Cardoso government focused its attention and resources on fundamental education. Federal

FIGURE 4-3. **Distribution of Enrollments, by Household Consumption Quintile, Latter 1990s**

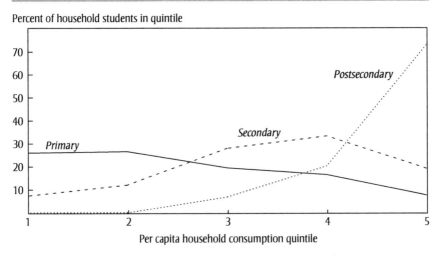

Source: José Márcio Camargo and Francisco H. G. Fereira, "The Poverty Reduction Strategy of the Government of Brazil: A Rapid Appraisal," Discussion Paper 417 (Rio: Pontifical Catholic University, 2000), p. 22.

universities obtained little in incremental funding, so the private sector stepped in. Most institutions offered only a bachelor's degree and employed few regular faculty. They emphasized evening classes, allowing students to continue working. Some were internationally financed. Their intellectual content and their ability to discriminate among applicants were not stellar. Stories abound about their readiness to admit all able to pay. What counted was private profit, not higher education.

Lula chose, through his initial focus on the ProUni program, to make these private facilities receptive to poorer students emerging from the expanded secondary track. Tax-free status was granted to nonprofit institutions in return for scholarship assistance and efforts to broaden the student body. Entrants so benefited, however, remained small in number. The majority had to pay the required fees. The capacity of these private institutions continued to expand, and potential places remained unfilled.

Partially as a result, the second Lula administration emphasized expansion of public universities. New units were started, as well as expansion of older facilities. The magnitude of change was considerable. Between 1995 and 2002, the number of federal universities and their enrollments remained the same; thereafter, the number went up and student bodies

TABLE 4-7. University Applicants, Attendance, and Graduates, 1995–2005

Thousands of students

Year	Applicants						Attendance			Graduates		
	Number applying		Vacancies		Vacancies filled		Public		Private	Public		Private
	Public	Private	Public	Private	Public	Private	Federal	Other		Federal	Other	
1995	1,339	1,255	178	432	158	352	368	333	1,059	46	49	159
1997	1,426	1,290	194	505	182	392	396	363	1,186	51	55	168
1999	1,832	1,603	228	741	217	570	443	389	1,538	59	53	212
2001	2,224	2,036	256	1,152	245	792	503	436	2,092	66	67	263
2003	2,367	2,533	281	1,722	267	996	567	569	2,751	84	85	359
2005	2,307	2,754	313	2,123	289	1,109	580	613	3,261	86	110	522

Source: Ricardo Luiz C. Amorim, André Gambier Campos, and Ronaldo Coutinho Garcia, Brasil: O estado de uma nação (Brasília: IPEA, 2009), statistical supplement.

increased as fast as those of private institutions. These recent gains have stabilized student proportions: about 30 percent public, 70 percent private. This is far different from the ratio in 1990, when the private sector was barely ahead.

Despite recent advances, the gross rate of university attendance remains low: 20 percent of those age eighteen to twenty-four, with the net ratio half as large. According to UNESCO comparisons, Brazil places at the bottom of the scale within Latin America and even more so internationally. The average for the Organization for Economic Cooperation and Development (OECD), including some developing countries, is close to 40 percent. The Brazilian target of 30 percent by 2010, as stated in the Plano Nacional de Educação (PNE) of 2001, was not met.

Nonetheless, Brazil is catching up. Cost continues to be a major problem. In 1995 expenditures for higher education were $12,000 per student. Comparable costs for primary and secondary students were $676 and $734, respectively.[15] More than a quarter of public outlays for education were allocated to fewer than 2 percent of students. This brought Brazil to the top of the international scale for universities and left it at the very bottom for primary and secondary education.[16]

Brazil, in a recent OECD report, is the country with the lowest public expenditure on education: $1,542 per student in 2005 purchasing power parity. At the tertiary level, however, it stands as one of the higher ranked. Brazilian public outlay, excluding research and development spending at universities, came to $9,808 compared to a simple OECD average of $8,102, and a weighted average of $13,141. Relative to primary and secondary education expenditure, the ratio is more than seven, twice as large as for any other country and more than five times the average. The devaluation of the *real* acted to minimize the Brazilian cost. The 2005 expenditure in dollars is 15 percent lower than in 2000, and more so since 1995.[17]

Reported costs in Brazil include pension payments to retirees and medical facility expenditures. Pension transfers alone represent more than a third of salary costs. Eliminating those elements, international comparison still leaves Brazil with expenditures inconsistent with income: positive deviation in any simple regression of the two variables stands out. One reason is generous salaries for the many faculty and employees.[18]

Policy Response

A national Education Development Plan has been operative since April 2007. An Index of Basic Education Progress (IDEB) now governs the distribution of federal resources to states and municipalities. IDEB consists of two components, equally weighted. The first is the rate of grade promotion; the second, the score of the new examination, Prova Brasil, a SAEB evaluation for urban public schools obtained on a near universal rather than sample basis.

Results for IDEB in 2007, as shown in table 4-3, have improved beyond the level anticipated, especially for the first four years of education. That has led Minister of Education Fernando Haddad, who has been reappointed by Dilma, to hope for future gains. Target values for 2022, the 200th anniversary of Brazilian independence, have been set to bring Brazil up to average OECD levels. This goal, extending over three presidential terms, is a plus. In the case of education, where results are not immediate, policy sustainability is essential.

As education at the secondary and tertiary level expands, so do resource needs. Managing that process is not easy. Governmental response has been to try to limit spending increases. Cardoso vetoed a provision in the 2001 PNE legislation requiring escalation within five years to 7 percent of GDP for public education. He also blocked a shift in pension payments from universities to the federal budget and negated a requirement for a minimal public share of 40 percent of tertiary enrollment.

Those measures had popular support; that is why they appeared in the proposed legislation. They benefited from lobbying efforts of school teachers and university employees—not a small group. An initial goal was public expenditure for education of at least 10 percent of GDP for a decade. Then there could be downward adjustment to 6 percent. That 10 percent is a recurrent but unrealistic goal.[19]

The Development Plan of 2007 offered an increase to 6–7 percent of GDP. Yet Minister Haddad, in later statements, returned to more realistic levels: "We are around 4.6 percent of Brazilian GDP today, but we have to reach 6 percent or even more than that. . . . I do not defend immediate achievement from night to day—that would even cause administrative problems."[20]

In the midst of the recent electoral campaign, Dilma promised a higher 7 percent, and a reappointed Haddad has made that his goal by 2014. Setting such targets is easy. The harder part is determining *how* to achieve the qualitative gains in education that Brazil requires, along with reducing the large regional differences. Opinion is divided over two important issues: one is the use of competition among schools and among teachers as a means of improving quality of instruction, and the other is establishing fees and compensating scholarships at public universities. Both matter over these next years.

Health

Central to the Brazilian health system after 1985 was a larger role for the federal Ministry of Health. A national structure evolved, with the cooperation and financial contributions of states and municipalities. Unlike the case of education just examined, there was no equalizing formula taking into account poorer regions.

Brazil also allowed room for the private sector. That was true from the beginning. Insurance firms became responsible for payments to physicians for private treatments outside of the national health scheme. This separation had significance. Survey data in 1998 showed that the upper classes especially utilized such facilities. Those with lesser income had no alternative but the long waits and sometimes inadequate care of the public system.[21]

What emerged in the constitution, in articles 196 to 200, was creation of the Sistema Único de Saúde (SUS). Previously, in article 194, the constitution set out the objectives and public responsibilities underlying social security: a combination of health care, pensions for past work, and social assistance that was treated as a comprehensive unit. The characteristics included universality—incorporating the total population; uniformity—ensuring the equivalence of urban and rural populations; a minimum value of benefits; equity through participation in expenses; and the democracy inherent in a decentralized system.[22]

There were three special features of the new SUS.[23] The first was a single point of responsibility at every level of government and increased importance for the Health Ministry. Second was the principle of decentralization in actual management. Last was the requirement of financing from each governmental unit—federal, state, and municipal. All of these emerged from discussions continuing since the early 1980s. These principles proved easier to specify than to implement fully.

The first legislation regulating the constitutional provisions, Law 8090-90 in September 1990, occurred amidst Collor's efforts to restrain public expenditure. Partially vetoed to eliminate sections specifying automatic, rather than negotiated, transfers, this bill was followed by Law 8142-90 in December of the same year. That restored automatic federal government transfer payments. There was also allowance for private health services.

The responsibilities set out for each of the three governmental levels were formidable: a bare summary would require pages to detail them. They could not be immediately applied. That explains the three basic operational norms (NOBs) promulgated in 1991, 1992, and 1993 intended to provide content to guide actual policy. Bureaucratic interests intervened to ensure a dominant federal role, even in the midst of explicit provisions to the contrary. Indeed, the Ninth National Health Conference, postponed from its scheduled meeting date of 1990, finally was convened in 1992 with the central theme, "Municipalização é o caminho" (municipalization is the way).

Decentralization became effective only after many years. At the end of 1997, 2,941 municipalities—out of about 5,100—were in partial compliance with the rules; they could receive federal and state resources to help pay for local hospital expenses. Only 137 municipalities—representing 16 percent of the total population—had a local health secretary able to assume responsibility for health care. The remainder of the municipalities, 40 percent of the total number, had not advanced even to the most preliminary level specified.[24]

Three years before, in 1994, conditions were more incipient: the number of municipalities receiving full resources was only twenty-four, representing less than 5 percent of the population; only 6 percent of support fell within scope of the program.[25] This expanding role of larger cities was central to progressive implementation of the SUS. Municipal participation increased from about 10 percent of total expenditure in the field of public health to more than 30 percent.

An expanded SUS integrated all the publicly funded subsystems. However, that did not eliminate, or even substantially reduce, the role of private medicine, much as some fervent advocates had hoped it might. Brazil functioned under a mixed system, and this structure did not alter. Indeed, based on the estimates in the 1996 Survey of Family Expenditures, private services dominated. Of the 7.7 percent of GDP spent on health care, more than half came directly from families; this was subdivided by thirds: health insurance, medications, and other services. Enterprises provided 9 percent, and the SUS, only 37 percent.[26]

There is a strong degree of inequity inherent in this dichotomous structure. Those with higher income were able to use the SUS free of charge for more elaborate procedures. They thereby reduced their average premium paid for private health insurance—such expenses could also be deducted from income taxes—while at the same time competing with the poor for limited public resources. The conflict inherent in this disarticulated joint system was confronted only later—and not to everyone's satisfaction.

Effective regulation of a national health service cum private medicine is not an easy task. During this initial period of the SUS, coordination was lacking. Brazil had evolved from a prior scheme where the private system, both for profit and not for profit, dominated in the availability of hospital beds and other medical services. Private insurance, provided both by enterprises and bought by individuals, was rapidly expanding. Most doctors worked both as private practitioners as well as for the national health plan. "Government and the medical community need to jointly ensure that private providers and payers of health care meet basic standards of access, quality and performance."[27]

In the early years, financing for the SUS, responsible for the care of more than 100 million persons, was far different than the 30 percent of the budget for social security that the constitution had specified. Firms obtained injunctions at the beginning of 1992 contesting their obligation to pay the designated tax for social security; only in 1994, after a positive declaration of constitutionality, was there resolution. In May 1993, the social security minister, fearing a deficit in his own funds, refused to pass along resources from the wage tax owed to the Health Ministry. These funds are now allocated to social security alone. In 1993 Itamar negated the 30 percent allocation, alleging its inconsistency with fiscal austerity required for price stabilization. Creation of the Fundo Social de Emergência in 1994–95 meant another demand on budget resources. Funds were available only as macroeconomic conditions allowed.

Previously, inflation represented a major challenge. Service providers were badly affected. A comparison of federal outlays for hospital and clinical services in 1993 provides a good example; inflation constituted approximately two-thirds of expenditures. If the domestic value is converted to dollars on the fifteenth of each month in which the services were performed, one arrives at a total outlay of $7 billion. If the value in *cruzeiros reais* is converted on the day that payment was made, the value is $4.4 billion, a difference of 40 percent.[28] This problem continued into 1994, when a comparison of deflation by month or year shows a large difference. Expenditures were postponed for payment to a subsequent calendar year, a common practice during this inflationary period. In 1993 this came to a full 12 percent of the Health Ministry's outlays.[29]

The effects of inflation therefore should be borne in mind when looking at expenditure data. Table 4-8 sets out a measure of public resources,

TABLE 4-8.   Health Receipts and Expenditures, 1985–94

Billions of 1990 dollars

Year	Receipts[a]			Expenditures[a]			
	Federal	State	Municipal	Federal	State	Municipal	Total
1985	8	1.9	1	7.4	2.6	1	11
1986	8.6	2.4	1.3	7.5	3.2	1.6	12.3
1987	12.5	1.1	1.2	9.4	3.6	1.7	14.8
1988	11.8	0	1.9	6.9	4.8	1.9	13.6
1989	13.3	1.4	1.9	9	5.5	2.1	16.6
1990	11.1	2	1.8	7.8	4.9	2.2	14.9
1991	9.2	1.6	1.3	6.3	3.6	2.2	12.1
1992	7.7	1.6	1.5	7.5	1.8	1.4	10.6
1993	8.6	1.6	1.5	7.3	2.3	2	11.6
1994	8.6	3	2.4	7.9	3.5	2.6	14

Sources: For 1985–90, World Bank, "Brazil: A Poverty Assessment," Report 14323-BR (Washington, June 1995), pp. 75–82. For 1991–92, federal figures from World Bank, distributed in accord with percentages for three levels from Medici, *O desafio da descentralização*, p. 131. For 1993, federal receipts, change in Ministry of Health receipts (net of debt and social security payments) projected backward from 1994 levels, in Reis and others, "Financiamento," p. 11. Total receipts calculated as 1.35 times federal, per Ricardo Cesar Rocha da Costa, "Descentralização, financiamento e regulação: A reforma do sistema público da saúde durante a década de 1990," *Revista de Sociologia e Política* no. 18 (June 2002): p. 55. Allocations to states and municipalities are same as 1992. Expenditures are approximated as intermediate between 1993 and 1994. For 1994, Medici, *O desafio*, absolute total value calculated as average of his 1990–92 values in 1999 dollars relative to 1990–92 values here in 1990 dollars. His distributional percentages are used.

a. May contain rounding errors.

at all three governmental levels, collected and spent upon health in this early period.[30] The pattern seems clear. There is a sizable but irregular increase in federal funds in the Sarney period, yielding a maximum in 1989 that is not matched subsequently.

Contributions by states and municipalities during these years are limited and irregular, only becoming more important at the end of this period. On the expenditure side, after transfers from federal and state levels are taken into account, there is a rise in the importance of state activity, followed by the beginnings of municipal ascent. Decentralization was later to become the theme.

Lack of predictable resources meant a troubled beginning for the SUS and the universal access enunciated in the 1988 Constitution. The World Bank provides a useful summary in mid-1994: "The dramatic changes that have occurred over the past decade effectively restructured health care in Brazil. The process has involved multiple steps, has occurred rapidly, and consequently has introduced a certain element of chaos.

Unstable financial flows, lagging legislation, uncertain authority and constant readjustments to new incentives and policies are to blame."[31]

President Cardoso inherited a universal health system in financial disrepair. Health was one of his electoral campaign's five issues. Inflation had diminished the value of federal allocations; states and municipalities directed their contributions to other ends. Despite the enthusiasm of SUS supporters, their efforts to construct a functioning network encountered constraints.

The minister of health, the distinguished physician Adib Jatene, had briefly served in the Collor cabinet and was familiar with the problems in making the SUS operational. Reformulation of the norms became a major task. There also was a difficult financial reality: borrowing could be continued in 1995, but repayment of past debt began reducing the net contribution. Some longer-lasting solution was necessary.

Jatene proposed reinstatement of the tax on financial transactions, at a rate of 0.2 percent; this time, all resources would go for health expenditures.[32] The Provisional Contribution on Financial Transactions (CPMF) began to bear fruit in 1997. Receipts went up, amounting to 28 percent of health expenditures during that year, increasing to more than 40 percent in 2002. These tied funds did not increase the ministry's expenditures one for one: past debts had to be repaid, and alternative resources were correspondingly curtailed. The SUS received an exclusive base, but real expenditures remained constrained. That was the reason for eventual passage of Constitutional Amendment 29 in 2000.

Equally important was decentralization. Productive interactions with state and municipal secretaries of health did not occur magically. Nor were agreements always implemented. Defining responsibilities and ensuring financial transfers for health and hospital care were necessary. The SUS focused on direct medical treatment as opposed to the ministry's historic concern with public health and epidemiology. A multiplicity of accounts had to be paid, very much delayed and sometimes inadequate, not to mention the demands of so many individuals eager to benefit.[33]

There were three interfaces with municipalities as defined by NOB 01-93: incipient, partial, and semicomplete; for the states, only the last two counted. For incipient municipalities, basic control over clinics and hospitals was envisaged, and funds were paid to individual facilities rather than to a municipal health council. With the partial interface, there was more local management and control involved, and a functioning health council. For the semicomplete interface, there was full local control, and resources were transferred through the bipartite state-municipal commissions. For the states, there were two categories: the partial classification received resources as a result of annual agreements, with corresponding lesser management; those in the semicomplete group received full transfers. These rules were operative until February 1998, despite another operational norm, NOB 01-96, after a year of meetings among officials of the ministry and state and municipal councils.[34]

The number of municipalities granted full transfer of resources at the end of 1997 was 144; the number of states, none. Something like 17 percent of the population was integrated as a result, involving less than a quarter of the resources transferred between the federal government and the municipalities. By the end of 1998, the situation altered. Almost all of the municipalities were included and two of the states. More than half of resource transfers acquired automaticity.[35]

Two factors contributed to this turnabout. One was NOB 01-96 entering into force at the beginning of 1998. It simplified earlier requirements and permitted decentralization to proceed apace. There were now two categories for recipients, partial and full. The original fixed sum made available to municipalities through the basic health care package (PAB) was modified. A variable component, conditional upon programs like community health, nutritional care, and pharmaceutical assistance, was added. There was finance for vaccinations and epidemiological care. Finally, there was a fund to deal with complex problems, with specific attention to AIDS.[36]

The second reason was the arrival of José Serra, the first nonphysican in many years to be appointed to head the Ministry of Health. A day after his installation, the weekly *Veja* painted a bleak picture of his prospects: "In a state of virtual chaos, health in this country has little money and spends badly the little it has."[37] Although he took office as economic problems were compounding and faced expenditure limits, he ensured that the SUS was able to proceed. Formerly the senator from São Paulo, Serra had the political experience to function within a ministry where many positions were assigned by patronage.

Serra expanded the Programa de Saúde da Família, begun in 1994. This consisted of a doctor, nurses, and community personnel working together in smaller areas. Another was the Programa de Agentes Comunitários de Saúde, led typically by nurses and focused on preventive and maternal care. There were other efforts to reach out geographically and functionally. A program providing food to the poor, Programa de Bolsa

TABLE 4-9. Projected Federal Expenditures for Health, 2004–07

Billions of 2003 *reais*, deflated by average IPCA index

Year	Constitutional Amendment 29	30 percent of social security funds	10 percent of federal taxes
2004	30,694	30,694	30,694
2005	32,429	65,656	39,873
2006	33,889	68,610	41,667
2007	35,114	72,041	43,750

Source: Rodrigo Pucci de Sá e Benevides and Ricardo Vidal de Abreu, "Financiamento da saúde pública no Brasil: A solução atual e o impacto da vinculação constitucional de recursos," unpublished document available on the Internet (dtr2001.saude.gov.br).

Alimentação, was established. Expenditures were modest. But these programs became an integral part of the ministry's agenda by extending the availability of care and contributed to the decline in the infant mortality rate over the period.[38]

Another success was Constitutional Amendment 29, passed in 2000, whereby specified resources at the federal, state, and municipal levels were committed to health. Like the required budgetary allocations for education, this guaranteed future finance. For the first year, 2000, the federal government had to contribute at least 5 percent more than in 1999; thereafter the budgetary allocation was to increase at the same rate as the nominal growth of gross national product. For the states, the proportion was to rise from at least 7 percent of state expenditures in 2000 to the steady state of 12 percent in 2004; for the municipalities, the minimum of 7 percent in 2000 was to grow to 15 percent by 2004.[39]

Table 4-9 displays the three different scenarios for health finance: Amendment 29, the constitutionally mandated 30 percent of the social security budget, and 10 percent of budgetary receipts.[40] One point stands out: future federal resources under the law are smaller than the two alternatives preferred by SUS proponents. Several supporters had recognized the impossibility of going back to an integrated social security budget and had mobilized in favor of a flat percentage. Actual outlays for health fell below both possibilities. But projected annual changes after the first year for the three options do not differ much. With pressure upon government expenditures, even the lesser guarantee, and greater state and municipal expenditures, avoided a worse outcome. That did not prevent pressures for further change in the Lula administration.

Serra encouraged Brazilian production of substitutes for antiretroviral medicines for treatment of AIDS. In 2000 Brazil threatened to issue compulsory licenses to produce generics; in January 2001, the United States entered a complaint against Brazil at the World Trade Organization. Brazil responded by seeking to change the rules. That culminated successfully in the November 2001 meeting initiating the Doha Round. Malaria, tuberculosis, and HIV/AIDS were designated as diseases exempt from patent rights on curative medicines. That meant generics, produced within developing countries at much lower prices, could substitute for exports from the developed world. Brazil, according to one account, saved $1 billion between 2001 and 2005.[41]

Integration and regulation of the private health system also occurred. This duality in Brazilian health care was very much a function of income, as the PNAD investigating health in 1998 reveals. In the top two income deciles in 1998, more than 60 percent of households had a health plan. In the bottom three income deciles, constituting more than 70 percent of the population, less than 10 percent of households had a health plan. Coverage was greatest within the industrialized southeast, extending there to the lower strata of the income distribution. Collective bargaining enabled workers to negotiate health coverage with larger enterprises before creation of the SUS. Those working for the government also had access; in 2003 they represented more than 20 percent of those insured.

There were a variety of private plans: group practices, akin to health maintenance organizations in the United States; cooperatives, owned by the doctors themselves; enterprise-centered clinics and care; and directly contracted insurance coverage for individuals. All persons had access to the SUS for complex procedures, thereby reducing their cost. There also was an income tax deduction for health premiums; that lowered the bill for higher-income recipients. As the SUS evolved, private coverage grew to about 30 million Brazilians by 1994, or close to 20 percent of the total population. That participation rate subsequently rose: in 2009 some 40 million Brazilians were enrolled, proportionally a bit more of the population.

Those favoring a national health system opposed a parallel private system. Nonetheless, this situation has persisted. One reason is organized labor's preference for such an arrangement. Unions retain ownership and management of some of the largest private plans, and their workers are unwilling to give up these privileges. Expenditures per person under private plans are more than two times the average outlays of the SUS.

Lula's election in 2002 and reelection in 2006 did not engender large modifications in the national health system.[42] The less expensive components of the health program such as family health, which entailed less than a tenth of total costs, continued to expand in geographic coverage. The portion of expenditures directly committed to public medical care did not change much. There were attempts to promote some new directions, as in the 2006 Pacto do Gestão, emphasizing more effective regionalization and planning, but these involved no fundamental change.

José Gomes Temporão's appointment as minister of health in March 2007 represented a return to professional health leadership. More resources from the federal government were indicated in the four-year plan, Mas Saúde, spanning 2008–11. That called for larger transfers to the northeast. Expenditures were justified as a commitment to economic development. However, there was one major difficulty: the Federal Senate voted down renewal of the CPMF in December 2007, an action that wiped out the source of almost half of ministry funds.

Other resources were substituted until the recession at the end of 2008. The question of reliable finance for the SUS then surged as an issue. The inability of Constitutional Amendment 29 to ensure a satisfactory flow of funds, by linkage to nominal GDP growth, is part of the problem. Despite a vocal contingent within congress calling for reconsideration of the SUS funding arrangement and a provision within the amendment calling for reevaluation at least every five years, nothing has happened yet. The possibility of a vote for a new CPMF in the current congress is under discussion.[43]

By way of conclusion, table 4-10 details governmental resources and expenditures for the years between 1995 and 2005, along with estimates for private contributions. When direct personal expenditures for medicines, physician services, and hospital care are included, as in the 1996 consumer survey or the special 1998 PNAD, and added to SUS expenditures, total outlays for health care come to around 7 percent of GDP. More recent data do not alter this picture. Three observations follow.

First, federal expenditures for health stabilize after Constitutional Amendment 29. They rise in real terms through 2007, with the rate of expansion dependent upon growth. The contributions of state and municipal governments increase; the minimum required allocations of 12 and 15 percent of revenues, respectively, are exceeded. Some units fail to meet the standard, but the wealthiest states and cities do. In 2005 these

TABLE 4-10. Receipts and Expenditures on Health, 1995–2005[a]

Billions of 2005 *reais* (average National Consumer Price Index) unless otherwise indicated

| Year | Public | | | | | | | Private (percent of GDP) | | Aggregate |
| | Receipts | | | Expenditures | | | | | |
	Federal	State	Municipal	State	Municipal	Total	Percent of GDP	Health plans[b]	Total outlay	percent of GDP)[c]
1995	26.5	7.7	8.3	8.6	10.2	42.5	3.0	n.a.	n.a.	n.a.
1996	23.3	8.5	8.2	8.8	11.1	40.0	2.7	n.a.	n.a.	n.a.
1997	27.1	8.1	8.7	8.8	13.0	43.9	2.9	n.a.	n.a.	n.a.
1998	25.9	9.4	9.6	10.5	17.5	44.9	2.9	n.a.	n.a.	n.a.
1999	29.7	8.4	10.4	9.8	20.3	48.5	3.1	n.a.	n.a.	n.a.
2000	30.8	9.6	11.2	12.3	22.2	51.6	2.9	1.4	5.0	8.1
2001	31.9	11.7	13.2	15.8	25.9	56.8	3.1	1.3	5.2	8.3
2002	32.3	14.0	15.7	18.1	28.5	62.0	3.2	1.4	5.1	8.4
2003	31.0	13.9	15.5	19.0	27.3	60.4	3.1	1.2	4.9	8.1
2004	35.0	17.1	17.5	24.9	31.7	69.6	3.4	1.2	4.9	8.1
2005	37.1	17.2	20.2	26.2	35.0	74.5	3.5	1.3	4.9	8.0

Sources: Benevides and Abreu, "Financiamento," for receipts 1995–99, adjusted to 2005 values; Sérgio Francisco Piola and others, "Estado de uma nação: Textos de apoio [saúde]," Discussion Paper 1391 (Brasília: IPEA, February 2009), for 2000–05 and transfers to states and municipalities for 1995–2005. See also Brazilian Institute of Geography and Statistics (IBGE), "Economia da saúde: Uma perspectiva macroeconomica, 2000–2005" (Rio de Janeiro, September 2008).

a. Federal statistics exclude debt payment and social security expenditures.

b. Health plans includes sum of entries for participation plus hospital services.

c. Implied total for 2002–03 using IBGE family budget study is 7.0 percent; PNAD data for 2002 give an implied total of medical outlays of 7.3 percent, with larger sums for health insurance.

contributions constituted about half the resources; indications are for a future balance in their favor.

Second, states and cities now spend more of the money. Through trilateral commissions, the federal government transfers resources. In 1995 this was 10 percent of federal health receipts; by 2005 it was two-thirds of revenues. States also contributed to cities through the bilateral agencies. Decentralization is a reality in the Brazilian health system, and the municipalities are the key component.[44]

This arrangement is a reason why regional inequality within the health system has not changed much. Federal expenditures per capita in 2005 differ between the richer southeast and poorer northeast only by 13 percent, but the corresponding difference for the sum of state and municipal expenditures is more than 70 percent.[45]

A third conclusion, evident in table 4-10, is the continuing importance, despite a slightly larger SUS, of private health expenditures. This
includes not only the health plans of some 40 million Brazilians but also
additional outlays for medicines, dental care, and private payments to
doctors and hospitals. A totally inclusive national public system of health
care does not exist. The lack of legislation to regulate Constitutional
Amendment 29, after almost ten years, reinforces this point.

This Brazilian duality is a reality. Those who wish for a more generous
revenue basis for the SUS are pursuing a chimera. Calculations showing that a designated 10 percent of federal revenues would mean greater
continuing contributions in the future are inaccurate. The historic rise
in taxes relative to GDP cannot be extrapolated. The gain has peaked:
the 2007 congressional failure to renew the CPMF on which the SUS
depended is practical proof. Future pressures against an increased governmental presence are likely to recur, even after its positive role in the
2009 recession.

Advocates for spending more on social services, including the SUS,
search for compensating reductions elsewhere. Interest payments on the
federal debt are a popular choice. Yet even those charges, as the real
interest rate has declined, have diminished. Defaulting, as some urge,
has consequences. There is no simple solution. Demands for government
services are not lacking; that is why overall fiscal deficits continue.[46]

Evolutionary progress in health reform is more likely. This is no trivial
task. Infant and maternal mortality, despite a large decline, remain com-
paratively high in Brazil compared to the rest of Latin America. As the
population ages, noncommunicable disease will rise in incidence. The
World Bank suggests that lower productivity as a consequence of inadequate treatment already matches health expenditures in cost. There are
diseconomies of scale, deficient management, distorted and diluted funding, and an absence of programs enforcing standards and ensuring quality. A World Bank program, the Health Network Formation and Quality Improvement Project (QUALISUS-REDE), joint with the Ministry of
Health, has been created to begin to cope with these issues.[47]

Retirement Pensions

The Constitution of 1988 extended social security coverage—making it
truly universal—and increased the retirement benefits for participants.[48]
Two comprehensive systems were established: the General Social Security

Regime (RGPS) covered all workers in the private sector; the General Civil Service Regime (RJU) was responsible for public employees. This was the first time there had been an attempt to unify the latter. All contracted federal civil servants—some 400,000—were transferred to this arrangement. They were entitled to unlimited pensions based on salary rather than constrained by the RGPS maximum of ten minimum wages.

Many states and municipalities took advantage of the opportunity in 1991, after constitutional provisions had been regulated, to enter this coverage. As a consequence, they no longer had to pay annual contributions for their employees, as required under RGPS, thereby freeing up resources in the short term. Eventually, those obligations would come due, usually in amounts exceeding expectations.

There were three categories for private sector old age pensions. One was a function of age, taking effect at sixty-five for men and sixty for women; for the rural sector, the requirement was less by five years. At retirement, payments were to be 70 percent of the individual's salary base of the last three years, with an additional 1 percent for each year of participation in the program. Another category comprised those who had a minimum length of service: thirty years for men, twenty-five years for women. Individuals in this category could increase their pension to a full 100 percent of salary by working an additional five years. A final category incorporated all those older than seventy years who had worked without making any contributions, to whom a minimum wage was granted. This same base pension was applicable to all other retirees. There was provision for full inflation adjustment as well as recalculation of benefits that had fallen behind in the surge of inflation in the 1980s.

Old age participants swelled between 1992 and 1994, the numbers increasing as the possibility of a pension became a reality. Rural sector pension recipients also increased and retirement payments doubled. The smallest old age pension paid in 1988–92 was only 27 percent of a minimum wage; the prospective increase was substantial.[49] By April 1993, more than half of beneficiaries received a minimum wage. Because the real value of the minimum wage had declined slightly between 1990 and 1993, costs did not rise proportionately. The number of retirees reliant upon length of service did not increase but augmented their receipts.

But the most important change was the increase in the retirement benefits of public employees, not only federal but also state and municipal. The gains available to this group grew as a result of the last monthly salary serving as the base for retirement benefits and the enrollment of

TABLE 4-11.   **Pension Receipts and Payments, 1988–94**

Billions of December 1998 *reais*

	RGPS		RJU[a]			
Year	Receipts	Payments	Receipts[b]	Payments[c]	Total balance	Percent GDP[d]
1988	30.8	17.8	1.2	11.8	0	0
1989	30.5	19	1.4	14	−1.1	−0.1
1990	31.5	19.5	1.8	18	−4.2	−0.5
1991	28.3	20.5	1.4	13.8	−4.6	−0.6
1992	27.9	22.3	1.3	12.6	−5.7	−0.7
1993	31.7	30	2.4	24	−19.9	−2.4
1994	33.9	33.1	3	30	−26.2	−3

Sources: RGPS from MPAS (Ministry of Social Security), as reported by L. A. S. Bertussi and César A. O. Tejada, "Conceito, estrutura e evolução da Previdência Social no Brasil," *Teoria e Evidência Economica* 11, no. 20 (2003): 36. RJU, federal government from MARE (MInistry of Administration and State Reform), as reported by Oliveira and others, "Reforma da Previdência," table 7.

  a. Includes states and municipalities.

  b. Receipts are treated as approximately 10 percent of total payments. Military paid 5 percent and civilians paid 6 percent of salaries until November 1993 when it increased to about 10 percent. This conforms to later years when there are data.

  c. Payments of states and municipalities estimated as equal to those of federal government, in accord with the approximately equal payments in 1997, 1998, and 1999 recorded in Francisco Eduardo Barreto de Oliveira and Kazio Iwakami Beltrão, "The Brazilian Social Security System," Discussion Paper 775 (Brasília: IPEA, December 2000), p. 7.

  d. GDP in 2007 prices from Ipeadata (www.ipeadata.gov.br), converted to a 1998 base; the implicit GDP used by MPAS is about a quarter smaller, with a slightly different annual evolution.

many public employees. In 1995 almost nine-tenths of federal employees were within the RJU; a corresponding two-thirds of state and more than half of municipal workers had comparable arrangements. By that time, the number of retired military, federal civil servants, and their dependents began to equal those in active service.

Table 4-11 provides a financial summary of the social security system between 1988 and 1994, restating these observations quantitatively. Although some estimates were necessary, the trend is certain.

First, there is a sharp rise in the deficit of the overall system in this period. It starts small until the negative balance balloons in 1993 and 1994. Private benefits increase by more than half between 1991 and 1994; public employee benefits rise more quickly. It is little wonder that from its very start in 1995, the Cardoso government sought changes as these pressures continued. Because the minimum wage was a base for the largest number of recipients, its determination took on special importance.

Second, while the magnitude of public sector benefits approximately matched those of private recipients, the number of beneficiaries in each

FIGURE 4-4. Average Retirement Benefits by Category, Early 1990s

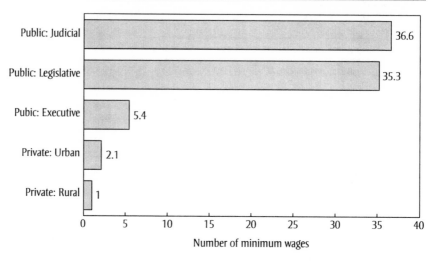

Source: Francisco Oliveira and others, "Reforma da Previdência," Discussion Paper 508 (Brasília: IPEA, 1997), p. 38.

group is very different. Those receiving federal governmental retirements and pensions constituted about 5 percent of RGPS recipients in 1996, implying an average public pension some eight times greater. Those within the legislative and judicial branches especially benefited.[50] Figure 4-4 provides a visual representation of this reality.

Third, because the number of retirees was rising, and the rate of population growth had much slowed, the ratio of workers to retirees would fall dramatically over time. Already between 1980 and 2000, that ratio declined by about a fifth. In addition, the projected increase in the age of mortality extended the benefit payment period. The consequence was progressive deterioration of the social security deficit. Changes in the retirement system became a necessity rather than an option.

The combination of more generous pensions and worse economic performance meant increasing outflows relative to receipts of social security taxes. One consequence was elimination of the transfer to the Ministry of Health of its presumed share of employer taxes in 1993, as discussed above. There was a joint project between the Economic Commission for Latin America and the Caribbean and the Social Security Ministry to seek acceptable solutions. Ending the requirement for readjustment of pensions by the minimum wage was one proposal; another was to limit the pensions granted on the basis of years of service rather than older age. More radical was the notion of creating a single national plan and incorporating public employees, who had just begun to claim their much larger pensions.

None of these obtained popular support, nor was there any legislative backing within the special congressional session devoted to constitutional reform. Instead, it was always popular to claim the deficit could be financed by ending tax evasion and illicit payments. These were hardly inconsiderable. The World Bank estimated an evasion rate in excess of 40 percent, with IPEA estimates only marginally less. In 1993 fraud involved an additional 5 percent of the actual claims.[51]

Even in the midst of a deteriorating social security surplus, with worse sure to come, full privatization à la Chile mustered little enthusiasm among reformers. The principal reason was obvious: the costs of absorbing the obligations of those already retired, and the many choosing to take benefits early, was too great. Brazil, with a small population then over sixty years of age, had undertaken large future commitments. There were estimates suggesting that the ratio of their present value to gross domestic product was as large as 200 percent. In the midst of the Real Plan, taking on an increase in the fiscal deficit above 5 percent was ruled out.[52]

By the beginning of 1995, Brazil was on the cusp of a significant problem. Previously, high rates of inflation had played a key role in equilibrating outflows and inflows. For an average monthly rate of inflation of 30 percent, the annual erosion of benefits was 20 percent, even with readjustment every four months. Positive interest receipts from social security deposits held in the Bank of Brazil regularly added to the value of contributions paid in. This temporary circumstance hid the underlying reality emerging after stabilization.

Retirement payments for the great majority of the elderly were marginal, but unlike in other developing countries, almost all were incorporated into the social security system. That is why measured poverty in Brazil among the elderly was less than in other Latin American countries. The greater problem was the cost of retirement by virtue of time of service. Already constituting about half the cost of urban pensions in 1980–92, this component grew to two-thirds of that cost by 1995. Such pensions amounted, on average, to more than two and a half times the amount received by the elderly.[53] When the rapidly mounting obligations to retiring governmental employees were added to the private RGPS system, prospects were bleaker still. Brazil required a major reform.

In early 1995, just a few months into office, President Cardoso sent to the National Congress a constitutional amendment to alter the Brazilian pension system. Unlike other proposals, this one met opposition. Not until the end of his first term, in mid-December 1998 after a loan from the IMF, did Constitutional Amendment 20 finally pass. Implementing legislation occurred over subsequent years.

That was not the end of the matter. In April 2003, shortly after assuming office, President Lula had to take up the matter again. Constitutional Amendment 41 resulted after eight months, this time because the PT was in power, and its support, along with that of many members from the opposition PSDB and PFL, provided the needed votes. An IMF loan—to which Lula had assented in the midst of the electoral campaign—preceded that rapid approval.

For some, the consequent logic is obvious. These modifications resulted from external forces. Greater globalization and neoliberal policies went in tandem; a relevant component was pension reform. The World Bank focused on this subject in the 1990s, resulting in a major report.[54] Its recommendation had three pillars: a minimum, public defined benefit component; a larger compulsory, defined contribution financed by employees; and voluntary savings managed privately.

Foreign investors made clear their desire for changes in the Brazilian retirement system before Cardoso's election in 1995. By 1998 the slow progress in pension reform was high among their complaints, as well as those of the multilateral agencies. A worsening economic climate in 2002 gave another impetus. IMF involvement on both occasions was not a matter of chance. In the Memorandums of Understanding of 1998 and 2002, when Brazil had to borrow, there is reference to the lack of actuarial balance in social security, both for the private and public systems.[55] Lula therefore had little choice but to introduce a proposal for reform early in his term.

However, that explanation is too simple. To be sure, there were pressures from outside forces. But Brazilian decisions regarding pension reform differed from the standard World Bank proposals. Domestic factors had greater weight, and they will continue to count as additional modifications become necessary to accommodate demographic realities.

The sequence of Brazilian social security reform is well documented. Cardoso mentions the internal political struggle that slowed advance over almost four years.[56] His account stresses a judgmental error in dealing with problems of the private and public sectors within a single piece of legislation. Those problems were different in character and therefore in resolution. Combination meant a united opposition from the private sector and public unions. Brasília was subject to overt and well-organized dissent.

Table 4-12 characterizes the amendment finally passed in December 1998, amid signs of the trouble that was shortly to befall the economy. The act offered less than had been hoped, after all the intervening congressional debate. Even a notionally capitalized system, as was occurring in Europe, was impossible.[57] For governmental employees, where much of the deficit emanated, the imbalance between payments and receipts was too large. A retention bonus to delay retirement helped, but only in the short run. Deficits would become larger in the long run.[58]

On the positive side, the amendment converted some constitutional details to regular legislative decision, thereby avoiding a requisite 60 per- cent majority for all subsequent changes. Law 9783 passed in January 1999. Three rates of taxation of civil servants were imposed, rising from 11 to 25 percent. Similar taxes were levied upon those who had already retired, with minor exemptions. Civil service employees experienced only minor changes: prior minimal employment was imposed, multiple pensions were eliminated, and a higher minimum age for retirement was set but applied only to future entrants.

In October 1999, the supreme court declared that levies imposed upon retired public employees and progressive rates imposed upon those working were both unconstitutional. What was left was the required contribution by government employees comparable to those in the private sector. This decision made inevitable a need for further amendment; the Cardoso government introduced an additional two, but there no longer was pressure for reform once the immediate economic crisis passed. Efforts to cope awaited the next administration.

For the private sector, results were better. A methodology for calculating pensions appeared in the implementing legislation, Law 9876, in November 1999. It involved an arithmetic average based on 80 percent of the highest covered wages over the months after introduction of the Real Plan; this was multiplied by a new *fator previdenciário* (actuarial coefficient). One component reflected the combined contribution rate of employers and employees (0.31); a second, the period (in years) that payments had been made; and the last, residual life expectancy. This was multiplied by an implicit interest rate, regularly rising to reward those working beyond the minimal period.[59]

TABLE 4-12. Pension Reform under Cardoso and Lula

Units as indicated

Program and characteristics	Prior	After Constitutional Amendment 20 and Laws 9783 and 9876	After Constitutional Amendment 41
RGPS			
Qualifications by age			
Urban	65M; 60F	65M; 60F	No change
Rural	60M; 55F	60M; 55F	No change
Length of service (years)	35M; 30F	35M; 30F Length of contribution	No change
Special groups[a]	30M; 25F	30M; 25F	No change
Partial pension[b]	30M; 25F	Abolished	No change
Minimum age	53M; 48F	53M; 48F	No change
Wage base	Average last 3 years	Average of 80 percent highest monthly contributions (inflation-adjusted)	No change
Benefit value			
Rural wage	Minimum wage	Minimum wage	No change
Urban wage	100 percent	Calculated by retirement factor	No change
Maximum	10 minimum wages	R$1,200 (inflation-adjusted)	R$2,400 (inflation-adjusted)
Contribution	20 percent employer	20 percent employer	No change
	8–11 percent employee	8–11 percent employee	No change

RPPS (Public Sector Pension System)

			Present employees	*New employees*
Qualifications by age	53M; 48F	53M; 48F current / 60M; 55F new employees	60M; 55F	No change / No change
Length of service (years)	35M; 30F	35M; 30F Length of contribution, minimum 10 years' contribution; 5 years in position	Minimum 20 years	No change
Special groups[a]	30M; 25F	30M; 25F	No change	No change
Wage base	Last month's salary, adjusted by successor's value	Same	No change	Average real salaries of working life adjusted by inflation
Benefit value				
Wage	100 percent or more	No accumulation of retirement pensions	Same (reductions of survivor's benefit over R$2,400 by 30 percent)	No change
Maximum	None	None	Ceilings for federal government, states, and municipalities	Ceiling for civil servants equal to RGGP
Contribution				
Employee	None	11–25 percent salaries progressively	11 percent[c]	No change
Retiree	None	Same as employee[d]	11 percent over R$2,400[e]	No change

Sources: Various, as cited in footnotes to this chapter.

a. Originally teachers, professors, judges, and legislators; subsequently, only teachers.

b. Proportional retirement based on years of service.

c. Exempted for those postponing retirement by time of service.

d. Declared unconstitutional in 1999.

e. Ruled constitutional in 2004, only above RGPS limit.

The effects were disappointing. The implicit interest rate was high, ensuring gains for working longer. Still, the number of individuals choosing to stay on beyond their minimum required years of service was small. The average age of retirement for males under this arrangement pre-1999 was 54.3 years; post-1999 it had increased only slightly to 56.9. For females, benefited by a five-year differential, the corresponding numbers are 49.7 and 52.2 years. There was a slight decrease in retirements based upon years of service after 1998. So some results were achieved. But the benefits were smaller than presumed. That was the reason for not imposing a minimum age requirement for the private sector in Amendment 41.[60]

In 2001 attention turned to the complementary pension schemes. These included the accounts of state enterprises such as Petrobras and the Bank of Brazil, privatized entities such as Vale do Rio Doce and CSN, and other large private firms. There were 362 authorized pension funds in operation as of early 2000. Older closed plans were defined benefit; newer ones were defined contribution. Open plans after 1994, linked to financial institutions, allowed private participation. More transparent regulation, through complementary Law 108 for closed plans and Law 109 for the open plans, had three effects. One was to establish new funds as defined contribution; another was to enhance portability and competition among open funds; and a final change was to require equal contribution for employees and employers within closed funds. By 2002 these funds amounted to more than 15 percent of GDP, and that proportion has continued to rise.[61]

Table 4-13 affords a quantitative view of the Brazilian pension scheme over the years since 1995. Over the Cardoso years, the increase in the RGPS deficits slowed. A similar pattern obtained for civil servants. Larger offsetting public contributions after 2001 enabled reversion to a smaller deficit. Overall, however, the consequence was alarming: Giambiagi and colleagues find an increase in the fiscal cost from 2.8 percent of product in 1996 to 5.2 percent in 2002.[62]

Soon after his inauguration, President Lula and state governors proposed further limits on civil service retirement benefits. After public discussion, the amendment went to congress by the end of April. Blanket PT opposition to social security reform reversed. A final version, less demanding than proposed, was adopted by the end of the year. There had been vigorous opposition by civil servants and unions, not to mention judges and prosecutors. Dissident PT members formed a new party, the Partido Socialismo e Liberdade (PSOL).

TABLE 4-13. Retirement Benefits and Receipts, 1995–2007

Units as indicated

	1995	1996	1997	1998	1999	2000	2001	2002	2003	2004	2005	2006	2007
Benefits (percent GDP)													
RGPS[a]	4.6	4.9	5.1	5.6	5.6	5.8	6	6.2	6.6	6.9	7.2	7.6	7.8
RPPS[b]	3.3	3.8	3.8	4.1	4.1	4.1	4	4.2	4	3.9	3.7	3.8	3.9
Federal	2.1	2.1	1.8	2	2	2	2.1	2.1	2.1	2	2	1.9	1.9
Receipts (percent GDP)													
RGPS	4.6	4.8	4.7	4.7	4.6	4.7	4.8	4.8	4.7	4.8	5	5.3	5.5
RPPS[b]	0.8	0.6	0.6	0.7	0.7	0.6	1.4[c]	1.5	1.3	1.1	1.3	1.4	1.7
Federal	0.3	0.3	0.3	0.3	0.3	0.3	0.5	0.6	0.5	0.6	0.6	0.7	0.7
Balance (percent GDP)													
RGPS	0	–0.1	–0.4	–0.9	–1	–1.1	–1.2	–1.4	–1.9	–2.1	–2.2	–2.3	–2.3
RPPS	–2.6	–3.2	–3.2	–3.4	–3.4	–3.5	–2.7[c]	–2.7	–2.7	–2.7	–2.4	–2.3	–2.2
Federal	–1.8	–1.8	–1.5	–1.7	–1.7	–1.7	–1.6	–1.5	–1.6	–1.4	–1.5	–1.3	–1.3
Beneficiaries (millions)													
RGPS	15.1	15.9	16.9	17.9	18.1	19.0	19.3	20.4	21.2	22.4	23.2	23.8	24.4
RPPS	n.a.	n.a.	2.9	n.a.	n.a.	n.a.	n.a.	2.8	n.a.	n.a.	3.0	3.0	3.0
Federal	0.8	0.9	0.9	0.9	0.9	0.9	0.9	0.9	1.0	1.0	1.0	1.0	1.0
Contributors/labor force, age 16–59 (percent)	43	44	45	45	44		45	45	45	47	48	49	51
Complementary pension assets (percent GDP)													
Closed	…	8.8	9.7	9.5	11.8	12.2	13.1	12.8	14.1	14.4	14.9	15.9	17.0

Sources: RGPS: Giambiagi, "18 Anos de Política Fiscal no Brasil: 1991/2008," *Economia Aplicada* 12, no. 4 (2008). RPPS: for total receipts and benefits for 1995–96, see Fabio Giambiagi and others, "Diagnóstico da previdência social no Brasil: O que foi feito e o que falta reformar," *Pesquisa e Planejamento Econômica* 34, no. 3 (2004), and for 1997–2007, see Ministry of Social Security and Social Assistance (MPAS), "Previdência no Serviço Público, Estatísticas" (www.previdenciasocial.gov.br/conteudoDinamico.php?id=423); data for federal benefits come from Giambiagi, "18 años," and for federal receipts for 1995–96, see Giambiagi and others, "Diagnóstico," PPE, and for 1997–2007, MPAS, "Previdência." Beneficiaries: data for RPPS come from World Bank, *Brazil: Critical Issues in Social Security* (Washington, 2001), p. 93, and MPAS, "Previdência"; data for RGPS are from MPAS, "Social Security plus Assistance Receipients, "Anuário Estatístico, various years, and Giambiagi and others, "Diagnóstico."

a. Includes RMV/LOAS (non-constributory pensions) in benefits.

b. Refers to sum of state and federal units. Municipalities would add about 0.2 percent to the deficit.

c. Rise in receipts (and decline in balances) as a result of assessing required governmental contributions.

At the end, as shown in table 4-12, that amendment was pared down. The pension remained the salary last received; future pay increases were passed along. Changes came in length of time served, with a minimum of ten years in public service and five in the position being vacated. Pension limits were set, based upon judicial salaries at the supreme court. A tax on active employees and retirees of 11 percent was established; the latter would be found constitutional if it applied to a level of income higher than the limit, then R$2,400, for the private system. One calculation measured the effect of congressional modification: the original proposal would have reduced the actuarial debt by 14 percent; the amendment managed only 8 percent.[63]

Nor have these changes ever been put into effect. The slowing growth in the social security deficit is the reason. That pause has come less by limiting benefits and more by accelerated economic growth and declining unemployment in recent years. Growth in formal employment and the resultant increase in contributions to the retirement system made a difference. Urban workers within the RGPS produce a surplus, offset by a rural deficit. As a consequence, short-term projections turned positive, showing—before the recession of 2009—a RGPS deficit continuing to fall, without further changes, until 2012.[64] That is a reason why the PT wanted to repeal the 1999 adjustment rule; but it was vetoed by Lula, who recognized its irrelevance for increasing pensions for the poor.

Future adjustments remain necessary. Delay has a calculable price: the longer the country waits, the more drastic the change that will be required. There is a list of proposals to confront the actuarial deficit and associated fiscal deficit that Brazil faces. These are enumerated in two studies published by IPEA. Giambiagi and associates use a simulation model to evaluate a variety of reforms; Rocha and Caetano show how provisions of the Brazilian system deviate from international norms. The Social Security Ministry itself has extended projections to 2050.[65]

These suggestions include setting the minimum age at sixty-five years, imposing the same age minimum for female retirement, increasing required years of contribution to retire by age, ending special treatment for school teachers as well as for rural workers, reducing access to LOAS (assistance for the elderly and disabled) benefits, and ending indexation of retirement benefits by the minimum wage, substituting only inflation adjustment. Rocha and Caetano add one more: less generous survivor's benefits, for this is where Brazil's deviation from current international practice is perhaps greatest. This had been a target of Amendment 41, where a 40 percent reduction was imposed on high-income beneficiaries.

The effect of such reforms is substantial. In their absence, the present value of the pension deficit increases relative to income; an exception occurs only when the real minimum wage remains constant while annual growth proceeds at 4 percent. Greatest sensitivity occurs within the RGPS, in particular to changes in the indexing rule for benefits. If the minimum wage were to increase at the future rate of the GDP— although recent increases actually have been greater—the effect would be a 2050 deficit of more than 7 percent, compared to an initial 4 percent. If pensions were instead to remain constant in real terms, the corresponding deficit would be less than 2 percent. The effect stemming from a generalized minimum age of sixty-five for retirement is also significant, likewise reducing the projected 2050 social security deficit. Other recommended changes, however equitable they seem, do not produce equivalent impacts.

Taken together, and with a constant real floor to benefit payments, "the present value of the actuarial debt for the period 2005–2050 [is reduced] from 2 GDPs of 2005 to something between 0.65 to 1.05 GDP. . . . These measures could reduce the current deficit of the order of 4 to 5 percent of GDP to something like 1.5 to 3 percent of GDP, around the year 2050."[66]

Long-term projections by the Social Security Ministry identify the problem but do not specify corrective actions. Retaining an annual rate of growth of minimum wages equal to per capita income, without any other significant changes, implies a deficit in the RGPS system of 5.6 percent in 2050; some modest but difficult to attain alterations reduce this value to 4.8 percent. The conclusion, however carefully phrased, is clear: "To ignore the structural factors that influence the behavior of the receipts and expenditures of Social Security . . . merely delays discussion of the needed adjustments in the system in order to alter the social process already in course."[67]

Brazil has developed a pension system that is sui generis: quite substantial in magnitude and dependent upon extensive public subsidy but hardly equalizing. In 2000 less than 1 percent of benefits reached the poorest 10 percent of the population; almost 50 percent of benefits went to the richest 10 percent. An older group has been rescued from poverty, but much larger payments have gone to those who are better off. The net welfare effect is negative. As Rodolfo Hoffmann has shown, "The

TABLE 4-14. Inequality and Poverty Measures, Various Years, 1981–96[a]

Units as indicated

Year	Gini coefficient	Headcount[b]	Poverty gap[c]	Mean income[d]
1981	0.574	39.9	16.3	336.7
1983	0.584	51.2	22.9	273.4
1985	0.589	43.5	18.3	331.7
1986	0.578	26.6	9.6	483.6
1987	0.592	40.5	17.1	362.6
1988	0.609	45.5	20.2	338.9
1989	0.625	43.7	19.4	382.7
1990	0.604	44.5	19.6	347.3
1992	0.573	45.6	20.9	302.3
1993	0.595	46.6	21.5	320.7
1995	0.591	38	16.4	385.7
1996	0.591	37.8	16.7	393.9

Source: Francisco H. G. Ferreira, Phillippe G. Leite, and Julie A. Litchfield, "The Rise and Fall of Brazilian Inequality," Policy Research Working Paper 3867 (Washington: World Bank, March 2006), tables 1 and 2.

a. No comparable data on inequality for 1994. Also no data available for 1982, 1984, and 1991.

b. Headcount is percentage of population falling below the poverty line, here regionally differentiated within Brazil.

c. Normalized poverty gap is equal to percentage of income required to eliminate poverty.

d. Monthly household income per capita measured in September 2004 *reais.*

limited progressive quality of income from private and official pensions in Brazil owes itself, in great part, to the duality of the retirement system, including the RGPS and the RPPS, with very distinct rules."[68] Only with difficulty has it been possible to tax civil service retirees, and only when their benefits exceed ten minimum wages. Changing the rules is not easy, but shortly there will be little choice.

Poverty and Income Inequality

Many hoped that the new constitution, with its assertion of social objectives, would mark the beginning of dramatic change. They were soon disappointed.

Table 4-14 sets out the record of inequality as measured by the Gini coefficient, which ranges from zero—perfect equality—to one—total inequality. Brazil scores among the most unequal countries in the world in accounts published by the World Bank. This same table adds two poverty measures: the proportion of the population that is indigent and the proportion of those with greater, but still inadequate, income. This table extends until 1996 to capture the full effect of the Real Plan, especially in the absence of comparable data for 1994.[69]

The most positive effect, both upon the distribution of income as well as the number of poor, derived from ending inflation. This was true for both the failed Cruzado Plan and the successful Real Plan. Effects on the Gini coefficient in both cases are quite small; large proportional gains for the bottom half of the population, representing a little more than 10 percent of total income, have modest consequence. Yet the move is in the right direction. This result is not limited to the PNAD data incorporating all sources of income but equally extends to the recipients only of wages recorded in the Monthly Employment Survey (PME).

Edward Amadeo and Marcelo Neri, and Sonia Rocha earlier, found that the proportion of those classified as poor decreased by 10 percentage points in the period between July 1994 and the end of 1995.[70] In their calculations, Amadeo and Neri attributed about half of income gains to the end of inflation, with its tax on cash holdings, and the other half to the rising minimum wage. There is a larger salary gain for informal workers—about twice as great as for formal employees over this same period. The inflation tax was imposed not just on individuals; some two-fifths of it was imposed on financial institutions holding cash. The bottom fifth of the income distribution could not have gotten the bulk of the aggregate 2 to 3 percent bonus received from the end of inflation.

Education has the largest explanatory power when disentangling the sources of income inequality. A variety of studies indicate that variation in educational attainment of the household head explains more than a third of total inequality. No other factor—age, gender, region, family type, race—has a third as large an effect.[71] Although one cannot attribute causality to education—past family income obviously enters into current school enrollment—the large income differentials attained by the small number of high school graduates, and by the much smaller number of university graduates, was part of Brazilian reality.[72] Rates of return to education merited greater public investment than occurred. In the post-1985 period, there was more attention to education but not enough.

High rates of economic growth have positive effects on the national poverty rate. As overall gains occur, even without redistribution, those at the bottom benefit. Fewer go hungry, and infant mortality can decline. That was the Brazilian past. After 1980 economic growth was inadequate for such automatic advance. In fact, with the great variability in economic performance between 1985 and 1994, involving more years of absolute economic decline than at any period of the twentieth century, the reverse occurred. Frustration, as well as poverty, mounted.

High inequality means that only a small income transfer from the rich would be needed to eliminate poverty. The World Bank found that a transfer of 1.6 percent of total income in 1995 would be sufficient to accomplish the task. That would translate to less than 5 percent of the income received by the wealthiest 10 percent of the population. Corresponding inequality declines from a Gini coefficient of 0.58 to 0.54—still a considerable concentration but a large change nonetheless.[73] Practical efforts to alleviate poverty are necessarily more inefficient.

Brazilian social expenditure in 1995, despite increases, had not moved far in benefiting the poor. Only in health expenditure, and that barely, did the poorest beneficiaries obtain a disproportionate gain. To the contrary, the largest public expense, for retirement benefits, went in the other direction: the richest gained more than the poor. Indeed, that assessment applies to social outlays as whole.

On the side of taxes, too, there was little if any gain for the poor. In Brazil receipts from indirect taxes exceed those levied upon income directly. While direct taxes are equalizing, indirect excises are not. Upper-income groups save part of their income, reducing their proportional consumption. One recent study, using later data, quantifies this point. The lowest 20 percent of income recipients are responsible for 16.9 percent of government revenues in 2002.[74]

New Policies to Improve Income Distribution and Poverty

Cardoso issued Decree 1366, establishing Comunidade Solidária, eleven days after he took office.[75] That was to be the pivot of his administration's campaign against poverty, and it was to be headed by Ruth Cardoso. Comunidade Solidária grew out of previous research conducted by IPEA, especially its geographic mapping of poverty. There were two objectives: one was to coordinate an array of overlapping federal efforts; the other, to engage civil society. The intent, simply put, was to enlist Brazilian society in a war against poverty.

This program continued for all eight years of the Cardoso presidency. At the beginning, 307 municipalities were engaged; at the end, the number had risen to 2,361. A set of flexible programs, ranging from reduction of infant mortality to creation of employment opportunities, were implemented, including an evaluation component. Interim reports coordinated by the Fundaçâo Getúlio Vargas's Brazilian Institute of Municipal Administration (IBAM), with participation by IPEA and the international agencies UNICEF, UNDP, and the Inter-American Development Bank, were released in 1998 and 1999.[76] Resources remained modest, particularly during Cardoso's second term, when stabilization impinged. Contributions from the World Bank and the Inter-American Development Bank helped.

In 2000 another federal program emerged to contend with poverty. Constitutional Amendment 31 authorized a Fund to Combat and Eradicate Poverty for a period of ten years, to the extent of R\$4 billion annually, with resources stemming from an 8 percent increase in the tax on financial balances, the CPMF. As with Comunidade Solidária, not all expenditures were new: outlays would be regrouped, and pressures plaguing the federal treasury would be eased.

As the presidential election drew near, Education Minister Paulo Renato and Health Minister José Serra sought support for the PSDB nomination. Programs financed by these incremental resources were a good start. In the instance of the Education Ministry, there was Bolsa Escola; for the Health Ministry, there was Bolsa Alimentação. Both were implemented beginning in 2001, using the new fund.[77] They focused on young children, a group increasingly exposed to poverty. At that time, approximately 35 percent of the population was classified as poor; but among those less than a year old, 55 percent fell into that category, a proportion that gradually declined to 46 percent among those age ten to fourteen years.[78]

Bolsa Escola dated back to 1994 when an initial program was put in place by the PSDB mayor of Campinas; later, in 1998 a parallel effort was implemented by the PT governor of Brasília, Cristovam Buarque. Other mayors followed. The basic idea was linkage of children's school attendance to transfer payments to poor parents, or more frequently, a single female parent. The goal was to reduce current poverty and diminish future recurrence. In 2001 the program began its national implementation, covering children age six to fifteen.

Bolsa Alimentação had as its target group families with less than half a minimum wage per capita. In return for income transfer, there were explicit obligations, such as prenatal examinations, vaccinations, and nutritional advice from an expanded corps of local health workers. The program covered the prenatal period through age six, with the objectives of lower infant mortality and better childhood health.

These innovations yielded neither a PSDB victory in the election of 2002 nor a palpable reduction in poverty. The reason for their minimal consequences is apparent: the resources applied were small relative to the need. Measured in terms of family PNAD income, total program expenditures in 2002 came to 0.2–0.3 percent of GDP compared to the 6.9 percent required to eliminate all poverty, assuming exclusive application to poor families.[79]

The Lula government substituted its own program in January 2003. In name and organization, the focus was elimination of hunger. Fome Zero combined three approaches: "(i) structural policies aimed at cases of extreme hunger and poverty; (ii) specific policies designed to directly help families gain access to food; (iii) local policies which can be set up by city halls and by society."[80] Twenty-five different policies encompassing more than forty programs were integrated.

Minimal per capita income, less than half a minimum wage, was the criterion for eligibility, as earlier, with a monthly transfer of R$50 via magnetic card. The regional focus was the semiarid northeast, where the first ministerial meeting of the Lula administration convened. Rural municipalities with the lowest human development index would be targeted. With tight budgets, the intent was a well-publicized beginning rather than total coverage; about a fifth of the eventual target group was to be covered during 2003. Management emanated from an office within the Casa Civil, an arrangement that demonstrated the program's importance.

Two circumstances influenced subsequent developments. One was the slow pace of implementation—1 million or so families by October—which elicited criticism from all sides, including nongovernmental organizations, the press, policy experts, and even the PT. A second was the opportunity for a World Bank loan for a conditional cash transfer program. The president of the World Bank, James Wolfensohn, had visited Brazil in November 2002, and met with Lula again in March 2003, this time along with Santiago Levy, then the head of Mexico's Progresa program. The World Bank provided short-term resources for Fome Zero and was a key participant in ongoing discussions in Brasília about its transformation to Bolsa Família. A loan of $574 million until the end of 2006 was approved in June 2004. That represented almost 10 percent of anticipated expenditure over the interval. More resources were available thereafter.

Bolsa Família emerged in October 2003, and a new Ministry of Social Development in January 2004. Both have continued and with considerable success. From its slow start in 2003, the program accelerated to

TABLE 4-15. Bolsa Família

Units as indicated

Rules and growth	2003	August 2007	July 2008	September 2009
Legal requirements and income transfers ($R per month)				
Maximum family per capita income	100	120	137	140
Up to 3 children age 15 and less	15	18	20	22
Up to 2 children age 16 and 17	n.a.	n.a.	30	33
Family income transfer (per capita income less than one-half maximum)	50	60	62	68
Maximum allowed per family	95	112	182	200

Expansion of Bolsa Família	Coverage[a] (millions families)	Expenditure (billions of R$)	Percentage of GDP
2002	5.0[b]	2.4	0.16
2003	3.6	3.4	0.2
2004	6.6	5.8	0.3
2005	8.7	6.8	0.32
2006	11.0	7.8	0.33
2007	11.1	9.1	0.35
2008	11.6	10.6	0.35

Sources: Legal requirements and income transfers, and coverage, see Ministry of Social Development, Bolsa Família, various years. Expenditure: for 2002–04, see Ministry of Finance, Secretary of Political Economy, "Orçamento social do Governo Federal, 2001–2004," p. 25; for 2004–07, see Doraliza Auxiliadora Abranches Monteiro and others, "Evolução dos gastos sociais e transferência de renda no Brasil: Reflexões sobre o Programa Bolsa Família" (www.ipc-undp.org/publications/mds/43P.pdf). Estimates in 2004 IPCA *reais* were converted to current values; for 2008, see *Folha de São Paulo*, May 5, 2009. GDP: Ipeadata, nominal GDP series (www.ipea.gov.br).
a. End of year.
b. Bolsa Escola.

include 11 million families by the middle of 2006. It remained around that mark until the end of 2008, subsequently adding another million families. Table 4-15 shows its evolution and eligibility rules.

The program's expenditures have grown but remain small.[81] A characteristic of Bolsa Família is its low cost. In 2002 the total spent on the original components came to 0.2 percent of GDP; by 2008 that doubled to about 0.4 percent. One of the reasons has been the low level of compensation set in 2003. That amount was not increased until August 2007, followed by additional increases in July 2008 and September 2009. Youth ages sixteen and seventeen were only included starting in 2008.

Regionally, the distribution of outlays has stayed the same: the northeast received more than half of the expenditures, with the southeast getting less than half as much. One sophisticated study, by municipality, suggests an absence of bias, as had a TCU probe in 2008. Two other articles point to a PT electoral advantage from Bolsa Família in 2006; another denies this result.[82] More econometrics will undoubtedly be forthcoming after last year's presidential race, where once more the northeast was a decisive factor.

At the beginning of 2009, Lula announced a higher target of 12.1 million families. A corresponding budgetary increase occurred, although fiscal revenues were falling. Some members of the opposition PSDB and DEM parties suggested political motives. Yet, technical arguments justify expansion of Bolsa Família. Families eligible in 2006 but not receiving funds were almost 80 percent as numerous as recipients. The income volatility of those on the margin of poverty is greater than average. Estimates suggested a need for expansion to 15 million—even 19 million—families.[83] However, coverage did not follow as the government's fiscal deficit went up in 2009 and income growth disappeared.

The effects of Bolsa Família have been studied. A generalized inquiry was undertaken by the Center for Regional Development and Planning in 2005. A recent study focusing on smaller farmers has been conducted by the Brazilian Institute of Social and Economic Analysis (IBASE), with additional participation by the UNDP. Positive and negative findings have emerged. Children have been attending school more regularly, but at the same time, rates of repetition have been greater. Food consumption has increased, including both healthful and less worthy varieties. Infant mortality has improved, but child mortality has apparently not. The adult labor supply grew somewhat.[84]

On balance, the impression is positive. International presentations about the Brazilian experience occurred with frequency, as conditional cash transfer programs have expanded globally. An impressive endorsement has come from the World Bank, which developed a second follow-on Adaptable Program Loan of $200 million, to begin in September 2010. According to the World Bank report, "The program has accomplished a *very good targeting of outcomes,* with low leakages to the non-poor (90 percent of benefits go to families in the poorest two quintiles and 68 percent were received by those in the poorest quintile). . . . The [Bolsa Família] beneficiaries have experienced *reductions in the rates of malnutrition,* especially in the younger populations." At the same

FIGURE 4-5. Evolution of Extreme Poverty in Brazil, 2001–07

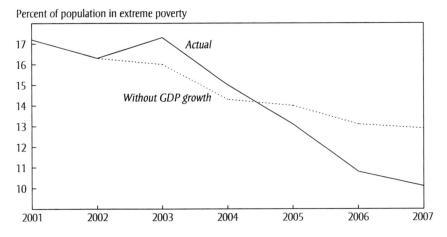

Percent of population in extreme poverty

Source: Ricardo Paes de Barros and others, "Markets, the State and the Dynamics of Inequality: Brazil's Case Study," UNDP Web, March 2009 (www.undp.org/latinamerica/inequality).

time, "evaluation results suggest impact on education and health outcomes could be strengthened."[85]

The amounts made available remain a small percentage of gross national product; approximately 0.5 percent is being spent. That is just the beginning of the story of poverty reduction. One must add in the consequence of post-2003 accelerated economic growth. Between that year and 2008, growth proceeded at a real annual rate of almost 5 percent, a result not achieved since the 1970s. Taken alone, that would have reduced Brazilian poverty by some 15 percent as per capita income rose in all deciles. Figure 4-5, based on the 2001–07 period, portrays these conclusions, focusing exclusively on the extremely poor.[86]

This impressive decline in poverty covers the period that Bolsa Família has operated. The program incorporates those denominated as poor by other definitions: in 2007 the overlap comes to almost 90 percent. The program's international prominence has good factual basis.

More precise analysis has been conducted using the data from 2004 and 2006. These studies assess the degree of inclusion: how many of the transfer recipients really qualify? Around 60 percent of the recipients of assistance in both these years fall within its defined boundaries; many of the remainder who do not qualify are quite close to the margin of eligibility. On a comparative basis, Bolsa Família performs a little better in 2004 than the comparable Mexican program, now called Oportunidades, in its coverage of the beneficiary poor.[87]

Over the longer period since 2001, the highest growth rates have come about in the bottom layers of the income distribution. The poorest 10 percent have expanded their incomes at 7 percent per capita annually; the richest, at 1.1 percent. Applying an average growth rate of 2.5 percent to the poor diminishes the poverty percentage by half its reported decline. The headcount falls from 39 percent to 28 percent, with growth explaining 5.4 points of the 11 point decrease. Those in extreme poverty decline from 17 percent to 10 percent. This time, lesser inequality constitutes an even larger share, 4.5 percentage points, of the total change.

These results can be phrased another way. For the poor, each percentage point reduction in measured inequality is equivalent to an increment of 2.8 percentage points in the per capita growth rate; for the extremely poor, that equivalence is 4.2 percentage points. There is no way that higher growth alone can eliminate poverty. That is why positive changes in the very unequal Brazilian income distribution count.

Impressive improvements in the income distribution have occurred since 2001. The Gini coefficient has declined from 0.594 in 2001 to .552 in 2007; the Theil index has declined proportionally more, from 0.72 to 0.61, respectively. The ratio of the richest 10 percent to the poorest 40 percent has fallen from 22.9 to 17.1; the share in the top decile has moved from 47.2 percent to 43.5 percent. The average rate of decline in the Gini coefficient has proceeded at a rate of 1.2 percent. Less than a quarter of seventy-four different countries for which comparable data were available had results as positive.

Much of this gain comes from an emerging middle class, category C in the five-group socioeconomic classification used in Brazil. Between 2002 and 2009 the top set (A and B) stays at around 15 percent of the population; the poorest set (D and E) falls from 43 to 32 percent; and the middle (C) goes up from 42 to 53 percent. Marcelo Neri, who heads the Center for Social Policy at the Fundação Getúlio Vargas, has emphasized the implications of this dramatic change: "Our Pelé is the new middle class."[88] In 2010, for the first time, category C constitutes a larger percentage of income than categories A and B. That translates into rapidly rising consumer demand.

Credit also goes to Bolsa Família, whose recipients represent almost a quarter of the population. Many IPEA papers have supported this conclusion, and a set of memoranda from its president on the improved

PNAD results reported in 2007 acclaims the program. Similar praise has come from the World Bank and the UNDP and, domestically, from the PT. A recent UNDP assessment exemplifies this mainstream endorsement: "Direct cash transfers from the state to families and individuals... improve secondary income distribution . . . a rise in the minimum wage leads to an increase in various transfers . . . conditional cash transfers, such as *Bolsa Família*, deliver substantial amounts directly to the poorest families. Together, these changes lead to reductions in inequality of . . . 0.2 Gini points per year."[89] Despite their small weight within total income, these social transfers are as important as higher wages.

Two components of assistance have produced these results: one is the increasing weight of LOAS transfers to the elderly and mentally disabled without much family support; the other is Bolsa Família. LOAS affords a per capita transfer of R\$107 in 2007, while Bolsa Família offers per capita outlays only a tenth as great. The minimum wage granted by LOAS, R\$465, is large enough to permit many families to escape poverty, however measured. LOAS expenditures expanded considerably after 2003. This led both to a decision to separate them from social security payments and to doubts by some about their legitimacy. The TCU has suggested that perhaps as many as 10 percent of the claims may be erroneous; 15 percent of new claims by the mentally deficient have come via judicial appeal.

Ricardo Barros has specified workable rules to separate LOAS grants from Bolsa Família payments. When these are applied, one obtains the following result: LOAS recipients, although a seventh of Bolsa beneficiaries, receive equal total income in 2007. Since 2001, moreover, the grant growth rate is higher than that for the Bolsa. This decomposition is preliminary to his assessment: "Despite representing just a tiny fraction of total income, each of these non-contributory benefits [LOAS and Bolsa Família] explains about 10 percent of the overall decline in income inequality."[90] Barros winds up assigning Bolsa Família a substantial, but more modest, role than claimed by others. So does Rodolfo Hoffmann, who had titled one paper with his conclusion, "Transfers are not the principal cause of the reduction in inequality."[91]

Why is there a difference? Other analyses, performed by IPEA and the UNDP International Poverty Center, utilize a different decomposition of the Gini coefficient (G):

$$G = \Sigma \phi k\, Ck,$$

where φ is the percentage weight of separate income components, and C is the coefficient of concentration of component k. This permits assessment of the relative contribution of different income sources to the measure of aggregate inequality. A problem emerges, however, when one assesses the effect of discrete, rather than incremental, changes; in the process, the overall level of inequality gets altered.

A recent application includes a presumed justification: "This decomposition by factor components . . . does not necessarily represent what the Gini coefficient would be if income source k vanished because the order of the individuals in the distribution might change and, if so, so would the Gini coefficient. While this critique is certainly valid, we believe this does not affect our results since our objective is not constructing counterfactuals, but decomposing changes."[92] Valid decomposition also requires infinitesimal changes, which are not always used. A 2008 IPEA report makes comparisons including and then excluding the large category of retirements and pensions.[93]

Information about the 2008 distribution of income has become available as well. Inequality has continued its decline. The fall in the share of income received by the poorest tenth of the population in 2007 has reversed. The indigent population has recovered from the large loss in average income reported in 2007 but remains below the 2006 level. As factors responsible for change, neither LOAS nor Bolsa Família has the importance of previous years. Instead, labor income variability was most significant.[94] So, the effects of the successful conditional cash transfer program are not the only factor operative.

In any event, Bolsa Família goes beyond ameliorating present inequality. Better health and more schooling also translate into greater future productivity. Even the World Bank sometimes focuses on the short-term results: "The program accounts for about 20 percent of Brazil's impressive reductions in its historically sky-high inequality (2001–2006) and about 25 percent of the recent fall in extreme poverty."[95] What happens to the young men and women when they leave the program is equally important.

This younger generation merits attention. Aggregate inequality has gone down, but poverty among the young has relatively increased. Such is its extent, despite Bolsa Família, that a 2007 age profile of extreme poverty reveals a positive segment from birth to nineteen years, turning negative thereafter. That is the reason why a simulated comparison between equivalent rises in minimum wages and Bolsa Família clearly favors the latter. Indeed, there is an *increase* in the number of extremely poor following a gain in the minimum wage. Ricardo Barros states the situation eloquently: "Moreover, poverty is still 10 times greater among children than among the elderly, but the average non-contributory public transfer for an elderly person is at least 20 times greater than the average non-contributory public transfer for a child. . . . [O]ptimizing social policy design gives Brazilian policymakers plenty of room to further reduce inequality, without the need for additional resources."[96]

Final Thoughts

When public outlays and private expenditures in the social area are added together, the current total comes to almost 30 percent of total product. That is larger than in many wealthier OECD countries. This is a substantial commitment, requiring increases in efficiency and not merely expansion.

There has been federalist decentralization. Except for expanded social security payments, municipal expenditures increased the most, followed by state outlays. The federal government contributed least. Mayors have a major influence on social expenditures and outcomes.

Future sustainability is a principal question. With demographic change, health and retirement outlays will inevitably increase. Expansion of higher education at current high costs will create additional pressures. These matters cannot be put off and ignored. Dealing with the problem now is better than waiting.

Economic growth is necessary but not sufficient to ensure the desired outcome. An improving income distribution will increase social demands. Intelligent social policy at all governmental levels is required to respond. This issue will test not only Dilma Rousseff but her successors as well. At stake is a more equitable Brazil over the next decades of the twenty-first century.

5

Foreign Policy in a Changing World

Brazilian foreign policy took on increasing importance as the country returned to civil leadership. Globalization had an impact economically and, subsequently, politically. During these years, four issues merit detailed discussion.

The first is closer convergence of Argentina and Brazil. Never before had these neighbors pursued joint policies as actively. This tale of Mercosul (known as Mercosur in Spanish) incorporates the boldness of the initiative but also stresses its limits: trade among the Mercosul countries, adjusted for inflation, has exceeded its 1997 level only recently. Differences in domestic macroeconomic policy in these two countries help explain why.

Second is regional policy. Response to U.S. efforts in behalf of a hemispheric free trade agreement occupied the Ministry of External Relations (hereafter referred to as Itamaraty) for more than a decade. A South American grouping took precedence and has continued to be favored. It is an arena in which an implicit contest with Venezuela's Chávez has evolved. Brazil has also tried to use Mercosul to reach out to the European Union (EU), earlier as a counter to the U.S. Free Trade Agreement of the Americas and now as a competitive alternative to China's rising dominance.

A third subject is Brazil's emergence as an important global player. Both Presidents Cardoso and Lula achieved international prominence and traveled widely. Foreign policy within the Lula years has extended to the India-Brazil-South Africa Dialogue

Forum, the BRICS grouping (Brazil, Russia, India, China, and South Africa), and even a presence in the Middle East. This extension, in turn, has created tensions in bilateral U.S.-Brazilian relations.

The last issue is Brazil's increased multilateral commitment. The country played a large role in the successful culmination of the Uruguay Round of the General Agreement on Tariffs and Trade (GATT) and has been central in the subsequent, but still incomplete, Doha Round of the World Trade Organization (WTO). Brazil hosted the 1992 Earth Summit in Rio, which focused on global warming, and has had to address global scrutiny regarding its subsequent environmental policies. Permanent membership in the UN Security Council has been a longtime goal, and those efforts accelerated during the Lula period.

Argentina and Brazil: The Beginning of Rapprochement

The return of democracy, first in Argentina in 1983 and then in Brazil in 1985, explains the origins of a more intense bilateral relationship.[1] With the end of military rule, the civil leaders, Alfonsín and Sarney, could reveal each country's experimental efforts to utilize nuclear power. Both presidents met in November 1985 and agreed to a Joint Declaration about Nuclear Policy. Full concordance, leading to eventual acceptance of UN nuclear control, was to take five years. In the interim, both countries proceeded toward economic cooperation.

Each country emerged from military rule in parallel fashion. Each experienced a run-up in external indebtedness and difficulty in paying interest due. Each suffered from limited access to foreign credit. Inflation in both had reached intolerable levels and had to be countered, not by orthodox IMF measures but by more heterodox means. That was the basis of the Austral Plan implemented in Argentina in June 1985 and the Brazilian Cruzado Plan in February 1986.

That close timing was no accident. Leading economists of the countries were in close touch. Many were intrigued by the possibility of a unified response to creditors. Debtor countries might enhance their negotiating power by acting jointly. The Cartagena Consensus in 1986, out of which the Rio Group developed, was a Latin American meeting calling for debt relief. Argentina and Brazil were active and equally frustrated participants searching for a solution.

In March 1986 came the Programa de Integração e Cooperação Econômica (PICE). Earlier there had been movement toward greater trade by means of the Association of Latin American Integration (ALADI), the regional trade association affording tariff preferences for specified products. Wheat and oil had come from Argentina, and some manufactured products had entered from lower-cost Brazil. But such exchange was limited, representing small percentages of each country's exports.

The PICE spoke of a "common economic space" rather than free exchange and began with a series of twelve protocols in potential areas for trade expansion, among them capital goods, wheat, iron and steel, and the automobile sector. Then, the intent was to utilize the ALADI. A dozen more protocols, extending even to the nuclear issue, were agreed upon in joint meetings through April 1988. The attempt was to "set goals that could be gradually achieved, and once consolidated, widened."[2]

When PICE was established, economic conditions in both countries were deteriorating badly—both the Austral and the Cruzado Plans had failed—and inflation was back and even higher. The two countries nonetheless went ahead in November 1988 to sign O Tratado de Integração, Cooperação e Desenvolvimento Brasil-Argentina, a formal treaty of cooperation and integration, ratified the next year. That established the intent to create, within ten years, an area of free trade in goods and services through removal of tariff and nontariff barriers.

This was a decisive step toward a common market and a different future. Prior discussions had dealt with resolving balance of trade surpluses and deficits, should they appear. A common bilateral currency, the *gaucho,* to alleviate need for scarce dollars, was considered. Each country was amenable to new rules to guide the relationship.

Both were moving away from trade protection. In Argentina the major change occurred with the Canitrot Reform of October 1988, reducing average tariffs from 45 percent in 1987 to 26 percent at the end of 1989. Additionally, import licenses for 3,000 tariff items were eliminated. World Bank loans were available and helped to motivate the process; opposition of internal groups was countered by the possibility of external financial support. Decline in protection continued: by November 1991, the average duty on Argentine imports amounted only to 19 percent, much less than half its level four years earlier.[3]

In Brazil the process of liberalization likewise began in the late 1980s. Both in June 1988 and September 1989, redundant protection and special tax regimes received attention. Due to pressure from interested sectors, the decrease implemented was less than had been planned: the average tariff, weighted by value added, of 55 percent in 1987 fell to 38 percent in the next year and to a still lower 29 percent in 1989. Nontariff barriers remained in place, however, and there was no change in special import regimes.[4]

Coming after extensive joint negotiations, the treaty was viewed by both Presidents Alfonsín and Sarney as critical to approximation. Both presidents were leaving office and hardly favorably. For each the political importance of the undertaking outstripped its economic significance. In the words of President Alfonsín, "The Treaty . . . between Argentina and Brazil not only incorporated the representatives of society in the process of decision making, but also created effective democratic control. Nevertheless, despite being approved by the Congresses and entering into effect, it would be other protagonists, *with other ideas,* who would take over the course of integration at the beginning of the decade of the 1990s."[5]

The reference was to Presidents Collor and Menem, who radically altered this original vision of progressive accommodation, sector by sector. The treaty, quickly ratified, did not last long. Instead, with changing political leadership in both countries, economic integration was accelerated and upgraded. From a ten-year agreement involving freer trade in a number of sectors, the objective scaled up to a common market within half that time.

Mercosul

This bold undertaking preceded later hemispheric efforts in behalf of freer external trade. Much energy was devoted to the process over the last twenty years. Yet concrete results have been more modest: a common market has not yet been attained.

The Good Years, 1991–1997. Both Collor and Menem sought greater foreign trade as a stimulus to domestic economic progress. An immediate opportunity, given the prior negotiations, was rapid bilateral liberalization. In July 1990, with the Act of Buenos Aires, the two countries moved creation of a full common market to the end of 1994. In December of the same year, Economic Complementarity Agreement 14, filed with the ALADI, spelled out in detail principles of forthcoming cooperation.

In March 1991 came the Treaty of Asunción with incorporation of Paraguay—no longer under General Stroessner—and Uruguay, but not Chile. Chile's absence was a disappointment. The country had participated in some earlier meetings, but its entry, then and later when asked again, was impossible. Chilean tariffs had fallen to lower levels than in Argentina and Brazil, and higher trade protection had little appeal.

The four member countries faced a need to eliminate all tariff and non-tariff barriers for Mercosul trade within a period of less than four years. Additionally, there was the fuller integration implied by a common market. That involved rules for free flows of labor and capital. Consistent monetary and fiscal policy were required to ensure little change in exchange rates among them. Europe had taken much longer to move to such economic conformity, despite post–World War II political convergence.

By January 1994, at the Colonia do Sacramento meeting, the four countries agreed that a common market by the beginning of 1995 was beyond their grasp. They redefined the immediate objective as a customs union. That required only a common external tariff. By so doing, they could ignore difficult issues such as trade in services, labor and capital movement across borders, and macroeconomic coordination. Expediency, and the domestic agenda within both of the principal countries, took its toll.

Even a customs union was not easy. Argentine officials began to display doubts about proceeding. Domingo Cavallo, the author of the successful Convertibility Plan in 1991 and a powerful voice, expressed opposition. He preferred a simple free trade agreement. That would have permitted Argentina to pursue a similar association with the United States. His view never altered: Cavallo advocated the same position again in 2001, during his brief return as minister of finance.

Already in 1991, during Collor's visit to Washington, there had been a four-plus-one agreement for Mercosul to pursue a free trade area with the United States. Guido Di Tella, then ambassador and later foreign minister, made clear that the Menem "government's exclusive center of interest is the United States. As a complement to that interest we will maintain relations with Western Europe. The rest of the World does not exist."[6] Argentina had already left the nonaligned group, provided minimal assistance to the United States during the first Iraq war, and was in search of "carnal" relations with the only world superpower. Its reward would be a special non-NATO status finally granted in 1998. That award was generally granted to countries closely engaged with the U.S. Department of Defense. However incompatible, that status did differentiate Argentina, which is all that seemed to matter.

In a final meeting at Ouro Prêto in December 1994, other subjects arose. First was an understanding that all tariffs and other limitations applicable to intra-Mercosul trade would not disappear. Each of the countries retained the right to define numerous exceptions. Higher average

Mercosul tariffs were established by Paraguay and Uruguay for some products than applied externally. All these exceptions were scheduled to disappear within five years. There was complete exclusion of sugar and the automobile sector from regular treatment. Large components of the capital goods and information technology sectors were separated; these sectors were not to be free for Argentina and Brazil until 2001 for the first and 2006 for the second.[7]

Furthermore, nontariff quotas on other products remained, as well as tariffs on imports from third countries destined for another within the group. National differences on antidumping and safeguard mechanisms also persisted. Although internal tariffs declined to zero for something like 95 percent of products, limitations to free exchange continued to prevail on January 1, 1995, when Mercosul officially came into being. Many of these impediments have lingered long after and still continue as a source of problems.

The timing was not propitious for Mercosul. Mexico's "Tequila Crisis" occurred, and Argentina and Brazil, newly stabilized, were ancillary victims. Argentina's fixed exchange rate attracted a surge of speculation betting on devaluation. There were consequences: Argentina experienced substantial capital outflows and rising interest rates as the money supply contracted. These caused relapse to negative growth during the year. However, the peso-dollar exchange rate did not alter.

Brazil also had to respond to capital flight and larger imports resulting from its appreciated real exchange rate. In June the country unilaterally increased protection in the automobile industry and imposed limits on other goods. Imports had risen during 1994 and into 1995, helping to ensure the stability of the *real*. Some of these tariff increases were subsequently disallowed by the WTO, forcing Brazil, but only later, to substitute lower rates. Argentina benefited by reason of its special access to the Brazilian market.

Mercosul's good years followed successful price stabilization, first in Argentina in 1991 and then in Brazil in 1994. Each involved immediate overvaluation, attracting increased imports to sustain stable prices. Geographic proximity worked to advantage. That favorable period, however, was rapidly drawing to a close.

Table 5-1 has the underlying data. Four conclusions emerge.

There is a phased expansion of trade between the two partners. Bilateral imports accelerate at the end of 1991 and in mid-1994 in response to the stabilization programs. Larger imports also came from

TABLE 5-1. Income and Trade, 1985–97

Units as indicated

Year	GDP (billions of 2000 dollars)		Imports (billions of 2000 dollars)		Real exchange rate[a]		Tariff (percent)	
	Argentina	Brazil	Argentina	Brazil	Argentina	Brazil	Argentina	Brazil
1985	186.6	417.9	3.8	14.3	58.1	71.3	39	51
1986	201.3	451.3	4.7	15.6	61.2	70.2	41	75
1987	207.1	467.6	5.8	16.6	55.7	73.7	45	75
1988	201.8	467.1	5.3	16.1	55.8	74.1	31	42
1989	186.7	482.4	4.2	19.9	33.8	115.1	23	32
1990	182.2	461.7	4.1	22.5	64.5	118.8	21	30
1991	205.3	467.7	8.3	23	85.7	92.5	14	24
1992	229.8	465.3	14.9	22.3	98.2	81.1	20	16
1993	243.4	488.1	16.8	27.3	105.6	81.9	16	14
1994	257.6	516.9	21.6	35.5	104.8	86.3	14	11
1995	250.3	538.6	20.1	53.7	98.9	93.7	12	13
1996	264.1	553.2	23.8	56.7	97.3	98.3	14	13
1997	285.5	571.4	30.3	65.1	100	100	14	15

Sources: GDP and imports of goods and services: IMF, "International Financial Statistics," online database (www.imfstatistics.org/imf/help/ifshelp.htm). Real exchange rate: Economist intelligence Unit online database (www.eiu.com/public). Brazilian tariff: Marcelo de Paiva Abreu, "Trade Liberalization and the Political Economy of Protection in Brazil since 1987," Working Paper 08a (Buenos Aires: Institute for the Integration of Latin America and the Caribbean [INTAL], 2004). Argentine tariff: Julio Berlinski and others, "Aranceles a las importaciones en el Mercosur," Working Paper 08/05 (Departamento de Economía, Universidad de la República, 2005). for 1985–91: Antoni Estevadeordal and, "The New Regionalism in the Americas," Working Paper 5 (Buenos Aires: INTAL, 2000); some intermediate values obtained from the chart in the paper.

a. Deflated by consumer prices.

the rest of the world to ensure price stability. Large foreign exchange reserves and access to international capital inflows made a difference. Stabilization was successful this time, unlike the previous failed Austral and Cruzado Plans.

Second, what had been irregular advance in the gross domestic product began to convert to regular growth. Domestic demand exceeded supply, stimulating import expansion and bilateral trade. Optimism replaced pessimism. That was especially the case in Argentina, where consistent growth and price stability seemed permanently elusive. In Brazil, too, after 1994 there was hope for a return to continuing progress.

Third, there is a regular decline in tariff levels from the late 1980s until creation of the Common External Tariff of Mercosul in 1995. Neither Alfonsín nor Sarney imagined a reduction of such magnitude when they first pursued a closer bilateral relationship. For the first time, both countries were opting for freer trade and benefiting from it. They had joined the rest of a globalizing world.

Finally, slowing trade growth is apparent by the mid-1990s. Each country confronted rising current account deficits uncannily like those that had led to stabilization failures. Both Argentina and Brazil would face, and eventually overcome, such later crises.

More than macroeconomics lies behind this early success of Mercosul. The automobile and automotive parts sectors, areas where no permanent agreement within Mercosul was ever to occur, were always a key component. Both countries required large foreign investment to underwrite participation in these sectors. Being larger, Brazil could benefit from economies of scale and accompanying domestic research and development. Its internal market was a principal virtue; imports and exports were always at the margin. By contrast, for Argentina, exports were a critical necessity to achieve efficiency. This fundamental difference was the engine driving constant changes in rules applying to bilateral automotive trade.

Argentina created a special arrangement for this sector back in 1991. There were two mechanisms. One was a quota on imports; this guaranteed a domestic market increasing more than proportionally with income growth. A second mechanism allowed producers to import vehicles as well as auto parts at preferential rates provided that they increased exports and invested domestically. Brazil, by contrast, allowed lower tariffs—20 percent at the end of 1994—to prevail. Imports rapidly escalated, and in June 1995 the duty was increased to 70 percent, followed by quotas. When that course was not allowed by the WTO, Brazil chose to replicate the Argentine rules, which were exempt from WTO regulation because they predated the Uruguay Round.

That helped to resolve the blowup occurring after Brazil imposed its *medida provisória* increasing tariffs unilaterally. Only direct presidential intervention, and six months of negotiation, settled the crisis.[8] An agreement was reached involving duty-free exchange between Argentina and Brazil up to specified limits, with reduced tariffs thereafter. This arrangement was to be valid until the beginning of 2000, subject, of course, to renegotiation.

In both countries, in the midst of liberalization, industrial policy was applied to revitalize this integral component of earlier growth. Multinational automobile enterprises had substantial negotiating power. Brazil went further than Argentina, allowing tariff reductions in 1997 for imports of capital goods for the sector, along with exemptions from local taxes. State and local governments also entered, providing not only fiscal incentives but direct donations of land and infrastructure. These were sizable and generated the desired expansion. Intended initially to help the poorer states of the northeast, these policies widened competition among state governments to attract investment, engendering subsequent problems.

Table 5-2 contains detailed data on bilateral trade in the 1990s. Trade mounts sharply from its 1990 base and more rapidly than total imports of each country. Brazilian imports of food and fuel from Argentina remain larger than those for automobiles and auto parts until the very end. Then, greater Argentine industrial capacity enters. Still, in these years, Brazil gains the initial advantage after Argentina commits to the fixed exchange rate in 1991. Brazilian exports much exceed imports in 1992 through 1994, and additionally show a surplus for the total of machinery, automobiles, and automobile parts virtually throughout.

This led to rising Argentine concerns. Only with creation of the *real,* and its overvaluation, do imports from Argentina expand, and then, the auto sector benefits. Larger automobiles, as opposed to the Brazilian produced "popular car," and not auto parts, make up the bulk of sales. Brazil remains less dependent on Argentina throughout. Something like a third of Argentine exports go to Brazil in 1997 whereas only a tenth of Brazilian exports find their way to Argentina. Moreover, in 1997 virtually all Argentine automobile exports are to Brazil; less than half of Brazilian exports in the sector are sent to Argentina. The larger trade partner is more diversified.

TABLE 5-2. Mercosul Trade, 1990–97

Units as indicated

	1990	1991	1992	1993	1994	1995	1996	1997
Relative Real Exchange Rate Argentina/Brazil (1997 = 1)[a]	0.54	0.93	1.21	1.29	0.21	1.05	0.99	1
Mercosul tariff (percent)								
Argentine	15	7	8	6	5	0[b]	0	0
Brazilian	12	10	4	3	3	0	0	0
Argentine imports (billions of dollars)								
Total imports	4.1	8.3	14.9	16.8	21.6	20.1	23.8	30.3
From Brazil	0.7	1.5	3.3	3.6	4.3	4.2	5.3	6.9
Machinery	0.06	0.12	0.25	0.33	0.41	0.32	0.46	0.57
Automobiles	0.06	0.09	0.36	0.21	0.18	0.13	0.27	0.64
Auto parts	0.05	0.12	0.38	0.48	0.5	0.49	0.58	0.6
Brazilian imports (billions of dollars)								
Total imports	22.5	23	22.3	27.3	35.5	53.7	56.7	65.1
Imports from Argentina	1.5	1.7	1.8	2.8	3.8	5.7	7.1	8.6
Food	0.87	0.86	0.84	1.05	0.38	2.04	2.3	2.34
Fuel	0.01	0.06	0.11	0.54	0.63	0.77	1.24	1.25
Machinery	0.06	0.06	0.05	0.06	0.08	0.15	0.15	0.19
Automobiles	[c]	0.03	0.1	0.15	0.15	0.21	0.78	1.36
Auto parts	0.05	0.07	0.12	0.25	0.39	0.46	0.37	0.34
Surplus-deficit ratio								
Bilateral goods trade (Brazil data)	-0.9	-0.3	1.2	0.8	0.3	-0.6	-0.3	-1.8
Total goods trade								
Argentina	8.3	3.7	-2.6	-3.7	-5.8	0.8	0	-3.9
Brazil	8.9	8.6	13.7	11.4	8.1	-7.2	-9	12.1

Sources: Exchange rate: Economist Intelligence Unit database (www.eiu.com/public). Goods trade and surplus-deficit ratio: UN Comtrade data (http://comtrade.un.org/db/default.aspx).
a. Deflated by consumer price indexes.
b. Mercosul tariffs go to zero, with exceptions cited in text.
c. Less than 0.01 billion dollars.

The bilateral trade growth achieved was not immune from criticism. Exchange of automobiles and auto parts expanded, but under special rules that were far from free. Nor are they the only capital-intensive goods to increase with high rates of protection. Some part of trade growth during this period was quite possibly trade diverting rather than trade creating. An article suggesting that conclusion emanated from World Bank research and quickly elicited replies from government officials and others committed to regional integration.[9] These correctly argued that the author used data on exports rather than imports, as well as ignored the possibility of economies of scale and more rapid technological gain, abetted by abundant direct foreign investment within the sector.

Nonetheless, the underlying issue remains. Trade growth alone does not guarantee efficiency. Mercosul does differ from earlier Latin American free trade attempts like the Latin American Free Trade Association (LAFTA) and the Latin American Integration Association (LAIA). This time there was a generalized opening to trade accompanied by progressively lower tariffs; moreover, transportation costs between the neighboring partners were lower than regionwide. There was scope for trade creation, or at least, lesser trade diversion. Increased imports over time within Mercosul received a stimulus from the falling levels of protection.[10] Even in the automobile sector, there was evidence of rising productivity from massive new investment—and hence future benefits—although the immediate short-term effects may well have been trade diverting.

The Crisis Years, 1997–2002. By the summer of 1997, expanding bilateral trade was drawing to a close. Brazil faced problems as total imports rose. The current account deficit amounted to over 3 percent of gross domestic product. Regulations to curtail financing of imports were decided upon. There was no special treatment, or even prior notice, for Mercosul partners. Once they complained, changes took place, but policy direction had altered.[11] Proex, a source of special benefits to exporters, incorporated new products. Taxes were raised to inhibit demand for consumer durables, and a 3 percent charge was added onto imports in the fall.

Those modest reactions pale in comparison to the effects of the Asian crisis. Thailand, Indonesia, and even South Korea were forced to devalue. Their growing foreign deficits had been financed by short-term borrowing. Brazil fought off a speculative exchange rate attack in the fall by raising interest rates to levels in excess of 40 percent. These fell before the presidential election but were soon to soar again. Brazil's exchange rate anchor, and therefore compatibility with Argentina's fixed rate, was coming to an end.

In August 1998, the Russian crisis affected Brazil as global financial institutions curbed their loans and reduced their exposure. Brazil's international reserves began to dissipate; there was a speculative attack in October. In November a massive loan of $41.5 billion was put together by the IMF, backed by the World Bank, the Inter-American Development Bank (IDB), the United States, and the European Union. In the midst of widening international economic unrest, a line in the sand had been drawn.

In such dire circumstances, Brazil was able to raise taxes. An initial primary surplus—the first of a continuing sequence—occurred in the last quarter of 1998. But that was not enough: in January there was a major devaluation, and another agreement with the IMF was drawn up.

The Argentine economy likewise slowed in response to international adversity and a strengthening real peso. Brazil's devaluation ran counter to Argentine hopes. All talk of policy consistency within Mercosul was forgotten as Brazil pursued stabilization on its own. In 1999 Argentina experienced the first of four years of continuing decline. Brazil began to be seen as a key causal factor in this loss of Argentine dynamism.

Subsequent to Brazilian devaluation, the Union Industrial de Argentina, the largest employer organization, called for a strong domestic response. A special report highlighted in detail the potential exit of 100 firms. In January 2000, an organization spokesman put the case simply: "Argentina ought to take measures to protect its industry."[12] In the same month, Brazilian ambassador José Botafogo was sent to Buenos Aires to deal with accumulating Mercosul issues.

This section does not detail the many specific disputes in industries such as steel, textiles, pork products, dairy products, wheat, chicken, rice, and shoes. These are all discussed elsewhere.[13] On the whole, the means of their resolution still holds today. An agreement between the private sector contestants, even if not entirely satisfactory, works for a short while; then the issue recurs. That sometimes led to a Mercosul arbitration panel, as with textiles; Argentina accepted that decision, but only after Brazil brought the dispute to the WTO. On another occasion, a special presidential meeting in Brasília occurred in July 1999 after Argentina used the ALADI norms to impose import quotas. That meeting, like others before at the highest level, achieved success.

Regarding automobiles and auto parts, instead of the agreed upon free trade at the beginning of 2000, another protective pact emerged in

August of that year. Long and difficult negotiations were involved. That arrangement did not last long: exports from Argentina were larger in 2001, in the midst of Brazilian decline. So another pact was substituted in 2002. That agreement applied the maximum WTO tariff level of 35 percent to entries from third countries, allowed greater reliance on local auto parts, and retained duty-free exchange of automobiles between Argentina and Brazil. The disproportion between Brazilian exports and imports would increase from 1.6 in 2001 to 2.6 in 2005.[14] Brazil, as the dominant car producer, benefited.

Economic conditions within Argentina, having survived Brazil's devaluation, turned worse in 2001. President de la Rúa, in desperation, turned to Domingo Cavallo. His second coming did not replicate his prior role as national savior. His decisions as finance minister disregarded Mercosul rules. Tariffs were unilaterally modified, raised on consumer goods and reduced on capital goods. Cavallo spoke frequently, as before, about ending the fiction of a Mercosul common market, much preferring a free trade agreement with the United States.[15] To the end, he believed that Brazil's pursuit of its own policy objectives contributed to Argentine failure.

In troubled joint circumstances after 1999, Mercosul was not of prime interest. Yet it absorbed time. There were two presidential meetings a year plus many by cabinet officials, apart from special efforts to resolve the many disputes. Discussions after 1999 returned to the need for a consistent macroeconomic policy. There was ready agreement on Maastricht-like requirements for acceptable levels of fiscal deficit, public debt, and inflation, but only for future implementation.

Table 5-3 presents data for the years between 1998 and 2002. It is not a pretty picture. After 1998 growth rates of gross national product decline, with modest improvement in 2000. Aggregate imports continue on a steady pace downward. Bilateral trade shows greater reduction. Results in 2002 are comparable to those almost a full decade earlier. The composition of trade altered. Brazilian imports of machinery, automobiles, and auto parts from Argentina decline from almost a quarter of the total in 1998 to about a seventh in 2000. Conversely, imports of food and oil hold up. Brazilian automotive exports to Argentina exceed imports for the first time, an advantage sustained in later years.

This change in the trade pattern coincided with Brazilian devaluation. That led some to argue that the other Mercosul countries would suffer because their production of "regional" goods, those without an external market, would be reduced by their increased relative price.[16] This

TABLE 5-3.   Mercosul Trade, 1998–2002

Units as indicated

	1998	1999	2000	2001	2002
Relative real exchange rate Argentina/ Brazil (1997 = 1)[a]	1.06	1.68	1.56	1.92	0.87
Argentine imports (billions of dollars)					
Total imports	31.4	25.5	25.3	20.3	9
Imports from Brazil	7.1	5.6	6.5	5.3	2.5
Machinery	0.56	0.39	0.36	0.33	0.12
Automobiles	0.66	0.34	0.42	0.23	0.12
Auto parts	0.59	0.4	0.37	0.27	0.15
Brazilian imports (billions of dollars)					
Total imports	60.8	51.7	55.9	55.6	47.2
Imports from Argentina	8.4	6.1	6.8	6.2	4.7
Food	2.58	1.99	1.83	0.56	1.32
Fuel	0.7	0.62	1.34	0.85	0.64
Machinery	0.2	0.16	0.2	0.2	0.14
Automobiles	1.53	0.61	0.6	0.8	0.34
Auto parts	0.27	0.23	0.25	0.19	0.17
Surplus-deficit ratio					
Bilateral goods trade (Brazil data)	−1.7	−0.7	−0.6	−1.2	−2.4
Total goods trade					
Argentina	−4.9	−2.2	1	6.3	16.7
Brazil	−9.7	−3.7	−0.7	2.7	13.2

Sources: See table 5-2.
a. Deflated by consumer price indexes.

exposure lies behind the proliferation of special cases. An increase in Brazilian exports of those regional goods should also occur. What table 5-3 shows, however, is no Brazilian trade surplus with Argentina in 1999 and the following years.

Income increases explain the rise occurring in both countries in 2000, but it is reciprocal, without disproportionate Brazilian advantage as a consequence of devaluation.[17] What seems to have happened is an expanded range of voluntary export restraints.

To put it another way, Brazilian exporters began to lose interest in Mercosul and turned instead to the growing global economy where their competitiveness had increased. Brazil allowed the Cavallo zero tariff on capital goods imports to persist until mid-2003, well after both govern-ments changed. Opportunities for Brazilian agricultural and manufactur-ing exports began to emerge. By 2002 there was a total surplus of more than $13 billion on the trade account, while the corresponding balance with Argentina registered a small deficit.

As Mercosul was downgraded, Itamaraty's focus shifted to other countries within the region.[18] This change was already under way. Bra-zil negotiated the border dispute between Peru and Ecuador, as well as played an active role in preserving Paraguayan democracy. A free trade agreement with the Andean countries had almost been reached in 1998. Brazil turned its attention to South American integration as a stepping-stone to eventual negotiation of the Free Trade Agreement of the Ameri-cas (FTAA) with the United States.

A first meeting of all South American countries took place in Brasília on August 31, 2000, with the intent of stimulating regional integration. Transportation projects among the countries, with IDB finance, were elaborated. Some were later realized. But, as economic problems soon proliferated in the region, this alternative forum provoked little immedi-ate followthrough. Only later did it reappear in the guise of UNASUR (Union of South American Nations).

A Potentially Vibrant Alternative to FTAA, 2003 Onward. With Lula's election in 2002, Mercosul received a new impulse. Celso Lafer, foreign minis-ter at the end of the Cardoso regime, emphasized that Mercosul, unlike FTAA, was not an option but rather Brazil's destiny. The entering admin-istration went further: as Lula argued during the presidential campaign, a major objective of foreign policy was "to reestablish Mercosul, to expand and deepen this process beyond *commercial interests.*"[19] The election of a Peronist successor in the Argentine presidential election, Néstor Kirch-ner, by a wide margin in March 2003 ensured that both countries were on the same political track. Roberto Lavagna, the Argentine minister of finance, had participated in the founding of the regional market and looked kindly on it.

Yet a closer bilateral relationship with Argentina did not evolve. Key was the different macroeconomic approach of the two governments. Brazil retained its pact with the IMF and raised its primary surplus target. Argen-tina, by contrast, rejected cooperation with the IMF and defaulted on its internationally held debt. Only in 2010, after suffering years of limited for-eign direct investment, has Argentina finally settled matters. Brazil utilized global export growth to recuperate after 2003. Argentina opted for import

TABLE 5-4.   **Mercosul Trade, 2003–06**

Units as indicated

	2003	2004	2005	2006
Relative real exchange rate Argentina/Brazil (1997 = 1)[a]	0.97	0.88	0.73	0.65
Argentine imports (billions of dollars)				
Total imports	13.9	22.4	28.7	34.2
Imports from Brazil	4.7	7.6	10.6	11.7
Machinery	0.41	0.71	0.78	.83[b]
Automobiles	0.41	0.96	1.29	1.48
Auto parts	0.19	0.33	0.54	0.91
Brazilian imports (billions of dollars)				
Total imports	48.3	62.8	73.6	91.3
Imports from Argentina	4.7	5.6	6.2	8.1
Food	1.42	1.38	1.37	1.83
Fuel	0.61	0.76	0.8	0.93
Machinery	0.14	0.15	0.17	0.2
Automobiles	0.21	0.22	0.33	0.88
Auto parts	0.18	0.3	0.4	0.44
Surplus-deficit ratio				
Bilateral goods trade (Brazil data)	–0.1	1.8	3.7	3.7
Total goods trade				
Argentina	16.1	12.1	11.4	12.3
Brazil	24.9	33.8	44.9	46.5

Sources: See table 5-2.
a. Deflated by consumer price indexes.
b. Disaggregated data are Brazil exports to Argentina for 2006.

substitution to revive stalled industrialization. Even exports of soybeans in both countries exhibited differences. Argentina accepted genetically modified seeds whereas Brazil did so reluctantly and only partially.

Since 2003 bilateral trade between Argentina and Brazil has been riled by disputes, not only about sugar and automobiles but also textiles, shoes, consumer durables, and capital goods. As earlier, the first solution was extensive negotiation and imposition of temporary quotas. That effort did not succeed, as shown in table 5-4. From 2003 forward to 2008, Brazil generated surpluses in trade with Argentina. As Argentina recovered, Brazil exported a range of manufactures, no longer offset by Argentine surpluses in food and petroleum. In 2009, as global trade diminished, bilateral exchange plummeted by more than 40 percent in the first nine months, virtually erasing the Brazilian trade surplus; with joint upturn and greater trade, the former imbalance reappeared in 2010.

Brazilian exports of automobiles and auto parts have especially benefited. These went up from $270 million in 2002 to $3.9 billion in 2008. There also has been a rise in exports of machinery and a range of other products. By contrast, Argentine exports of automobiles and parts to Brazil were larger in 1998 (even in non-price-deflated dollars) than in 2006. Subsequent results show a slightly higher rate of growth in these products for Argentina than Brazil, but that had little effect upon the net balance, at least until 2009.

This trade surplus provoked changes in regulation of bilateral exchange. The auto sector rules expired in 2006. Instead of the 2002 provision permitting Brazil more than twice as many exports as imports, Argentina, not surprisingly, wanted to return an equal number of cars. That amendment, "after prolonged and difficult negotiations," was agreed upon in June 2006. Brazil's auto industry was oriented globally. While exports mounted to a third of production, less than 30 percent went to Argentina in 2006. Those cars came to more than half of Argentine sales. By contrast, Argentine exports made up less than 5 percent of the larger—by more than four times—Brazilian consumption.[20] Productivity within the two countries had diverged: since 1999 labor productivity and scale of production had risen in Brazil.[21]

Back in 2003, protests from Argentine industry led to the creation of a Bilateral Commission for Monitoring Trade to facilitate private sector negotiation. A year later, Minister Lavagna pressed for safeguards to counter macroeconomic asymmetry and differential competitiveness. More than fifteen months of negotiation passed before these were added to treaty provisions.

This Mechanism of Competitive Adaptation was more a legalistic step to satisfy domestic Argentine pressures for protection against import competition than a practical solution.[22] Difficulties regularly continued. As a share of Brazilian imports, Argentina has yielded to China, while Brazil continues to command a third of the Argentine market. The disparity produces constant suggestions for modifying the rules and repeated presidential statements—the last in June 2010—about forthcoming improvement. Discussion about how to implement Banco Sur, advocated by Venezuela as a substitute for the IMF and approved in 2007, has persisted. Brazil and Argentina have agreed to trade in their currencies, but implementation lags. Meetings and apparent decisions recur, but action is lacking.

Mercosul no longer lives up to past hopes. What changes might help? One direction is a true common market with a single currency and a consistent macroeconomic policy. That was the destination originally envisaged.

Fabio Giambiagi proposed a bilateral common market between the two countries, thereby excluding Paraguay and Uruguay, as well as Venezuela. The latter could switch to a free trade agreement, as Bolivia, Chile, and Peru currently have. A real common market requires universal sectoral inclusion, ending the special position of automobiles and sugar, not to mention many other protective arrangements; a common tariff; and common institutions governing economic activity, regulatory rules, and industrial policy. Only at the very end do macroeconomic coordination and monetary unification enter.[23]

Logically sound, this option sharply clashes with reality. The automobile sector, responsible for more than a fifth of bilateral exchange, will not quietly acquiesce. The earlier promise of free bilateral trade was left out of the 2006 agreement. Other sectors involving a range of consumer goods, consumer durables, and capital goods have managed their own solutions.

Corporatism still reigns. Trade associations are involved at the microeconomic level, sector by sector, and influence their respective governments. As the director of ABECEB, an Argentine consulting firm, put it, "The first steps of the negotiations [in the 1980s] advanced on a sectoral basis: bilateral agreements in previously identified sectors. . . . The original methodology permitted detection of asymmetries and discussion case by case of the possible solutions which could facilitate mechanisms of industrial complementation and integration of chains of production. The later methodology hid the asymmetries behind the great macro objective of the Customs Union."[24] Sudden reliance on market forces through a decline in tariff protection under Menem and Collor accelerated trade but hardly eliminated domestic resistance.

This reluctance to negotiate has come to the fore as the economic strategies of Argentina and Brazil diverged. Brazil sanctifies low rates of inflation but needs a consistent fiscal and monetary policy. Its fiscal deficit remains, forcing high real interest rates and an overvalued exchange rate. Foreign capital inflows and imports depend on domestic priorities. These far outweigh any priority for bilateral trade.

Argentina, on its side, has been trying to reconstruct its industrial sector. Foreign investment has not returned, and Argentina's credit rating is well below Brazil's. Inflation has been greater for some time and more than officially reported, despite a continuing fiscal surplus. The exchange rate has progressively appreciated as a consequence. Trade intervention is a necessary balancing instrument.

Ultimately, therefore, one returns to the present imperfect trading arrangement. Mercosul policy is slow to change; costs are too high. Ardent regionalism has ceded to globalism. Brazil has entered the global market more vigorously than anyone imagined twenty years ago. Exports have grown and diversified by type as well as destination. Argentina no longer is the preferred choice. Today, China and India are the desired economic and political partners. Their size and growth are without parallel. Brazil is reaching out to both, aware that they are competitors as well as complements.[25]

Perhaps there is a third, and much more radical, alternative: a global future free from the hassles of Mercosul. Marcelo Abreu and Winston Fritsch asserted that at its very start, making light of the economic opportunities afforded by commercial ties to Argentina that others were touting.[26]

Brazil, the United States, and the EU

The idea of extending the North American Free Trade Agreement (NAFTA) did not emerge in the United States until almost a year after the Clinton administration began. A hemispheric summit was promised.[27] The crucial question, unresolved until a month before the meeting, was whether President Clinton would make free trade a centerpiece. Failure to do so would disappoint the larger countries; many had little interest in the ancillary agenda of political and social cooperation being put together. There were fourteen initiatives in the final package, ranging from reinventing government to development of compatible environmental standards.

Key negotiations before the Miami meeting were held between Brazil, representing itself along with the Rio Group, and the United States.[28] A direct encounter occurred only two weeks before the scheduled summit. Discussions covered a number of issues. There was an alternative Latin American draft, involving multiple changes.

For Richard Feinberg, from the United States, these bordered on the trivial and were modest concessions, at best: "The Brazilians and some of the other Latin Americans were intent in using the [Airlie] conference to render the plan of action more modest in its ambitions, less exact in its objectives, less specific in its timetables, and less accountable in its implementation." For Simas Magalhães, a Brazilian diplomat, "Brazil introduced elements that had been omitted, or treated superficially by the United States, among them the principles of non-intervention in the internal affairs of countries, the interrelationship between democracy and development, and perhaps most relevant of all, recognition of the convergence of existing regional agreements as consistent with FTAA."[29]

The divergence was wide, and that became evident as later negotiations took place. For the United States, the FTAA was a generalization of the successful NAFTA outcome. Mexico had been elevated in status; others in the region could emulate that accomplishment. For Brazil the FTAA created an unwelcome distraction. Its preferred strategy was different: a process beginning with Mercosul, followed by a South American Free Trade Area (SAFTA) and culminating in direct negotiations between NAFTA and SAFTA. Even the personal friendship of Presidents Clinton and Cardoso could not narrow that gap.

In 1995 negotiations about the Free Trade Agreement of the Americas were in full sway. An intensive program of hemispheric meetings and creation of working groups continued in Denver and Cartagena. In imitation of GATT operating procedures, some eleven working groups were established. Some reflected Brazil's eagerness to focus on U.S. agricultural subsidies as well as antidumping and countervailing duties; others groups focusing on services, intellectual property rights, government procurement, and competition policy reflected the U.S. desire to broaden the regional trade agreement beyond previous Uruguay Round results.

Brazil hosted the 1997 ministers' meeting in Belo Horizonte. There, signs of lingering Brazilian dissatisfaction emerged. There was insistence upon Mercosul's right to negotiate as a group and to survive any regional agreement that might be reached. The negotiation was to be a single undertaking: all countries were to take full part, just as with formation of the WTO. Any final decision required unanimity. These discussions enhanced Brazil's position as leader of the Latin American bloc. Impatience with the lack of U.S. fast-track authority was growing, and other countries went along. Brazil ensured a public presence at the conclave, making clear the domestic popularity of these positions.

The summit next year in Santiago moved to actual negotiation, despite the Clinton administration's inability to obtain fast-track authority. The United States argued that such a provision was important only for final congressional approval and that discussions should continue. Brazil remained engaged, but only marginally. Extension of Mercosul to South America as a whole occupied Itamaraty. Any final FTAA negotiation would occur between Brazil and the United States, each representing its neighbors. That arrangement was already implicit since the two countries would serve as co-chairs in the final round.

Brazil also reinitiated negotiations with the European Union, as agreed in 1995.[30] Right after conclusion of the Uruguay Round, there was little incentive for another major effort to expand international trade, but facts began to argue differently. Exchange with Europe was growing, as was foreign investment, in the midst of privatization and Brazilian economic realignment. By 1997 the EU exceeded the United States in direct foreign investment. Spain and Portugal had taken the lead.

As the FTAA moved ahead after the Santiago Summit of the Americas, so did discussions with the EU. An EU–Latin America summit in June 1999 became the focal point: "Brazil . . . made clear that the summit could be a success only if EU-Mercosul free trade negotiations were launched."[31] That discussion did begin but only after considerable effort and compromise within the EU Council. The concluding text excluded reference to a free trade area, agreeing upon "expansion . . . and development of free trade" in its stead. Chile was to be included in the talks.

These negotiations began in Buenos Aires in April 2000 and continued thereafter. The moment was not propitious. Argentina was in dispute with Brazil about whether Mercosul should revert to a free trade area rather than move ahead to a common market. In December 2001, the Argentine government collapsed and its successors were forced to devalue. Political chaos and income decline ensued before stability returned at the end of 2002. Brazil, recovering from its own devaluation in early 1999, was afflicted by an energy crisis in 2001, slowing economic growth, and rising inflation. Furthermore, a presidential election loomed in 2002. This was hardly the moment for negotiating a comprehensive trade agreement.

George W. Bush became U.S. president with a Republican congressional majority in 2000. He obtained his version of fast track, Trade Promotion Authority, by the middle of 2002. At the Quebec City Summit of the Americas in April 2001, in the midst of contrary public demonstrations, Bush encouraged a drive to completion.

Cardoso, approaching the end of his term of office, and aware of domestic opposition from labor unions, industrialists, academics, and diplomats, was less positive in his prepared remarks: "FTAA will only be of interest to Brazil if it offers effective access to more dynamic markets,

establishes anti-dumping rules, reduces nontariff barriers . . . if, in pro-
tecting intellectual property, FTAA promotes at the same time the technological capacity of our people. . . . If not, it would be irrelevant, or in
the worst of hypotheses, undesirable."[32] U.S. Trade Representative Robert Zoellick's response, in a post-conference press gathering, was more
pointed: "Brazil will have to choose between being a global player and
being the largest country in the Southern Cone."[33]

Once fast-track legislation actually passed, Brazil engaged in negotiations more actively. A second draft of a potential agreement emerged
from the Quito ministerial meeting in October 2002. Brazil and the
United States officially became co-chairs of the process moving forward.
Specific trade proposals from individual countries were to be received by
February 15, 2003. Brazil, after the Lula election and with little preparatory time, opted to present a modest list of possible tariff reductions limited to goods, proposed a later terminal date, and reiterated a preference
for negotiation as a Mercosul group. The United States gave evidence of
its increasing impatience with Brazil by offering a differentiated proposal,
with larger tariff cuts for one group of participants and lesser reductions
for Mercosul.

The FTAA discussions were rapidly coming to an end but not with
the positive conclusion foreseen in 1994. Brazil had already decided,
before the Cancún WTO ministerial meeting in September 2003, to opt
out. That emerged during Zoellick's preparatory trip to Brazil in May,
where he rejected Brazilian hopes for a postponed 2007 termination and
separate bilateral negotiations with Mercosul. Foreign Minister Celso
Amorim elaborated publicly in July the Brazilian position:

> President Lula has approved the blueprint of the Brazilian posi-
> tion on FTAA negotiations. . . . [It] can be described as follows: 1)
> the substance of access to the goods market, and in limited form,
> for services and investments, would be treated in a 4+1 negotia-
> tion between Mercosul and the United States; 2) the FTAA process
> would focus on some basic elements, such as resolution of contro-
> versies, special and differential treatment for developing countries,
> compensation funds, sanitary rules, and commercial trade facilita-
> tion; 3) the more sensitive themes that would represent new obliga-
> tions for Brazil, such as the normative part of intellectual property,
> services, investments, and governmental purchases, would be trans-
> ferred to the WTO.[34]

After the September failure in Cancún, an "FTAA light" solution emerged in November.[35] Its basis was division of negotiations. Mercosul could pursue its limited interests, as already defined, while other countries could seek comprehensive arrangements. As the agreed ministerial declaration put it: "Countries may assume different levels of commitments . . . [with a] common set of rights and obligations applicable to all countries . . . [and may also] choose, within the FTAA, to agree to additional obligations and benefits."[36] A country's benefits were thus linked to the obligations it was prepared to undertake.

Although a third draft text was exchanged at Miami and a subsequent meeting was held at Puebla, Mexico, the negotiations had effectively come to an end. Brazil and the United States, leading the trade negotiating committee, did not organize another encounter. The extent to which FTAA had become unrealizable was clear by the fourth and final summit in Mar del Plata, Argentina, in November 2005.

For Brazil ending the FTAA talks rewarded not only PT supporters frustrated with Lula's conservative macroeconomics but also local entrepreneurs concerned with the threat of increased import competition. The Federation of Industry of the State of São Paulo (FIESP) and other local manufacturing associations had opposed the agreement; they produced estimates showing potential losses if Brazilian business adhered to its conditions. At a moment when a trade surplus was only just emerging, evidence of greater imports than exports as a consequence of FTAA participation provided a powerful argument in favor of retreat.[37]

These quantitative effects are not indisputable. Some results assert the opposite: a larger gain in exports than imports and an increase in Brazilian GDP.[38] Everything depends on the particular assumptions of the models. Such projections are hardly decisive evidence, even when increasing returns and various dynamic feedbacks are included.

The effects of a free trade agreement with the EU have been calculated, and the results have been compared with those for the FTAA. They are presented in a little volume, provocatively titled *The Costs of Opting Out*.[39] What one model shows—assuming total free trade except in agriculture—is that the FTAA and an EU free trade agreement come out fairly even as alternatives. A second shows that "the FTAA agreement enables the Mercosur countries to increase their manufactures exports more than the FTAA + Mercosur-EU agreement." In a third scenario, there is elaboration of the last result: a free trade agreement with the EU, without limitations, enables great expansion of Mercosur exports of sugar, meat, wheat, rice, and other foodstuffs; exports of manufactures increase at a lesser rate. By contrast, the FTAA generates a more balanced increase across sectors.[40]

These results did not influence policy. The Lula administration chose to focus on the Doha Round and later, to revive Mercosul discussions with the EU. Neither has produced anything conclusive. Formal discussions with the EU involved twenty negotiating sessions between May 2000 and October 2004, when the Doha talks superseded them. Agreement to resume negotiations was reached in May 2010. On that occasion, Cristina Fernandez, serving as head of Mercosul, asked for an agreement that would "constitute a real association in which both parties . . . start seeing each other as partners. . . . Everyone must obtain some advantages so that it does not become a burden for any of our economies."[41]

A Bolivarian Alternative

Brazil, with its decision to host the first-ever meeting of South American leaders in 2000, has made little secret of its hopes for continental leadership. A South American free trade organization would bolster negotiating power vis-à-vis the United States and extend the earlier organized Rio Group. Despite continuing efforts and the support of the IDB for highways and other unifying projects, a formal free trade combination of the Andean and Mercosul groups never has taken form. UNASUR has gradually come to substitute, without showing signs of practical progress. As a result, Brazil oriented its foreign policy more broadly. Greater Brazilian trade has nonetheless evolved within the region, and it has been a growing and large market for manufacturing exports.

Venezuela has, from time to time, contested this Brazilian role. Since that country's formal, but still non-ratified, entry into Mercosul in 2006, President Hugo Chávez has wanted to incorporate the scheme within his vision of continent-wide socialism. He is uninterested in the old Mercosul, geared to economic exchange and motivated by "savage" capitalism.[42] The prize for him is leadership of South America, and he has used his country's petroleum resources to that end.

When the price of oil soared in 2008, he had foreign exchange to distribute. Argentina, Bolivia, Cuba, Ecuador, Nicaragua, and others benefited. Petroleum was made available to Caribbean countries at lower cost. His assistance exceeded U.S. foreign aid, and his promises were greater still. Now, in 2011, with oil prices again higher, but Venezuelan national income barely greater, those prospects have dimmed—but not Chávez's rhetoric nor his efforts to try to enlist Brazil in his Bolivarian dream.

Chávez preaches freedom from U.S. and IMF imperialism. He wants to go beyond his association with Cuba, Bolivia, Ecuador, and others within the Bolivarian Alternative for Latin America (ALBA)] to South America as a whole. He renamed UNASUR, but that grouping has not yielded much gain to his ambitions. Within Mercosul Chávez has sponsored far-reaching ideas such as continental length natural gas networks and the Bank of the South. Little beyond regular meetings and discussions about this twenty-first-century socialist alternative has yet transpired. It has not served his intent.

Differences between the countries have emerged, as at the 2007 Energy Conference when Chávez argued against ethanol as depriving the people of the food they need.[43] In Copenhagen at the end of 2009, Brazil was a key signatory to a preliminary agreement on global warming. Venezuela was much opposed and openly dissented. On the other side, there has been an occasional alliance. In the case of the 2009 Honduran exile of its president, Chávez's efforts received backing from Brazil, in whose embassy ex-president Zelaya stayed. There was also seeming concordance during Iranian president Ahmadinejad's visit to Venezuela, Bolivia, and Brazil at the end of 2009.

This variable relationship reveals the diplomatic sophistication of Brazil as opposed to Venezuela's narrower agenda. Chávez's concerns are predictable and do little to advance the independent status he seeks. He now must deal with a new Brazilian president and foreign minister at a moment when his popularity, both domestically and internationally, has been in decline. He has stepped back in his feud with Colombia and no longer is a factor in Peru. Forces seem to be moving against Venezuela's efforts to play a larger regional role, just when Brazil's are expanding. Statements in favor of Bolivarian unity are one thing; followthrough is another.

Brazil and the India-Brazil-South Africa Dialogue Forum

The India-Brazil-South Africa Dialogue Forum (IBSA) was organized soon after Lula's inauguration.[44] This alliance extended discussions with South Africa, ongoing since the end of apartheid in 1994, to encompass India as well. A series of meetings during the first part of 2003 led to creation of the forum at a meeting of foreign ministers in Brasília. That was followed by a presidential conclave in September.

Two elements explain the unusual speed of this undertaking. One was the launch of a major effort by Brazil and India, along with Germany and Japan, to secure permanent membership on the UN Security Council. The IBSA leaders met in New York at the beginning of the General Assembly session. South Africa—not yet part of the Group of Four (the African Union was representing that continent's interest)—clearly had this objective in mind. This IBSA grouping helps define their claim, as opposed to alternatives such as Pakistan, say, or Argentina and Mexico, or Egypt and Nigeria.

The second factor was Brazil's search for support at the WTO Cancún meeting, where Indian assent was key. The country was an ally within the Uruguay Round and supported the amendment allowing production of generic drugs for critical diseases like HIV/AIDs, tuberculosis, and malaria. At Cancún, while the Group of Twenty (G-20) leadership fell to Brazil, India and South Africa were important members. Brazil and India participated in later meetings with the United States and the EU trying to move the Doha Round toward completion, and India's refusal to go along in 2008 prevented agreement.

Neither of those aims has yet come to fruition, but IBSA has. Annual rotating meetings of the three executives began in 2006 in Brazil. There is a logic to IBSA: all three countries are functioning democracies, are regional leaders, span wide cultural and racial differences, are populous, seek to accelerate their rates of economic growth, are active members of the UN, participate in the new G-20 dealing with the world economy, and emphasize a global diplomatic presence.

Differences, however, also abound. In military terms, India is prominent. That comes from historic and ongoing conflict with Pakistan and China. As a result, India has nuclear capability, now accepted by the United States, but a direction both Brazil and South Africa have rejected. That is not its only distinction. India provides more personnel for various United Nations peace missions than other countries.

In economic terms, Brazil's purchasing power parity per capita income is three times as large as India's and equals South Africa's. India has grown at a high rate and specialized in increasing service exports over the last fifteen years. Its rural poverty and educational needs are recognized problems. South Africa has managed continuing, if lower, growth without an inflationary surge. Its need to cope with high unemployment—more than a quarter of the labor force—and high inequality of income is a constant pressure. South Africa is the most open economy of the three, with total external trade amounting to 60 percent of income, versus 45 percent for India and 25 percent for Brazil. All of the countries have much reduced their levels of protection over the last twenty years. Brazil started first, with South Africa following in the 1990s, and India has rapidly caught up thereafter.

Yet intra-IBSA trade is limited, despite recent expansion. There have been efforts to create a preferential trade agreement. Mercosul and India signed a trade treaty in January 2004, where modest preferences were reciprocally granted in certain sectors. Those amounted to only a tenth or so of the items within the tariff code. And in December of that year, Mercosul also signed a trade agreement with the South African Customs Union (South Africa and its immediate neighbors). That treaty had its beginnings in 2000, and it, too, was minimal and quite partial.

At the 2007 summit in Cape Town, talk of a genuine free trade agreement among the three parties surfaced. Since then there is little to report. The trade histories of these countries are not very complementary. Each went through intense, and highly protected, import substitution to create a domestic industrial sector. Within agriculture each is more than self-sufficient. And within services, where India has concentrated its trade efforts, the other two prefer to develop their own capabilities.

Table 5-5 presents data on trilateral trade that support this conclusion. First, the level of interchange is small; export of gold from South Africa to India is the dominant entry. Distance enters as an explanation. Contrast the also reported trade between neighboring Brazil and Argentina. Second, Brazilian commerce with the other two IBSA countries has grown but not very differently from trade totals. Recent information does not alter this result. When one examines the specific composition of trade, this conclusion of marginal importance is reinforced. Brazilian imports from India are largely diesel oil; more than half the exports are copper sulfates and crude soy oil. Trade with South Africa is more diversified, but barely. Imports are ferromanganese, organic chemicals, and platinum and rhodium. Exports include automobiles—a third of the total—as well as machinery, sugar, and chicken and meat products.

Each of these middle powers looks elsewhere for its principal alliances, despite flowery speeches at annual IBSA summits. Each of the individual countries is better integrated with rich countries than poor ones. The grouping exists more as a product of active foreign offices than a response to market impulses. India, more proximate to the United States, may desert Brazil, as it did in the Uruguay Round and once again in the

TABLE 5-5. **IBSA Trade versus Argentina-Brazil Trade, 2003 and 2006**
Billions of U.S. dollars

| Country | 2003 Imports | | | Total |
	Argentina	India	South Africa	
2003 Exports				
Argentina	. . .	0.6	0.3[a]	29.9
Brazil	4.6	0.6	0.7	73.2
India	0.1	. . .	0.5	63
South Africa	0.4	2.0[b]	. . .	31.6
Total	13.9	77.2	34.5	. . .

	2006 Imports			
2006 Exports				
Argentina	. . .	0.9	0.9	46.4
Brazil	11.7	0.9	1.5	137.8
India	2	. . .	2.2	126.1
South Africa	0.1	2.5[c]	. . .	53.2
Total	34.2	185.4	69.2	. . .

Sources: UN Comtrade data (http://comtrade.un.org/db/default.aspx); Ministry of Development, ALICE-Web (Internet-Based Foreign Trade Information Analysis System).
a. Calculated as imports from Argentina for this year.
b. Includes gold; excluding, US$0.4 billion.
c. Includes gold; excluding, US$0.8 billion.

Geneva talks in July 2008. South Africa, more integrated economically with the EU, may decide to turn its attention northward.

Future collaboration can provide a stronger basis for engagement. There are a dozen areas where joint working groups exist. Energy is one: all three countries look to alternatives to petroleum to satisfy energy needs. This remains true for Brazil, despite the substantial presalt oil fields discovered offshore. Ethanol, based on sugar, has promise for India, the second-largest global producer of cane sugar; there is also jatropha as a potential source for biodiesel. South Africa has specialized in transforming coal to liquid gas. If real collaboration were to evolve, this international grouping could begin to make sense.

The IBSA will continue, as it should. It conveys an important message: the virtue of political democracy. The organization offers a base for South-South activism and a claim for global UN leadership. Will it remain just a minor appendage? That depends. Some laud IBSAC, incorporating China, as the next step,[45] The IBSA, however, could entail a common diplomatic force vis-à-vis China, a direction that might soon become relevant.

Brazil and Multilateralism

During the decades since civilian government resumed, Brazil has been a major participant in multilateral endeavors concerning economic growth and trade, global warming, and international security.

The GATT and WTO

The Uruguay Round was formally proclaimed in 1986 at the GATT ministerial meeting held in Punta del Este. Its conclusion came eight long years after, in April 1994, at Marrakesh.

The Uruguay Round was the first occasion when developing countries achieved an influential voice within GATT. Previous negotiations had focused on the industrial sector and limits to trade among the industrial countries. Post–World War II globalization owed much to that process. Average tariffs on manufactures declined by approximately two-thirds between the 1948 Geneva Round and the 1979 Tokyo Round. Europe and Japan recovered rapidly from their post-1945 disrepair, aided by the U.S. foreign assistance and openness to imports. In the midst of the cold war, politics trumped economic considerations alone.

As Asian countries such as South Korea and Taiwan began to grow rapidly through industrial exports in the latter 1960s and early 1970s, import substitution came under critical fire from the World Bank, OECD, and elsewhere. International trade was expanding at a rate twice as great as world gross domestic product. Openness offered another, and more efficient, route to manufacturing specialization. The oil shocks of the 1970s, which slowed the growth of the industrialized countries and increased the availability of cheap external debt, gave import substitution a final chance. Outward orientation was beginning to take hold in developing countries.

In 1982 GATT was asked by the United States to expand its agenda from goods alone to new areas, such as the service sector, and to new rules to govern foreign investment and intellectual property rights. The Brazilian response was quite negative, and its opposition persisted in subsequent ministerial meetings.[46] India also joined in resistance to such an agenda during 1984. At that time, the so-called Group of Ten took shape, inclusive of other developing countries, notably Argentina, Egypt, and Yugoslavia; its aims were broad.

These countries sought to block extension of GATT into areas of primary interest to the United States and to ensure attention to agriculture and the Multi-Fiber Arrangement governing textiles and clothing. Both of these issues were also novel for GATT: agriculture had not been discussed since concession of a 1955 U.S. waiver, and the Multi-Fiber Arrangement was a special regime and therefore technically beyond regular GATT rules. The Group of Ten insisted upon a "standstill," thereby averting new restrictive rules sought by developed countries, as well as a "rollback," elimination of all practices at variance with established procedures.

Another alliance of countries took shape in 1985, ahead of the Punta del Este meeting a year later. The Cairns Group consisted of leading world exporters of agricultural products. Brazil became a member, as did eight other developing countries. Three high-income primary producers—the former U.K. colonies of Australia, Canada, and New Zealand—also joined. This group wanted explicit treatment of the agricultural issue, favoring freer exchange, and saw itself as mediator between the United States and the European Union. Brazil's goals, however, were different. It viewed agricultural exports as secondary to industrial exports, and its claims for special and differentiated treatment for manufactured products dominated any concern it had regarding liberalization of primary products.

In 1986 the Uruguay Round was launched. That involved a delicate compromise, already signaling future changes within GATT. New areas proposed by the United States were included on the agenda but so were protection of the agricultural sector and of textiles and clothing. Brazil finally yielded, in part because of ongoing bilateral trade issues with the United States, and in part because other developing countries had not rallied in support. These lessons were not forgotten in later Doha Round negotiations.

Services were allowed consideration but were to be discussed in a two-track fashion: negotiations on freeing up their trade were to take place within a special GATT committee. This was a pyrrhic victory for Brazil, despite the considerable diplomatic skill and effort invested. Conclusions reached on services were later to be fully incorporated into international trade rules with the metamorphosis of GATT into the WTO.[47]

The Uruguay Round did not reach consensus until the end of 1993, largely because of differences between the EU and the United States. The outcome within the agricultural sector proved disappointing; some progress did occur regarding tropical products, which are noncompetitive on the whole with developed country exports. Rules were established for the first time, however, to limit agricultural governmental subsidies. These were not terribly constraining, and a later round would have to revisit that subject. Agreement banning protection on textiles and clothing was attained, with accelerating effect in future years; only in 2005 would free trade begin to prevail, giving particular advantage to low-wage Asian countries. By that time, the issue was irrelevant for Brazilian textiles.

Tariffs on manufactures continued to come down. They fell by close to 40 percent, as in previous rounds. Of equal importance, a variety of "voluntary trade restrictions," prominent forms of protection in sectors such as computer chips, automobiles, and steel, disappeared. Consolidation of tariff structures occurred, embracing 97 percent of specific items in the developed countries and 65 percent of those within developing countries. Special and differential treatment remained, imposing fewer demands on developing countries for conformity. Zero-tariff entries within the codes of the developed countries doubled.

Advances to increase trade within the service sector did occur, but only modestly. Foreign investment was treated in the Trade-Related Investment Measures (TRIMs) agreement. There were to be no preferences for domestic firms or special export requirements. The Trade-Related Aspects of Intellectual Property Rights (TRIPs) agreement enforced rules governing intellectual property rights, benefiting producers of pharmaceuticals especially. These shortly became a source of controversy. Progress toward a comprehensive regulatory structure within the WTO required far more sophisticated technical and diplomatic interaction than was needed within GATT.[48]

For Brazil the path toward compromise eased with the selection of Ambassador Rubens Ricupero as the Brazilian representative in Geneva in 1988. His personal leadership contributed to exits from impasses in Montreal in 1988 and in Brussels in 1990. Agriculture was a divisive and decisive issue, and the United States and the European Community held contending views. Indeed, final agreement was delayed for almost a year as a result. This theme has again emerged as a dividing line in global trade discussions and has now become even more difficult to resolve.

The Doha Round Negotiations

The Seattle Ministerial Conference at the end of 1999, a supposed prelude to yet another WTO round, proved a failure. Amid organized public opposition, police enforcement, and tear gas, no agenda could be agreed upon. Opponents included nongovernmental organizations (NGOs) and U.S. steelworkers in surprising unison. The former wanted fair trade for the developing countries whereas the latter wanted greater protection against imports. World trade was expanding at an historic pace, twice as great as global output, but prospects for multilateral agreement appeared dim. Growing interest in bilateral arrangements gained force within the developed world. That was a way to help services and technologically advanced sectors while conceding ground in manufactures to the developing countries.

The Doha Development Round was a successful follow-on to the Seattle fiasco. One important reason was the prior September 11, 2001, disaster. Countries wished to show unity, and concessions were made; there was attention to the special needs of developing countries. The TRIPs accord was modified to permit developing countries to manufacture generic medicines, regardless of existing patent protection, for serious epidemics like HIV/AIDS, tuberculosis, and malaria.

Brazil played an important role in the launch of the Doha Round. Both Celso Lafer and José Serra were actors moving the negotiations forward. Successful conclusion became a focus for Itamaraty over the Lula years. For Celso Amorim, the new minister of foreign relations and former ambassador in Geneva at the end of the Uruguay Round, this took priority.

However, success proved elusive. An early ministerial meeting occurred in Cancún in 2003. Brazil took the lead, organizing a group of developing countries—the G-20—to reject the last-minute agreement between the United States and the EU that slighted agriculture. Several developing countries wanted freer agricultural trade and insisted on significant concessions. The World Bank had been suggesting that free trade in agriculture could provide significant gains to several food exporters such as Argentina, Brazil, and Thailand, among others. Ironically, the EU was the largest beneficiary, followed by Japan and South Korea: lower food prices would mean gains for their consumers. Unfortunately, those stakeholders are not organized.[49]

World Bank studies and other research have emphasized a number of key points relating to agriculture over the last years. One is that the widely cited level of $300 billion dollars a year of OECD agricultural support is primarily the consequence of tariff and quota protection rather than domestic subsidies or special assistance to exports. A recent calculation yields a distribution of 75 percent, 19 percent, and 6 percent for

TABLE 5-6.   Support of Agriculture, 2001

Billions of U.S. dollars

Policies	Primary OECD	Primary Non-OECD	Food processing OECD	Food processing Non-OECD	Total	Welfare consequences
Domestic subsidies	90	7	0	0	97	8
Export subsidies	3	1	26	0	30	10
Import tariffs	43	75	172	82	372	111
Total	136	83	198	82	499	129

Source: Anderson, Martin, and Valenzuela, "Market Access," tables 1 and 3.

the effects of these three policies. Tariff protection is most utilized by the EU as a sure way of ensuring profitability to its less efficient agricultural sector. Under such a regime, imports cannot lower prices, and consumer welfare is reduced.

Another finding is that non-OECD countries, most especially the Asian countries, are also important sources of distortion. Efforts by the Group of Thirty-Three for exemption from agricultural liberalization are reflective. This translates into significant political power in a WTO environment requiring generalized consensus.

A third point is that price distortions within food processing approximately double the primary agriculture results. Agricultural activity goes beyond a narrow definition to accommodate later stages of value added. In low-income countries, activities such as flour milling, meat production, and dairy output are among the largest industrial sectors.

Finally, the net welfare consequences of these price distortions, taking account of the demand and supply elasticity that determines how economies readjust to these various interventions, come to about a quarter of the gross support levels: $129 billion (in 2001 dollars and based on 2001 quantities) compared to an initial level of total support of $499 billion.[50] Table 5-6 incorporates all of these factors.

After critical outbursts from both sides following Cancún, discussions began anew, leading to another ministerial meeting in Hong Kong.[51] The United States proposed large reductions in agricultural tariffs, utilizing more than proportional cuts increasing with the level of protection. A new maximum tariff of 75 percent would apply. The EU, where tariff protection is more important, countered with a less generous offer. Under the U.S. plan, its average tariff rates would decline by more than 50 percent, from about 9 to about 4 percent; under the EU proposal, the decline would be in similar proportion, but leaving a higher 18 percent average.

There were other differences, especially in specifying sensitive products: 1 percent of tariff lines could be indicated in the U.S. proposal and 8 percent in the EU's. There is the rub: many highly protected sectors satisfy these exemptions and so limit gains. Additionally, because bound rates are much higher than applied rates, even large reductions of the former can mean little actual liberalization.[52]

The WTO G-20, led by Brazil, tried to intermediate between these opposing U.S. and EU positions but was unsuccessful. At Hong Kong, a smaller immediate reduction of agricultural protection was accepted, in return for EU continuing liberalization. The final date for agricultural subsidies was set at 2013, as the EU insisted, rather than at 2010, which the majority of countries preferred. There was also an important commitment made to the Group of Thirty-Three: the final Hong Kong text recognized the need, and the right, of developing countries to specify which products are essential for food security, rural development, and the income of the poorest farmers, and to establish special safeguards.

This encounter offered sufficient progress to schedule meetings in 2006 to take up the other areas, manufactures and services. But both the Left and the Right were unhappy with these Hong Kong advances. According to the Heritage Foundation of the United States, "The modest progress made . . . at the [Hong Kong] ministerial meeting is disappointing. Although the United States introduced a strong proposal to liberalize trade, other countries held back . . . preventing . . . a substantive conclusion."[53] According to Oxfam, "The WTO Hong Kong ministerial meeting was a lost opportunity to make trade fairer for poor people around the world. Rich countries put their commercial interests before those of developing countries."[54] This difference in views mirrored the divergence among participants. Later meetings failed to achieve agreement.

A last effort was made in July 2008, at the end of the Bush administration, when high agricultural prices prevailed. That made concessions from the United States and the EU easier. Brazil was ready to accede. At the last minute, India demanded the right to limit trade in foodstuffs when international prices soared; that was the moment when farm prices were moving sharply upward. This insistence impeded any further progress. The Great Recession and U.S. presidential elections then imposed a hiatus. In meetings of the UN and the new G-20, Brazil has made completion a primary issue. Now, 2012 may see one more try.

Agriculture remains center stage. The sector represents around 4 percent of global gross product but only 2 percent of output of the developed countries. Even as a proportion of world trade, it is less than a tenth. For the poorest countries, agriculture and the rural economy are focal, accounting for more than a third of output and engaging more than half of the population. A group of large developing country exporters, where Brazil is preeminent, has now come to the fore. As a result, resolution of the agricultural question is a sine qua non for the Doha Round to conclude.

This search for a viable agricultural outcome has dominated trade negotiations. Statements recur about the great welfare gains from complete liberalization of trade of agricultural and food products through the next decade. As was seen in table 5-6, there is an annual value of $129 billion (in 2001 dollars). That presumes elimination of *all* barriers to agricultural exchange. The reality, unfortunately, is otherwise: no one has been negotiating anything close to that type of change.

Table 5-7 illustrates this point using estimates prepared by the World Bank.[55] At the high end, presuming elimination of export subsidies and cuts in applied agricultural tariffs in only four developed country markets—the United States, EU 15, Norway, and Australia—and with smaller reductions for developing countries (none for the least developed), one comes up with a welfare gain of about $70 billion in 2001 dollars. If one adds exceptions for sensitive products—2 percent for the developed countries, 4 percent for the developing—that estimate declines to less than $20 billion, only about a tenth of the rewards from agricultural free trade. And this 2 percent exclusion is more of a concession than the EU has been prepared to make.

Table 5-7 includes additional estimates from another exercise, published in 2006 for the Carnegie Endowment for International Peace.[56] These figures, beyond being based upon a different econometric model of the world economy, incorporate the potential concessions emerging from the Hong Kong meeting in December 2005. As a result, the calculated total welfare gains emerging from agriculture—had final agreement been possible—are palpably smaller than what the World Bank estimates.[57] But it is fair to say that these magnitudes, however different in scale, add up to relatively modest agricultural gains as soon as any acceptable limitations on trade are included.

The results make sense although they underestimate the expansion of the Chinese market and miss the gains of commodity exporters after 2001. The poorest developing countries do not benefit. They do not offer

TABLE 5-7. **Estimates of Liberalization Welfare Gains in 2015**

Billions of 2001 U.S. dollars

Sector	World Bank			Carnegie		
	Free trade	Significant tariff reductions	Doha	Free trade	Doha	Hong Kong
Agriculture and Food	182	74	18	(68)[a]	5	5
Developing	54	7	0	. . .	0	0
High income	128	66	18	. . .	5	5
Manufacturing	105	45	21	(100)[a]	53	38
Developing	32	14 (28)[b]	7 (13)[b]	. . .	30	22
High income	73	31	14	. . .	23	16
Total	287	119	39	168	59	43

Sources: World Bank: Anderson and Martin, *Agricultural Trade Reform*, table 12.16. Carnegie: Polaski, *Winners and Losers*, table 3.1, and figures 3.1, 3.2, and 3.3.

a. Approximated on the basis of text discussion.

b. Includes the higher-income developing countries, such as South Korea and Singapore.

subsidies to their subsistence farmers. Some would lose out by erosion of trade preferences they presently enjoy in the EU and U.S. markets. Others will confront alternative, and more efficient, sources of supply, enhancing imports rather than production. All current net importers, and many remain, have to pay more in a competitive agricultural world. That is another side to the complex negotiations involved in this Doha Development Round.

Manufactures have been neglected in the Doha Round due to the need for prior agreement on agriculture before moving ahead. At Hong Kong, the need to advance was recognized but could only occur jointly with agriculture: "The text links the level of ambition in market access for agriculture and NAMA." Special and differential treatment was specified, as well as greater reduction of higher tariffs utilizing the Swiss formula.[58]

What kind of gains might be anticipated from eliminating trade barriers in industrial goods? After all, there is a much larger base. Global trade in manufactures now runs about nine times greater than exchange in agriculture, amounting to more than $7 trillion in 2005. Prices have remained relatively stable in recent years. The elasticity of demand is greater than for agricultural products. However, applied tariffs within both the developed and developing countries have moved lower, and limitations to trade from textile quotas have finally been eliminated, so new concessions will mean smaller gains than in the past.

Table 5-7 also contains differing estimates made by the World Bank and Carnegie Endowment for the consequences of liberalization within manufacturing. According to the World Bank, global welfare improves by more than $20 billion as a result of a 50 percent cut in tariffs by developed countries, accompanied by a reduction of 33 percent in developing countries, excluding the least developed. A reduction of 50 percent for all countries more than doubles the gain to $45 billion. The Carnegie estimate, on the other hand, shows a greater benefit of $53 billion. Under modest liberalization of 36 percent and 24 percent for the two groups, the benefits decrease to $38 billion. Whichever estimate one chooses, the prospective gains exceed those likely from agriculture.

For services, already constituting almost 20 percent of global trade, these particular quantitative models literally have nothing to say; neither, in essence, did the Hong Kong declaration. A single appendix, modified from its original Geneva form, was tabled. For many of the developing countries, the area was irrelevant. But for some, like India, this category has now become important. Estimates of potential gains from temporary migration, treated under Mode 4, come to $200 billion current dollars, shared almost evenly between developed and developing countries.[59] This level of benefit is equivalent to that from totally free agricultural trade and would be even greater for the developing countries.

For developed countries, parts of the service sector offer their principal opportunity for gain. That helps to explain why developing countries have been so reluctant to negotiate. Banking, insurance, and other financial services have expanded internationally. Construction activities in infrastructure and energy provision across borders are equally relevant. Telecommunications is a third related area. These are sectors subject to internal regulatory provisions, which vary substantially. As a consequence, negotiations differ from those in agriculture and manufactures. They consist of bilateral requests and offers. The WTO appendix requires countries to consider such requests but without obligation to participate. Potential gains from full liberalization are large: one recent estimate, including only transportation, trade, and business services, shows them exceeding the welfare benefits of free trade in agriculture.[60]

Predicted geographic and sectoral gains from agricultural and manufacturing liberalization are fairly independent of the particular model chosen. Production winners from the modest agricultural reform discussed at Hong Kong include Argentina, Brazil, and to a lesser extent, Thailand, India, and South Africa. Many producers are losers. The largest gains go to consumers within Japan, South Korea, the EU, and the United States. Overall, the importance of manufactures declines for the developed countries and increases in the developing ones. In metals, motor vehicles, electronics, and machinery, larger redistribution occurs. Regionally, China, India, and other Asian countries gain export share, as Africa and Latin America lose out to these lower-cost providers.[61]

These patterns are observable now, without reduction of trade barriers. As Asia has vaulted forward in the industrial sector, there has been national reaction, whether by the United States and the European Union, or by advanced developing countries like Brazil and Mexico. Claims of export subsidies, utilization of low-paid labor, violation of copyright privileges, and other infringements are likely to multiply in the next years. This nonagricultural market access (NAMA) sector will be more troublesome when negotiations eventually resume. Already, under the pressure of increasing unemployment, a wave of antidumping measures threatens—and not just in the United States and the EU.

Table 5-8 gives estimates of potential gain for Brazil, Argentina, China, India, and South Africa. While the Carnegie results show greater progress from comparable reductions of protection within the industrial sector, the country relative magnitudes are quite consistent. What impresses is how small the benefits are. There is less than a single percentage point of real gain by 2015 in all cases. That may help to explain why agreement in the Doha Round has not emerged as a compelling strategy even for these principal beneficiaries.

The possibility of a Doha agreement before 2012 has disappeared, despite a sequence of meetings where Brazil is always present but never able to prevail. Domestic interests within Brazil are not unhappy. Agriculture, after all, continues its trade growth, and favorable prices have returned. New industrial and construction markets within the oil-rich Middle East and a recovering Africa beckon industrial exports without imposing greater competition domestically. Brazilian tariffs have failed to move downward, and with Chinese imports threatening, have begun to rise. Ethanol, for which Brazilian production is second only to the United States, is encountering an expanding market. Future petroleum exports, a new focus, do not require Doha reforms.

TABLE 5 - 8 .   Estimates of Country Real Gains, 2015

Billions of 2001 U.S. dollars unless otherwise indicated

| | World Bank | | Carnegie | | Total gain in |
Country	Agriculture and food	NAMA	Agriculture and food	NAMA	real income (percent)
Argentina	1	0	0.3	0.2	0.2
Brazil	1.1	0.3	0.2	0.9	0.2
China	−1.5	2.2	-0.3	10.5	0.8
India	0.2	2	0.6	2.2	0.5
South Africa	0.3	0.3	0.5	0.2	0.3
Developing countries	−0.4	7.1	-0.1	21.4	
Total	17.7	21.6	5.4	38.1	0.1

Sources: See table 5-7.

Global Warming

The first international conference on global climate change was hosted by Brazil in Rio de Janeiro in June 1992. Sponsoring this event was intended to show the distance Brazilian foreign policy had come on the environmental question since the Stockholm meeting two decades earlier. That would counteract accumulating bad publicity about Brazil, ranging from the deadly Cubatão oil fire in 1984 to destruction of the Amazon rainforest area through proliferating ranching projects. Data suggested vast deforestation was occurring, contributing to global greenhouse gas emissions. Considerable land clearing was under way in the 1980s, giving rise to extensive tree burning. An annual average loss of 21,500 km^2 was estimated over the decade.[62]

For Brazil, unlike the other major contributors to greenhouse gas emissions, the source was not energy generation. Because of abundant water resources, electricity generation was largely renewable. Moreover, Brazil's commitment to ethanol as a fuel source for automobiles meant less use of gasoline; in the early 1990s, as oil became cheaper, production of multi-carburetor vehicles had slowed, but that could, and would, reverse. The principal problem was deforestation of the Amazon region.

Matters deteriorated with the assassination of Chico Mendes, a rubber tapper and union leader, at the end of 1988 in the state of Acre. Mendes had achieved global notice by virtue of his resistance to Amazon development projects, some funded by the multilateral development banks. His death helped to link the international environmental and internal social opponents of such undertakings. Rubber tappers and indigenous groups joined to emphasize the destabilizing character of encroachment.

The Mendes story was the next morning's lead in the *New York Times*—and the publicity did not stop there. Between 1987 and 1990, "the number of articles in the major American newspapers on the tropical forests more than tripled, the vast majority of them focusing on . . . Brazilian Amazonia."[63] Cattle ranchers responded by defending themselves, seeking to focus instead on the virtue of economic development.

The military had always been averse to external interest in this unoccupied area. That was why it had supported construction of a trans-Amazon highway back in the 1960s and resisted Herman Kahn's Hudson Institute plans for a massive reservoir flooding the Amazon Basin. In 1990 the Escola Superior da Guerra released a document defining "pro-indigenous and environmental movements as agents of the 'international forces that are attempting to undermine the Brazilian sovereignty over Amazonia.'"[64] Some of the domestic press was sympathetic to this assertion.

Collor selected the environmental issue as one of his priorities. He appointed José Lutzenberger, a leading ecologist, to his presidential staff. Soon after, there was announcement of the Earth Summit in 1992. "The Collor administration made a deliberate political decision to assume a high-profile leadership in global environmental affairs, in part to blunt criticism of its environmental record."[65] Over the next two years, Itamaraty would play a central role in hosting the event.

As with commercial policy, Itamaraty's views were not uniform. Secretary General Paulo Tarso, for example, had argued against the "international campaign to impede the exploitation of natural resources in order to block Brazil from becoming a world power."[66] At the 1979 Climate Conference, Brazil had insisted on no foreign involvement in environmental questions—developing countries had a need to catch up with the developed world, negative environmental effects notwithstanding. Now Itamaraty would have to alter that view somewhat to achieve the desired consensus. A successor secretary general, Ambassador Marcos Azambuja, announced that "Brazil [should] shoulder its responsibilities, conscious that its actions have repercussions for the whole planet."[67]

Itamaraty's position failed to satisfy everyone. Amazon state governors feared a loss of sovereignty. Lutzenberger, on the other side, wished to go farther, linking an international forest agreement with a climate change convention. Lutzenberger's differences led him to announce to the international press that the additional funding sought by Brazil would not halt deforestation. They also led to his dismissal just two months before Brazil was to host the UN Conference on Environment and Development.

Nonetheless, Brazil's stance had altered. Collor's inaugural speech to the Rio Earth Summit made clear the more active direction Brazilian foreign policy would take, in place of the defensive posture previously assumed.[68] Now there was recognition of externalities and common, but differentiated, responsibilities. Brazil would take its place as a country deeply involved in global environmental issues, but one insistent upon national sovereignty and economic advance. Environmental imperialism would be resisted.

After the Rio meeting, Itamaraty retained its principal role in defining Brazilian policy on global warming. The Ministries of the Environment and of Science and Technology were relevant but secondary. Brazilian NGOs dealing with the issue grew substantially in number but without great domestic influence. International NGOs captured an expanding world audience, aided by increasingly pessimistic assessments by scientists in successive Intergovernmental Panel on Climate Change reports in 1995, 2001, and 2007.[69]

The Kyoto Treaty of 1997 was subsequently modified in 2002. Its original aim of reducing greenhouse gas emissions by 5.2 percent of 1990 levels was reduced to 2.2 percent in 2002. It went into effect in early 2005, providing a basis for an expanding market in carbon emission credits, one in which developing countries and Brazil have claimed an increasing share in recent years. The EU led the way; the United States never ratified the treaty.

Within Brazil, as agricultural production and profits expanded, "between 1996 and 2005 some 19,500 sq km of the Brazilian Amazon were cleared each year. At that rate, a third would be gone by 2050 and the rest might wither."[70] Subsequently, the rate of loss slowed to 7,000 sq km in 2008–09. Declining prices aided but so did increasingly effective federal policy. Appointment of Marina Silva as minister of the environment in 2003 made a difference.

The Amazon area is difficult to control. Ranchers desire access to more land; local and state officials have private interests that supersede conservation. Nor is the government always united, as evidenced by Silva's later resignation when pressured to approve new hydroelectric projects.

Yet significant advances—and pressure from NGOs—continued.[71] There was the REDD (Program on Reducing Emissions from Deforestation and Forest Degradation in Developing Countries) agreement with the Norwegian government in 2008, and in 2009 the World Bank granted a near-record loan of $1.3 billion to finance the difficult task of helping "Brazil attain sustainable development goals linked to economic growth: from Amazon sustainable development to climate change as well as the water sector."[72]

Brazil played a central part in the Copenhagen Conference in December 2009 and in the Cancún follow-up a year later. Brazil (and China and India) have emerged readier to accept national responsibilities to limit global warming to a maximum increase of 2 degrees Celsius. Brazil's National Climate Change Policy is illustrative. A new law set a "voluntary" target for greenhouse gas reduction of between 36.1 and 38.9 percent of projected emissions by 2020 and allowed outside verification. At the same time, Lula vetoed the part of the text calling for abandonment of fossil fuels: presalt oil reserves counted more.[73]

Brazil has come far from its early position on the environment and global warming. These issues will only grow, and the Amazon rainforest will be fundamental to any solution. That ensures in the future both Brazil's larger international presence and wider internal participation. Managing that combination will be a central task of foreign policy.

Brazil and the United Nations

Brazil has sought recognition of its diplomatic importance. Twice the country has come close, once in the 1920s in the League of Nations and again during the formation of the United Nations in 1944. On both occasions, however, permanent membership in the Executive Committee or Security Council was not achieved. Instead, Brazil has become the country most often selected for temporary Security Council service, despite the two decades of absence coinciding with military rule between 1964 and 1985.[74] Brazil initiates the annual meetings of the General Assembly, which provides Itamaraty with an opportunity to assess foreign relations from its perspective.

After 1985 Brazil renewed its claim for permanent inclusion in the Security Council. President Sarney did so in his last appearance in 1989, and Foreign Minister Celso Amorim reiterated it in 1994.

Meanwhile, the UN has changed. Now there are special sessions on the environment, human rights, population change, the role of women, and still other issues. UN peacekeeping forces were called in during the dissolution of Yugoslavia, independence struggle of East Timor, and elections in Cambodia. Tellingly, the Security Council—which had met formally 69 times in 1989—had 171 sessions in 1993.

Violent breakdown of internal legal processes now provokes UN action. More peacekeeping activities have occurred than had ever been envisioned. Some have gone beyond, to peace enforcement. Here there is a dilemma. The General Assembly in 2005 passed a resolution calling on members to intervene if nation-states did not protect their citizens from mass atrocities. This provision tried to deal with the inconsistency between state sovereignty and state actions beyond civilized limits. Many governments are reluctant to open that gate, as the ambiguity about Darfur demonstrates.

For more than fifteen years an enlarged Security Council has been discussed but without resolution.[75] In December 2007, another working group was convened. Two alternative enlargement schemes emerged. One expands the council to twenty-four members, through six new permanent slots, without veto powers, allocated to Brazil, Germany, India, Japan, and two African countries, plus three temporary two-year appointees. The second is creation of eight new seats for a period of four years, renewable, and one two-year slot. Brazil, not surprisingly, is inclined to the first option. Other Latin American countries like Argentina and Mexico prefer the latter, where they see a better chance for participation. They are joined by the large countries in other regions fearful of exclusion: Pakistan and Indonesia, for example, or Nigeria and Algeria as opposed to Egypt and South Africa.

Foreign Minister Amorim gave Security Council candidacy great emphasis. Brazil's economic emergence has enhanced historical arguments based upon national size and commitment to international law. Brazil used its speech inaugurating the General Assembly to make its case more strongly. In 2003 it backed a battle against world poverty using a variant of the Tobin Tax, a levy on financial transactions, to provide the resources; in 2005 the successful efforts of India, Brazil, and South Africa in combating internal poverty served as the basis for a broader UN undertaking.

Of even greater consequence for its international standing, Brazil entered into peacekeeping activities as head of the UN Stabilization Mission in Haiti. Since 2004, 1,200 Brazilian soldiers, aided by other Latin American countries, participated. This effort has been more successful than earlier attempts to stabilize and democratize Haiti. Violence has diminished and modest increases in foreign assistance have followed. Brazil's involvement has been successful, if seemingly unending. Hurricanes in 2008 and the earthquake early in 2010 have racked up immense unanticipated costs. Most recently, there has been the cholera epidemic. Sufficient international funds have yet to become available.

These efforts have promoted Brazil. *The Economist,* at the beginning of 2007, recognized the value of a broader Security Council and the permanence of new members.[76] Brazil is a global player not only by virtue of its diplomacy but also because of its emergence as a global trader. Growth in its agricultural exports, accompanied by a diversifying trade in manufactures, has resumed. Brazil's presence in world financial markets has likewise increased. Outside perceptions have been changing, aided by Brazil's rapid recovery from the Great Recession. As Celso Amorim said, "Rome wasn't made in a day. The reform of the Security Council doesn't take one day. . . . It will happen."[77]

Not everyone agrees. A prominent academic dissenter is the American Edward Luck. He argues that the UN "doctrine of the responsibility to protect" runs counter to the Grotian basis of Brazilian (and Indian) foreign policy. Pressure for UN reform has been aided by earlier U.S. dismissal. That is no longer the case. But as Luck notes, "The very divisions among members . . . ensure that a radical restructuring is not in the cards."[78]

Brazil had tried to avoid the ongoing issues of Afghanistan, Pakistan, Iraq, and Iran, where costly UN and U.S. involvement continues. The Middle East and South Asia were seen to lie outside Brazil's interests. But now that seems to have changed.

In March 2010 Lula traveled to Israel and Palestine on a peace mission, without success. In May he went to Iran where, jointly with Turkish prime minister Erdogan, Lula signed an agreement that produced headlines around the world. The deal seemed to replicate an earlier one reached with the five permanent members of the Security Council plus Germany in October 2009, which Iran later rejected. In the May 2010 agreement, Iran was to ship low-grade uranium to Turkey and receive in return, within a year, fuel rods enriched to a level of 20 percent for its Tehran medical research facility. President Ahmadinejad shortly added a decisive addendum: Iran was to continue its domestic enrichment, involving approximately half its nuclear stock, some of which already had reached the 20 percent mark.

U.S. response was negative at the outset. Soon afterward, when Iran's intent became clear and the UN Atomic Agency was denied authority to pursue free investigation, the Security Council approved a punitive resolution before it, with only Brazil and Turkey voting to the contrary, and Lebanon abstaining. Lula's effort, partially motivated by the Brazilian presidential campaign under way, came to naught. In place of prominent global ascent, Brazil had to publicly retreat.

This new foreign policy "realism," required for greater engagement in global matters, somewhat contradicts the long-standing principle of non-intervention undergirding Brazilian foreign relations. Autonomy has been an enshrined value, even as Itamaraty strategists have redefined the concept over the last two decades. Autonomy has enabled Brazil to pursue national interests without concession or compromise. That will be more difficult if its Security Council participation becomes permanent. Then Brazil will be under pressure to take positions on all issues; abstention has its limits. Acceptance of peacekeeping and rejection of peace enforcement may not prove a simple rule to implement on a continuing basis.

Closing Comments

The world was transformed soon after Brazil returned to civil governance. The struggle between the United States and the Soviet Union ended. Communism dissipated, and Eastern Europe moved to freedom. Germany was reunified. Economically, the United States accelerated, leaving Japan and the EU in its wake. Latin America began to recover from the Lost Decade of the 1980s. China and India surged forward. Globalization began to impinge, posing challenges.

This chapter has dealt with Brazil's changing foreign policy over the last twenty-five years. The discussion has ranged widely from Mercosul to the United Nations. Brazil has been an active participant in international relations as its size and growing economy merit. Not all initiatives have yet shown success, but it has attained growing importance within the world. In particular, Cardoso and Lula have received merited plaudits for their considerable efforts. They have shaped an active Itamaraty agenda by virtue of their personal involvement.

In the Cardoso years, Brazil successfully asserted its claims for hemispheric leadership and played a significant role in launching the Doha Round. In the Lula years, Brazil intensified its efforts within the UN and the WTO, rejecting the FTAA and reaching out to the developing world as a priority. Brasília emerged as an important capital. Indeed, Lula engaged actively within Africa and the Middle East.

Tullo Vigevani and Gabriel Cepaluni have entitled this policy "autonomy through diversification." They stress outreach to the South as a way to reduce past "asymmetries in external relations with powerful countries."[79] Within Itamaraty, Samuel Pinheiro Guimarães emphasized competition with the existing blocs—the United States, the EU, and China.[80] As he has written, "Brazil . . . has to react to the political initiatives of the great powers, especially . . . the United States. Brazil has to articulate political, economic and technological alliances with peripheral states of the international system to defend and protect its interests."[81]

Relations with the United States deteriorated rather than strengthened over much of this period. Obama's election signaled a potentially positive turn. That was not immediately evident in the midst of Brazil's efforts in Honduras and Iran, but subsequent resolution of the WTO cotton subsidy case has been a more encouraging sign. Final arbitration in 2009 ruled in favor of Brazil and granted a retaliatory penalty of some $830 million. In late April 2010, agreement was reached, providing for U.S. annual payment of $147.3 million. Related developments include U.S. permission for meat imports from the Brazilian state of Santa Catarina, and higher interest costs and shorter maturity periods on farmer loans from the U.S. export credit program. Full resolution of the dispute depends on the content of legislation for the 2012 renewal of farm subsidies in the United States.

Antonio Pátriota, then secretary general of Itamaraty, led these negotiations for Brazil, and he is now foreign minister. Meanwhile, U.S. treasury secretary Timothy Geithner went to Brazil in February 2011, and President Obama visited in March. Dilma is scheduled to come to Washington later this year. Perhaps, in the midst of concerns about unfair Chinese competition with Brazil and an undervalued renminbi, there will be an opportunity to reconstruct a more positive relationship.

6

Evaluating the Past and Looking to the Future

Anticipating Dilma Rousseff's election as Brazil's president, *The Economist* stated: "Success has bred an atmosphere of hubris in Brasília. With the outlook for the world economy so uncertain, that is potentially dangerous. . . . [T]here are three difficult sets of issues . . . Ms. Rousseff will have to deal with. The first is corruption. . . . The second concerns the role of the state in the economy. . . . The third test . . . will be in foreign policy."[1]

There are questions regarding Brazil's capacity to sustain its surge forward. Abiding Brazilian evolution within a problematic world is not a sure thing, but the past yields an optimistic appraisal. Important obstacles to cumulative progress arose in the last twenty-five years. Sometimes their origin was internal, such as episodes of political corruption, and sometimes external, as with the economic crises in Mexico, Asia, and Russia in the 1990s or the recent Great Recession. These episodes imposed real costs and delayed attention to more fundamental problems. Yet, as previous chapters have stressed, transformation has been comprehensive and far reaching.

There has been a perceptible change in relative power of the executive, legislative, and judicial branches of government. Brazil returned to civil governance in 1985 with a powerful presidency as a heritage of prior military rule. While the 1988 Constitution seemingly diminished that influence, the reality was otherwise. The *medida provisória* and popular rejection of a prime ministerial alternative in 1993 meant presidential authority dominated. Presidents Cardoso and Lula productively used that power to achieve advances.

That singular position has been slowly eroding. The National Congress has acquired greater say and increased its institutional capacities. This has happened not merely because constitutional amendments—and there have been many—require a three-fifths vote but for other reasons as well. Rules explicitly constraining executive authority have passed, such as the limit on the use of the *medida provisória*. There has been evident reluctance, especially in the absence of an economic crisis, to accept exactly what the executive has proposed. Congressional engagement might have moved faster if the political party structure were more consolidated and able to offer greater leadership. In its absence, a vigilant press has stood ready to inform the public, not always entirely accurately but sufficiently on the mark to ensure eventual governmental response.

Judicial authority has been on the ascent. Efficiency has improved, although the number of court cases has risen significantly. Modern technology has helped the system cope. Recourse to injunction as a means of delay became less prevalent once privatization ceased. Constitutional Amendment 45 introduced a better organized legal structure. The *súmula vinculante* will help to ensure consistency in decisions on important matters. The Public Ministry has widened its prosecutorial focus; no matter of significance eludes its engagement. The Brazilian judiciary is one reason why reversion to democracy since 1985 has been able to work so well.

The thrust toward federalism inherent in the 1988 Constitution partially turned into centralization because of economic circumstance. That trend has since reversed. States and municipalities are active political entities. Federal resources have regularly been transferred to local authorities—and so have responsibilities. What has failed to happen, despite frequent promises and draft laws, is real fiscal reform. Numerous charges and taxes are imposed, with consequent inefficiencies in their collection and subsequent redistribution to lower-level units. While the distortion engendered by state and local competition for investment seems to have abated, this issue calls out for permanent resolution.

Brazil has experienced alternation in political leadership at all levels—municipal, state, and federal. Lula's succession was facilitated by full cooperation from the Cardoso administration. Dilma, formerly head of the Casa Civil and also from Lula's PT, has assumed office without problem. In a Latin America where popular leaders are tempted to stay beyond reasonable limits, President Lula wisely chose to desist. That decision strengthened Brazilian democracy and merits acclaim.

Within the economic arena, there has been a virtual revolution. Objective data verify the change. Here is the simplest summary. In the last twenty-five years, real per capita income has gone from $7,318 to $10,607, a gain of 45 percent. Annual inflation of more than 200 percent has given way to price increases of around 5 percent. This impressive dual result really takes shape with the Real Plan in 1994. It has been sustained by consensual acceptance of taxes required to pay for government expenditure. There is constant complaint about the magnitude of taxes, which are more comparable to an OECD average than to Latin American levels. But Brazilians have complied. Transparency of the fiscal accounts has increased over time, and the 2001 Fiscal Responsibility Law has remained a decisive institutional advance. The central bank has become de facto independent, regularly imposing an essential monetary brake to impede inflation.

Privatization has modernized Brazil. Dominant state enterprises have substantially been sold off. A new class of entrepreneurs has emerged. Export capability has extended progressively to all sectors: agriculture, industry, and mineral products. Imports have entered in return, helping to restrain prices when internal demand has exceeded product and ensuring access to a range of new capital goods. Foreign investment has been welcomed, bringing advanced technology. Globalization, while criticized by some, has become inherent in Brazilian economic growth.

This path was not entirely smooth. Initial attempts to curtail inflation failed. Even after apparent success, an altered, and more durable, macroeconomic structure became necessary in 1999. It relies upon three components: inflation targeting, a flexible exchange rate, and a primary fiscal surplus. All these have persisted, despite political change and occasional deviation, such as the exaggerated primary surplus reported in 2010. In the presidential campaign, and right afterward, Dilma was quick to recognize the significance of these policies and pledge their continuance. She has emphasized a need for tighter fiscal policy to aid the central bank and has introduced reductions in outlays.

Governmental economic leadership has become more stable: key appointments remain in place for years rather than months, as before. Regulatory authorities likewise continue, with new appointees to be sure and sometimes modified objectives, but with their independence substantially intact. Some PT supporters lamented this constancy. The Programa de Aceleração do Crescimento, set out at the start of Lula's second term, was responsive. Its implementation, other than by Petrobras, was slower than hoped. What characterizes this initiative, moreover, is the importance of private participation. Federal funds were limited. A coherent industrial policy and greater expenditure for science and technology remained hopes more than reality.

Active governmental response to the Great Recession brightened the interventionist mood. The fiscal deficit widened and the primary surplus sank to lower levels as compensatory policies took hold. Tax rebates and other incentives encouraged private expenditure; government consumption rose. The SELIC rate fell, and public institutions such as the Bank of Brazil, Caixa Econômica, and BNDES issued a larger share of credit. Economic recovery occurred at a rapid pace, validating this approach. Brazil in 2010 has grown at a rate of 7.5 percent, although projections for the future are lower. Additionally, inflationary pressures have begun to quicken and have led to rising interest rates compounded by an appreciating currency.

Social policy has seen equivalent far-reaching advances. That was Lula's intent from the beginning. Cardoso, hampered in his second term by the need to retrench, was more limited in his options. He made important gains in education, health, and social security that served as a basis for Lula's initiatives. The most popular of these is Bolsa Família, consolidating the earlier Bolsa Escola and Bolsa Alimentação. This program has yielded high social returns. Its small expenditure, about half a percent of gross domestic product, has benefited a target group in excess of 45 million persons. More than a fifth of Brazilians receive assistance from it. Brazil's conditional cash transfer program became an international model that other developing countries eagerly imitate.

Policies to advance education, health, and social security have been more expensive to implement. In large measure, rights to these services stem from constitutional reform in 1988, which guaranteed them to all citizens. Brazil has tried to meet this ambitious objective, not always successfully. Each of these areas has shown significant progress, but problems persist. Overall, while Brazil spends great sums, the quality of services is low and improves only slowly.

Social security underwent systemic expansion as greater numbers of the elderly were progressively incorporated. More public expenditure was an inevitable consequence. So was an attempt to reduce larger deficits. Two constitutional amendments in the Cardoso and Lula administrations tried to control outlays and increase the revenue stream. Both helped to slow the tide but not to reverse it. The real minimum wage serves as the private system's anchor, and this has gone up much faster than GDP. At the same time, the number of beneficiaries expands more rapidly than the population as a whole. More than 10 percent of GDP is now spent annually on social security, with a shortfall almost a third as great. That is one reason why tax revenues must continue to be high. Future projections suggest this imbalance will only get worse over the next generation.

Education has advanced. Brazil started far behind. Now, everyone goes to primary school. Progress has also been occurring at the secondary level. That is the good news. The bad news is that this result is deceptive, as performance in domestic and international evaluations reveals. Functional illiteracy is high among poorer students. Average outlay per primary and secondary student is small, especially in the poorer regions. Brazilian public expenditure favors state and federal universities. Much is spent on the favored few, preventing universal education from contributing as much as it should to bettering the income distribution.

The availability of health care has expanded as the SUS evolved from its ambitious 1990 start. Public provision of health care has improved, especially for those with limited initial access. Costs have also gone up, putting pressure on the public fisc. Brazil spends a lot on medical expenses: the sum of public and private outlays is more than 8 percent of GDP. That lies above the international norm. Because average age is increasing, these pressures upward will persist. At the same time, there is a need to implement more effective federalism. Unlike educational allocations, poorer regions receive no special help from the central government for provision of health care.

A very positive outcome in the social area is continuing reduction in the level of Brazilian income inequality, long a matter of concern. That decline has gone on for almost a decade, with greater improvement in recent years. This equalizing process stems from a combination of policy and higher rates of growth, an ideal long preached by development texts. Simultaneously, a new lower middle class has emerged as employment has increased and the number of poor has fallen. Optimistic projections indicate the possibility of ending absolute poverty—incomes below $1.25 a day—within a relatively few years.

Brazil, finally, has become an involved global player. Sarney visited the United States in 1986. His disappointing trip illustrated how little serious attention Brazil then received. In 2009 Obama welcomed Lula to the White House and publicly acknowledged a Brazil whose views and support mattered a great deal.

In this interval, Brazil moved from an emerging bilateral engagement with Argentina to an impressive international presence. Itamaraty has widened its reach. Foreign policy now actively extends to Africa, the Middle East, and Asia. The UN and the WTO count. In bilateral trade and investment, and as a global partner, the United States has clearly lost out. The EU, in the midst of its own difficulties, is seeking to retain a role. Unequivocally, China has risen in importance—as a potential collaborator, but even more, as a future competitor.

Brazil has turned down a more nationalistic path in recent years. South-South interactions have moved up on its agenda, through membership in UNASUR, IBSA, and the BRICS, as well as extension bilaterally. This direction is a response to new economic realities. However, rhetoric still exceeds concrete gains, and there is the danger of excessive ambition.

The Future

President Dilma Rousseff, the first woman so elected in Brazil, received the presidential standard from Lula on January 1, 2011. She enters in better circumstances than any of her New Republic predecessors. Her congressional majority is firm, as a consequence of PT victories and having a PMDB vice president who formerly led the Câmara. Economic growth has been strong; indeed, it requires slowing. External reserves are overflowing. Social policy is firmly ensconced and contributed to her great majorities in the northeast. Foreign policy, with the U.S. cotton dispute out of the way and Iran a lesser focus, is prepared to resume its outward thrust.

What policy priorities should she emphasize at the beginning? The continuity she has committed to, evidenced by her cabinet and key administrative appointments, is hardly inconsistent with fundamental change. Indeed, some modifications are vitally necessary if Brazil is to ensure further progress.

A first possibility relates to politics. This is an ongoing but unresolved issue. Lula has indicated a desire to lead in this direction, promising to fight "like a lion" for reform. Later, in his two-hour interview with bloggers at the end of November, he said, "It is inconceivable that the country go on without political reform." He called for a Constituent Assembly, as he had done in 2009, to take place within the first year of the Rousseff administration. Real commitment by the president at the very outset might make the difference. She mentioned the possibility in her inaugural address, but barely.

The basic proposals are well known and have long been debated. They include moving to a closed electoral system for the Câmara, with a slate of candidates in specified order. Voters would then choose among political parties. How far one goes down each list, and thus selects the individual winners, depends upon the party's share of votes. This revision strengthens parties: individual popularity matters, but party identification counts. Such a change can be applied at the municipal level as well.

Related reform sets geographic districts as electoral units within states. A fraction could be elected statewide as well, as in Germany and elsewhere. While studies suggest that a geographic base characterizes the present system, thereby approximating a district system, electors continue to confound political parties when they vote for individuals. Minimal levels of voter support can be imposed to determine party eligibility in future contests. A reduction in the over twenty parties included in the present Câmara can make the policy platform a better basis for choice.

A larger congressional role in governance is the desired outcome. Instead of reacting to executive proposals, legislative initiatives could surface. Instead of medidas provisórias, positive programs for needed legislation can take shape in congressional committees. Perhaps these changes could help ameliorate the present negative public evaluation of the National Congress.

Economic policy equally needs revision if higher growth is to persist into the future. Two issues stand out: one is a need for steady increases in investment; the other is elimination of the fiscal deficit to permit a steady decline in real interest rates.

Fixed investment required to sustain annual growth of at least 5 percent has not received much notice. Figure 6-1 provides data since 2000 on its varying amount, along with domestic savings and current account balances. Investment is currently less than 20 percent of national product, despite its recent rise. The BNDES presumes a future increase of about 2 percent. Yet a minimal level closer to 25 percent, and perhaps beyond, is needed. It is encouraging to see that the report for 2010 from the Finance Ministry seems to agree.[2] Other successful developing countries—and not only China, at greater than 40 percent of national product, and India at a slightly lower level—regularly achieve these higher rates.

FIGURE 6-1. Capital Formation in the 2000s

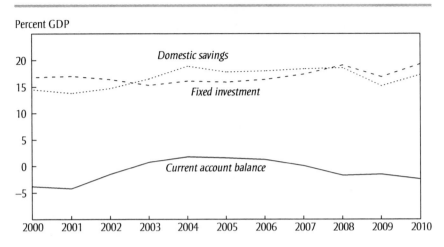

Source: Economist Intelligence Unit (www.eiu.com/public).

In the case of Brazil, capital for infrastructure— beyond planned off-shore petroleum development—is critical. Roads, port development, and airports, not to mention new housing in urban areas, are all needed. The 2014 World Cup and 2016 Olympics only elevate the cost, especially when ancillary investment, such as a new bullet train, is included. These requirements have long investment maturities and entail a higher capital-output ratio.

Achieving that target cannot be left to foreign participation. Brazil, along with other Latin American countries, has painfully learned this lesson multiple times in the past. Net foreign inflow of no more than 3 percent of gross national product is a prudent rule. Some projections suggest that Brazil will shortly need much more. Foreign investment is important not so much because it adds to domestic savings but because it allows access to technological innovation.

More domestic savings means smaller private (and public) consumption. Such a transformation is not easy; for Brazil, it is novel. Larger private consumption has stimulated recent income gains. So have public outlays—and not only at the federal level. In the midst of primary surpluses, it is simple to ignore the continuing fiscal deficit. That adds up to little, if any, public contribution to domestic savings.[3] Increasing taxes to get there is not a meaningful way to go. Political opinion on all sides is opposed to that approach. People rightly suspect any increase will all wind up being spent, and only partially for investment.

Resolving this challenge is an essential task for the new administration. Otherwise, sustainable growth at higher rates will not be possible. The surest solution is increased public sector savings. Admittedly, this choice turns past Brazilian practice on its head: historically, in the 1960s and 1970s, the government invested and the private sector saved. Now, those responsibilities have to be reversed. Since an active industrial policy, with attendant public expense, is slated as well, larger public sector savings become more necessary.

Where can they come from if higher taxes are impossible? One feasible source is eliminating the social security deficit. That now comes to about 3 percent of GDP. Greater income growth and formal employment has recently helped by increasing contributions, but that is not enough. Too much is being paid out, and that is bound to worsen as retirements accelerate with demographic change. Public sector workers have a privileged position. Their average pension receipts on retirement are multiples of those in the private sector. Already, by constitutional amendment, future obligations when regulated are diminished, but not enough. Indexing private gain fully to the minimum wage further worsens the situation (see chapter 4 for the details).

When the new administration offers another amendment to stem the social security deficit, as it eventually must, there is the chance to be bolder. It should try to ensure that the resultant savings translate exclusively into investment. Some funds can go to Petrobras: it will need considerable resources to extract and market prospective oil beneath the salt layer. Indeed, for several years, outflows will exceed inflows. Some resources can go to expanding public housing projects. Part will have to be recycled back to private sector projects through the BNDES.

This policy simultaneously moves to eradicate the omnipresent fiscal deficit. Reducing the government's current spending—rather than planned PAC decline—can further help. Fiscal expenditures and increases in public sector jobs will have to be controlled. Monetary policy cannot be the sole or primary source of restraint. Lower real interest rates will follow, and the pressure of capital inflows on the exchange rate will diminish. Capital controls can contribute, but only temporarily and not as a substitute for real domestic reform.

With expanded public savings assured, there is no reason to insist upon a smaller state as the only way to go. That goal is improbable. Dilma and Luciano Coutinho at the BNDES are committed to an active industrial policy. What must accompany such a move is adequate supervision and limited market intervention. An efficient state is required. Otherwise, one runs the risk of replicating the past: larger expenditures without ongoing domestic technological advancement.

Undoubtedly, not everyone will find such an economic strategy appealing. Some will prefer only to attack a bloated government. Others will not want to begin to cut growing pension benefits. Still others will insist upon increased social services to compensate for past neglect. Perhaps President Dilma can persuade the majority of the need for some compromise. If not, then future development begins to look less certain.

Within the social area, the magnitude of Brazilian expenditures has often and erroneously been taken as a marker of success. The best counterexample is Bolsa Família, whose achievement has yielded a high rate of social return at small cost. Brazil spends substantial amounts on SUS. As more families enter the lower middle class, demands for better health care will increase. Allocations for preventive, as opposed to therapeutic, care will expand. Effective and professional administration, and better management of federalism, will have to compensate.

Education needs attention. That is the secret behind economic success elsewhere in the world. Regional differentiation within the country has been narrowed but not eliminated. Secondary school completion is rising and, along with that, pressures for greater access to universities. But expenditure favors public higher education excessively. Brazil spends more for education than most developing countries, but the qualitative results do not correspond. More resources are scheduled to come from Petrobras profits in the future, but one cannot wait.

In foreign policy, Brazil is reaching out in many directions, and its enhanced international status is clear. In New York, Geneva, and Basel, Brazil now has a prominent voice. Cardoso and Lula have both contributed to this heightened stature. Within the multilateral platform, on a variety of subjects, Brazil has influence. Within the region, Brazil is a leader, and the country is rapidly expanding its bilateral contacts within Africa and Asia.

Perhaps this is a moment for Itamaraty to reconsider its priorities. Lula is an impossible act to follow. An excessive agenda remains behind for

President Dilma. But selectivity may enable tangible gains. One early issue is the problematic relationship with the United States. Strengthening that, while retaining an orientation toward the South, should become a focus.

Government in Brazil will not, and should not, vanish. Dilma will have to ensure its efficiency. Simple recipes, for all their appeal, are inadequate. Dramatic and bold changes are no longer the answer; however, deepening the institutions that have been emerging over the last years is. Enduring, evolutionary reform in the twenty-first century under a democratic New Republic is a result that everyone wants.

Notes

Chapter One

1. "A Special Report on Business and Finance in Brazil." *The Economist*, November 14, 2009, pp. 15 and 18.

Chapter Two

1. For a useful summary of the question, see chapters 2.1 and 2.2 by Antônio Octávio Cintra in *Sistema político brasileiro: Uma introdução*, 2nd ed., edited by Lûcia Avelar and Antônio Octávio Cintra (São Paulo: Editora UNESP, 2007). An earlier source is Scott Mainwaring, *Rethinking Party Systems in the Third Wave of Democratization* (Stanford University Press, 1999). Both are relevant for subsequent sections as well.

2. Carlos Pereira, Timothy J. Power, and Lucio Rennó, "Under What Conditions Do Presidents Resort to Decree Power? Theory and Evidence from the Brazilian Case," *Journal of Politics* 67, no. 1 (2005): 185.

3. Ibid. Sarney, in his last year and a half, and Collor, shortly after his start, were highly unpopular, but this interpretation would be much more convincing had the authors separated out the Itamar years, when a return to broad inclusion occurred in the aftermath of Collor's impeachment and when many of the MPs were associated with the successful Real Plan.

4. Avelar and Cintra, *Sistema político brasileiro*, p. 138.

5. Mainwaring, *Rethinking Party Systems*, p. 278.

6. David Samuels, *Ambition, Federalism, and Legislative Politics in Brazil* (Cambridge University Press, 2003), p. 58.

7. In 2010, 408 out of 513 deputies ran for reelection. Of these, 286 won—about 70 percent—representing 56 percent of the new Câmara. That ratio is higher than in 2002 or 2006, when it was less than half.

8. See, among other joint works, Argelina C. Figueiredo and Fernando Limongi, "Processo orçamentario e comportamento legislativo: Emendas

individuais, apoio ao Executivo e Programas de Governo," *Dados* 48, no. 4 (2005): 737–76. Among the followers, there is the recent publication in English, of Santos and Vilarouca, mentioned below.

9. Fabiano Santos and Márcio Grijó Vilarouca, "Political Institutions and Governability from FHC to Lula," in *Democratic Brazil Revisited*, edited by Peter R. Kingstone and Timothy J. Power (University of Pittsburgh Press, 2008), p. 97.

10. Alfred P. Montero, *Brazilian Politics* (Cambridge, United Kingdom: Polity Press, 2005), p. 66. See Barry Ames, *The Deadlock of Democracy in Brazil: Interests, Identities, and Institutions in Comparative Perspective* (University of Michigan Press, 2001), and Mainwaring, *Rethinking Party Systems*.

11. See Carlos Haag, "With One Eye on the Fish and Another on the Cat: Brazilian Mistrust of Democratic Institutions," *Revista Pesquisa FAPESP*, no. 153 (November 2008): 96–101.

12. Ibid.

13. Monthly payments were provided to legislators who supported the PT, provoking a much covered congressional investigation. Very limited expulsions (still under appeal) and resignations followed.

14. Quoted in the excellent discussion of different views about congressional performance by Antônio Octávio Cintra and Marcelo Barroso Lacombe, "A Câmara dos Deputados na Nova República: A visão da ciência política," in Avelar and Cintra, *Sistema política brasileiro*, pp. 168–69.

15. In this section I have had the benefit of access to Rogério Bastos Arantes, "Judiciário: entre a justiça e a política," in Avelar and Cintra, *Sistema política brasileiro*, chapter 3.

16. Fiona Macaulay, "Democratisation and the Judiciary: Competing Reform Agendas," in *Brazil since 1985: Politics, Economy and Society*, edited by Maria D'Alva Kinzo and James Dunkerley (London: Institute of Latin American Studies, 2003), p. 86.

17. Rogério Bastos Arantes, "Direito e política: O Ministério Público e a defesa dos direitos coletivos," *Revista Brasileira de Ciências Sociais* 14, no. 39 (1999): 90.

18. Macaulay, "Democratisation," p. 98; Arantes, "Judiciário," p. 103.

19. In Constitutional Amendment 3, of 1993, the supreme court was authorized to declare measures constitutional, through an *ação declaratória de constitucionalidade*. This was thought to enable rapid decisions; the executive, both houses of congress, and the federal prosecutor were given authority to file. It has only been used rarely. The reason seems clear: why would those who have just approved legislation seek to find out whether it is constitutional? Those adversely affected have much more reason to seek an answer.

20. Celso Fernandes Campilongo, "Judiciário e a democracia no Brasil," *Revista USP* 21 (March–May 1994): 120–21.

21. Matthew Taylor, *Judging Policy* (Stanford University Press, 2008), pp. 30, 33. Of the fifteen members of the National Judicial Council, nine are judges themselves. The lower courts seemingly remain insistent upon total autonomy and filed an ADIN asking the supreme court to declare the amendment invalid.

22. Ibid., p. 31. *Súmula vinculante* had been present within the court system even earlier but could be applied only on a limited basis.

23. Matthew Taylor, "O judiciário e as políticas públicas no Brasil," *Dados* 50, no. 2 (2007): 237.

24. *The Economist*, March 28, 2009, p. 46.

25. In these paragraphs I have relied upon Aloisio Araujo and Bruno Funchal, "A nova lei de falências brasileiras: Primeros impactos," *Revista de Economia Política* 29, no. 3 (2009): 191–212, and Bruno Funchal, "The Effects of the 2005 Bankruptcy Reform in Brazil," *Economics Letters* 101 (June 2008): 84–86.

26. *Gazeta Mercantil,* June 9, 2008.

27. Lesley McAllister, *Making Law Matter* (Stanford University Press, 2008), p. 76.

28. Rosangela Batista Cavalcanti, "Civil Society and the Public Prosecution in Brazil," in *Enforcing the Rule of Law,* edited by Enrique Bruzzotti and Catalina Smulovitz (University of Pittsburgh Press, 2006), p. 37.

29. *Estado de São Paulo,* April 1, 2009.

30. McAllister, *Making Law Matter,* p. 196.

31. Matthew M. Taylor and Vinícius C. Buranelli, "Ending Up in Pizza: Accountability as a Problem of Institutional Arrangement in Brazil," *Latin American Politics and Society* 49, no. 1 (2007): 65.

32. Fabio Kerche, "Autonomia e discricionariedade do Ministério Público no Brasil," *Dados* 50, no. 2 (2007): 260. Italics in the original.

33. Avelar and Cintra, *Sistema político brasileiro,* p. 216.

34. Maria Hermínia Tavares de Almeida, "Recentralizando a federaçáo?" *Revista de Sociologia e Política* 24 (June 2005): 33, available in translation on the Internet as "Decentralization and Centralization in a Federal System: The Case of Democratic Brazil" (socialsciences.scielo.org/pdf/s_rsocp/v1nse/scs_a02.pdf).

35. Marcos J. Mendes, "Wrestling with States and Municipalities: Brazilian Federalism," Braudel Paper 23 (São Paulo: Fernand Braudel Institute of World Economics, 2000), p. 51.

36. Ibid., p. 16, citing Janos Kornai, "The Soft Budget Constraint," *Kyklos* 39, fasc. 1 (1986): 4.

37. Almeida, "Recentralizando a federaçáo?" p. 24.

38. Kurt Weyland, "The Brazilian State in the New Democracy," in Kingstone and Power, *Democratic Brazil,* p. 43.

39. There are even different tax rates for exports from the southern states to the north and northeast than for the reverse: 12 percent for the former and 7 percent for the latter.

40. Valeriano Costa, "Federalismo: As relaçôes intergovernamentais," in Avelar and Cintra, *Sistema político brasileiro,* p. 226.

41. José Antonio Cheibub, "Political Reform in Brazil: Recent Proposals, Diagnosis, and a Suggestion," in *Brazil under Lula,* edited by Joseph L. Love and Werner Baer (New York: Palgrave Macmillan, 2009), p. 15.

42. A comprehensive guide to the preparation of the legislation passed within the key areas can be found in Edson de Oliveira Nunes and others, *Agências reguladoras e reforma do Estado no Brasil* (Rio de Janeiro: Garamond, 2007).

43. Ibid., p. 183.

44. Aline Diniz Amaral, Peter R. Kingstone, and Jonathan Kneckhaus, "The Limits of Economic Reform in Brazil," in Kingstone and Power, *Democratic Brazil,* p. 153, citing a report in *Folha de São Paulo,* September 9, 2002.

45. Bernardo Mueller and André Rossi de Oliveira, "Regulation during the Lula Government," *Brazil under Lula,* pp. 96–97.

46. Ibid., pp. 103–04. That decision was later upheld by the supreme court at the beginning of July 2004.

Chapter Three

1. For Brazil, see particularly the original contributions of Pérsio Arida, André Lara Resende, and Francisco L. Lopes, all of whom played a large role in the eventual Cruzado Plan. I refer here to their early work: Pérsio Arida and André Lara Resende, "Inertial inflation and monetary reform," in *Inflation and Indexation,* edited by John Williamson (Washington: Institute of International Economics, 1985), pp. 27–45; and Francisco L. Lopes, "Inflação inercial, hiperinflação e desinflação," *Revista da ANPEC,* no. 7 (1984): 55–71. But there was a broader international discussion involving economists within the United States, Israel, Argentina, and elsewhere, as can be seen in the book edited by John Williamson.

2. I have chosen to follow André Lara Resende's treatment in "A moeda indexada: Uma proposta para eliminar a inflação inercial," *Revista de Economia Política 5,* no. 2 (1985): 130–34.

3. Ibid., p. 131. My translation.

4. Ibid., p. 134. My translation.

5. The principal factual source for details on the Cruzado Plan and its successors during the Sarney period is Eduardo Modiano, "A opera dos trés cruzados: 1985–1989," in *A ordem do progresso,* edited by Marcelo de Paiva Abreu (Rio de Janeiro: Editora Campus, 1990), pp. 347–86.

6. Carlos Eduardo Carvalho makes a persuasive case that the German postwar experience had little to do with the origins of the development of the Collor Plan. Rather, he traces the basic idea back to more casual perceptions arising during the presidential campaign preceding Collor's election. Since the deviations from the historical antecedent were substantial, this amendment seems correct. See Carlos Eduardo Carvalho, "As origins e a gênese do Plano Collor," *Nova Economia* 16, no. 1(2006): 101–34.

7. See Luiz Carlos Bresser-Pereira, *Crise econômica e reforma do estado no Brasil* (Sao Paulo: Editora 34, 1996), chapter 13, and World Bank, *Brazil: An Agenda for Stabilization,* Report 13168-BR (Washington, 1994), among other sources.

8. Bresser-Pereira, *Crise econômica,* p. 237.

9. For treatments of the Real Plan, see the recent book by Alkimar Moura, ed., *Paeg e real* (São Paulo: Fundação Getúlio Vargas, 2007), and the references there cited. For an interesting comparison of the intellectual bases of the Cruzado and Real Plans, see Carlos Pio, "A estabilização heterodoxa no Brasil," *Revista Brasileira de Ciências Sociais* 16, no. 46 (2001): 29–54. For a key participant's view, see Edmar Bacha, "Brazil's *Plano Real*: A View from the Inside," in *Development Economics and Structuralist Macroeconomics,* edited by Amitava Krishna Dutt and Jaime Ros (Cheltenham: Edward Elgar, 2003), pp. 181–205. Bacha headed up the Cardoso economic advisory team.

10. Fernando Henrique Cardoso, *A arte da política* (Rio de Janeiro: Civilização Brasileira, 2006), chapter 3.

11. This had the advantage of requiring only a majority vote within the congress rather than the 60 percent ordinarily necessary. Of some 30,000 potential amendments, only 6 were approved.

12. Fabio Giambiagi and Mario Ronci, "Brazilian Fiscal Institutions: The Cardoso Reforms, 1995–2002," *CEPAL Review,* no. 86 (2006): 71.

13. Bacha, "Brazil's *Plano Real,*" p. 12.

14. See Maria Clara R. M. do Prado, *A real história do real: Uma raiografia da moeda que mudou o Brasil* (São Paulo: Editora Record, 2005), for a full discussion

of this initial divergence, and the subsequent ones as time passed and interest rates remained high.

15. I am using here, and elsewhere in this chapter, the data contained in Fabio Giambiagi, "18 anos de política fiscal no Brasil: 1991/1998," *Economia Aplicada* 12, no. 4 (2008): 547.

16. Fabio Giambiagi and Marcio Ronci, "Fiscal Policy and Debt Sustainability: Cardoso's Brazil, 1995–2002," Working Paper 156 (Washington: IMF, 2004), p. 38.

17. International Monetary Fund, *The IMF and Recent Capital Account Crises: Indonesia, Korea, Brazil* (Washington, 2003), p. 125.

18. Rudiger Dornbusch, "Brazil's Incomplete Stabilization and Reform," *BPEA*, no. 1(1997): 367. Interestingly, the major limitation of policy he emphasizes is the large increase in the minimum wage that was allowed in 1995, hardly ever cited in discussions about the exchange rate.

19. These accounts come from a *New York Times* article by Diana Jean Schemo, on January 4, 1999; the IMF, "Brazil Memorandum of Economic Policies," March 8, 1999 (www.imf.org/external/np/loi/1999/030899.htm); and Macroplan, *Cinco cenários para o Brasil, 2001–2003*, report (Rio de Janeiro, 2001), p. 23.

20. Claudio Hamilton dos Santos, Márcio Bruno Ribeiro , and Sérgio Wulff Gobetti, "A evolução da carga tributária bruta brasileira no período 1995–2007: Tamanho, composição e especificações econométricas agregadas," Discussion Paper 1350 (Brasília: Instituto de Pesquisa Econômica Aplicada [IPEA]), August 2008).

21. The formulation can be written as $D = D (1 + i)/(1 + \pi)(1 + g) + \varepsilon w/(1 + \pi)(1 + g) - s$, where D is the level of the net debt; i, the nominal rate of interest; π, the rate of domestic inflation; g, the real rate of domestic growth; ε, the percentage change in the nominal exchange rate; w, the share of debt linked to the dollar; and s, the annual primary surplus attained. I was among those musing about alternative strategies; see Albert Fishlow, "Brazil: What Kind of Future," *Revista de Economia e Relações Internacionais* 1, no. 1 (2002): 19–34.

22. Some, critical of the continuing primary surplus, put together such calculations comparing the neoconservative and neo-Keynesian options. They have no problem proving—with this one equation model—that the latter comes out better in growth and real domestic interest rates, and the same in real exchange rates and final debt ratios. See José Luís Osorio, João Sicsú, and Luiz Fernando de Paula, "Controle da dívida pública e politica fiscal: Uma alternativa para um crescimento autosustentado da economia brasileira," in *Agenda Brasil: Políticas econömicas para o crescimento com estabilisdade de preços*, edited by João Sicsú, Luiz Fernando de Paula, and Renaut Michel (Barueri: Manole, 2003).

23. I have benefited from the earlier work of Armando Castelar Pinheiro, Fabio Giambiagi, Ben Ross Schneider, and Licinio Velasco Jr. in this section. Specific references will be provided as particular issues are treated.

24. *The Economist*, August 21, 1993, p. 18, as cited in Armando Castelar Pinheiro and Ben Ross Schneider, "Fiscal Impact of Privatisation in Latin America," *Quarterly Review of Economics and Finance* 34, special issue (Summer 1994): 25.

25. Rogério Wernick emphasized this point early on in the Brazilian case. See, for example, "Aspectos macroeconômicos da privatização no Brasil," Discussion Paper 223 (PUC-Rio, Departamento de Economia, April 1989).

26. Armando Castelar Pinheiro and Luiz Chrysóstomo de Oliveira Filho, "Privatização no Brasil: Passado, planos e perspectivas," Discussion Paper 230 (Brasília: IPEA, August 1991), p. 16.

27. Paragraph I of Law 8031, as cited in ibid., p. 28.

28. Armando Castelar Pinheiro and Fabio Giambiagi, "Brazilian Privatization in the 1990s," *World Development* 22, no. 5 (1994): 741–42.

29. Armando Castelar Pinheiro, "The Brazilian Privatization Experience: What's Next," Discussion Paper 87 (Rio de Janeiro: BNDES, November 2000), p. 18.

30. BNDES, "A nova fase da privatização" (www.planalto.gov.br/publi_04/COLE CAO/Fase.htm).

31. See Alfred P. Montero, "State Interests and the New Industrial Policy in Brazil: The Privatization of Steel, 1990–1994," *Journal of Interamerican Studies and World Affairs* 40, no. 3 (1998): 52.

Montero argues that there was greater attention to the subject during the Cardoso period. Cardoso did speak about it, but as is evident from the actual sales—which continued to be low in 1995—his focus was elsewhere.

32. Ibid., p. 53. Montero suggests a total of only $2 billion in sales during the Itamar period and asserts that there was much greater change in the program after his ascension to the presidency. The data used here are from the BNDES, *Privatização no Brasil: 1990–94, 1995–2002* (Rio de Janeiro: July 2002). Montero's evaluation incorporates a large prior adjustment to receipts, a procedure common among critics of the privatization process.

33. For a recent view, especially critical of the larger sales in the later Cardoso years, see Guido Mantega, "O programa de privatizações brasileiras e sua repercussão na dinamica economica," Research Report 53 (São Paulo: EAESP/FGV/NPP, 2001).

34. Montero, "State Interests," p. 53, seems to assert exactly that when he states that "the use of live money efficiently funded government without the *desâgio* [discount] that subsidized firm buyers and penalized public accounts." In fact, although the quantity of cash rose dramatically in 1994, it still made up little more than a third of total sales in the Itamar years. See table 3-4.

35. Armando Castelar Pinheiro and Fábio Giambiagi, "The Macroeconomic Background and Institutional Framework of Brazilian Privatization," in *Privatization in Brazil: The Case of Public Utilities,* Ensaios BNDES 10, edited by Armando C. Pinheiro and Kichiro Fukasaku (Rio de Janeiro: BNDES, April 1999), p. 12.

36. See Montero, "State Interests," pp. 47–48.

37. Pinheiro, "The Brazilian Privatization Experience," p. 18.

38. See the long treatment in Cardoso, *A arte,* pp. 353–62.

39. For a good discussion of the program, see Geraldo V. S. Maia, "Reestruturação bancária no Brasil: O caso do Proer," *Notas Técnicas do Banco Central do Brasil,* no. 38 (2003).

40. Both Banespa and BANERJ were not incorporated in the original PROES legislation, but the cost of the recuperation of these banks has been conventionally included in the valuation of PROES. In table 3-8, I account for this in assessing the magnitude of the federal intervention.

41. Municipal debt was similarly restructured in 1999, to the special benefit of São Paulo and Rio de Janeiro, although almost 200 municipalities were involved. In what follows, I do not discuss this smaller component of restructuring.

42. The assertion, in early January 1999, of the former president and new governor of Minas Gerais, Itamar Franco, that he was no longer going to pay the state's debt interest sparked the beginning of the subsequent crisis. Governor Olívio Dutra of Rio Grande do Sul deposited the interest but did not forward it. No one seemed to notice

that these decisions were irrelevant since the federal government was able to withhold payments owed to the states.

43. See Afonso Bevilacqua," State Government Bailouts in Brazil," Latin American Research Network Working Paper R-441 (Washington: Inter-American Development Bank, 2002). The totals for the states specified in the particular years can be found on pp. 13, 20, and 33; the regression results are found on pp. 40–45.

44. Cardoso did not discuss PROES, and cites the 3 percent for PROER commonly claimed. The article relating to the CPI on Banking is dated November 26, 1999, and available on the Internet; interestingly, it cites a study by the Comision Economica Para America Latina y el Caribe about the costs of PROES but fails to note that the ultimate source is Gustavo Franco, former president of the central bank.

45. This value for the central bank charge is given in Maia, "Reestruturação bancária," and it is the same as the estimate of 0.88 percent of income cited by Ilan Goldfayn, Katherine Hennings, and Helio Mori, "Brazil's Financial Sector: Resilience to Shocks, No Currency Substitution but Struggling to Promote Growth," Working Paper 170 (Stanford Center for Research on Economic Development and Policy Reform, June 2003), p. 16.

46. The initial figure of R$40 billion comes from the special budgetary allocation to the Ministry of Finance for PROES at the end of 1997; Gustavo Franco's estimate of R$54.5 billion is contained in his testimony before the CPI on Banking in August 1999, and reported in the *Gazeta Mercantil;* a R$61.5 billion gross value appears in Cleofas Salviano Junior, *Bancos estaduais: Dos problemas crônicos ao PROES* (Brasília: Banco Central do Brasil, 2004), pp. 129 and 130. See also Goldfayn, Hennings, and Mori, "Brazil's Financial Sector."

47. These values come from Francisco Rigolon and Fabio Giambiagi, "A renegociação das dívidas e o regime fiscal dos estados," in *A economia Brasileira nos anos 90,* edited by F. Giambiagi and M. M. Moreira (Rio de Janeiro: BNDES, 1999), p. 129. There was additional state debt remaining from the earlier federal redemptions.

48. Ibid. Their assessment presumed an initial high SELIC interest rate in 1998, followed by an immediate rapid reduction and continued decline in 2002–07 to 6 percent in the lowest case and to 9 percent in the highest. I have chosen to use the actual high SELIC rates in 1998–2006, followed by conversion to a 6 percent real rate thereafter. Both results are very different from the calculations of Monica Mora, "Federalismo e dívida estadual no Brasil," Discussion Paper 866 (Brasilia: IPEA, 2002), p. 31 , where she finds that a real interest rate of 8 percent implies a present value cost of 27 percent of gross national product. That would be more than twice the value of the initial state debt: simple immediate default would represent less than half that sum and logically is the limit to any cost measure.

49. Afonso Bevilacqua and others, "The Structure of Public Sector Debt in Brazil," Latin American Research Network Working Paper R-424 (Washington: Inter-American Development Bank, 2001), p. 35.

50. See, for example, the article by Vinod Thomas and John Nash, "Reform of Trade Policy: Recent Evidence from Theory and Practice," *World Bank Research Observer* 6, no. 2 (1991): 219–40.

51. I have benefited from the writing of Honório Kume, who was directly engaged in the process of tariff reform at this time as well as subsequently. This section, and some of the following paragraphs, is based on Kume's work with Julio Berlinski and others, "Aranceles a las importaciones en el Mercosur: El camino al arancel externo

común," Working Paper 08/05 (Montevideo: Departamento de Economía de la Facultad de Ciencias Sociales, November 2005), pp. 12 ff.

52. Armando Castelar Pinheiro and Fábio Giambiagi, "Padrões de proteção na economia brasileira," Discussion Paper 355 (Rio de Janeiro: IPEA, October 1994), p. 10, echoing Winston Fritsch and Gustavo H. B. Franco, "Trade Policy Issues in Brazil in the 1990s," Discussion Paper 268 (PUC-Rio, Departamento de Economia, October), p. 48. Sectoral effective protection rates do not fully bear this out, as shown in table 3-10, perhaps as a result of the limited weight of imports in such sectors.

53. Berlinski and others, "Aranceles a las importaciones," p. 26.

54. Andre Filipe Z. de Azevedo and Marcelo Portugal, "Abertura comercial brasileira e inestabilidade da demanda de importaçoes," *Nova Economia* 9, no. 1 (1998): 46.

55. The data involve use of the monthly indexes of real aggregate imports as well as the monthly real exchange rate, adjusted to reflect the annual changes in the level of aggregate protection from table 3-9. Initial quarterly values were used in the regression, thus allowing for a short lag. Effective protection was slightly more significant than nominal in adjusting the exchange rate, and that is the result given here. An adjustment was made for autocorrelation of the residuals, thus explaining the AR variable. Student t values are in parentheses below the coefficients; $R^2 = 0.67$; DW = 1.99.

56. Donald A. Hay, "The Post-1990 Brazilian Trade Liberalisation and the Performance of Large Manufacturing Firms: Productivity, Market Share and Profits," *Economic Journal* 111 (July 2001): 634. Using 1990, a year of negative growth, as a base yields a very large subsequent gain in productivity that exaggerates the real change in this period, which is much closer to 1–2 percent, and for some intervals, even less. There is wide variance in the results of individual authors.

57. The implicit tariff for consumer goods in 1989 was already only 3 percent, and 21 percent for intermediate and capital goods. As a result, there was still redundancy except in a few sectors. As Kume notes, "The non-tariff barriers do not provide additional protection." See Honório Kume, "A reforma tarifária e a nova política de importação," in *O Brasil e a nova economia mundial*, edited by João Paulo Velloso (Rio de Janeiro: J. Olympio, 1991).

58. See Mauricio Mesquita Moreira and Paulo Guilherme Correa, "A First Look at the Impacts of Trade Liberalization on Brazilian Manufacturing Industry," *World Development* 26, no. 10 (1998): 1869–71.

59. See Rafael Azul, April 23, 2003 (www.wsws.org/articles/2003/apr2003/braz-a22.shtml).

60. See Ben Ross Schneider, "Big Business in Brazil," and Edmund Amann, "Technology, Public Policy, and Brazilian Multinationals," in *Brazil as an Economic Superpower?* edited by Lael Brainard and Leonardo Martinez-Diaz (Brookings, 2009), chapters 7 and 8, respectively.

61. See the translated statement of Gustavo Faleiros, "Plano econômico de Lula é insustentável," May 14, 2007, replicated by the Americas Program, Center for International Policy (www.ircamericas.org/port/4041). There he points out Lula's position that "environmental and social issues hindered the country's growth."

62. These targets were based upon the national accounts before their revision a few months later. Under those circumstances, the correct figures would be some 10 percent lower, but the future projections would be unaltered.

63. These comments go back a long way. See, for example, her statements during congressional hearings on December 18, 2007, about the lack of planning and

macroeconomic management in the Cardoso government. These criticisms intensified during the presidential campaign.

64. See Fábio Portela, "PAC," *Veja*, June 10, 2009.

65. These results come from the final Four Year Report of the PAC, published in December 2010, and available on the PAC site now hosted by the presidency (www. presidencia.gov.br/pac/relatorios).

66. Fabio Stefano Erber, "Development Projects under Finance Domination—the Case of Brazil during the Lula Years (2003–2007)," *Third World Review*, no. 195 (2008): 607–08. Erber had participated in the preparation and implementation of the PITCE as a member of the BNDES in 2003–04.

67. See Glauco Arbix and João Alberto De Negri, "Ampliação da faixa de empresas que inovam e diferenciam produtos," in *Porque o Brasil não é um país de alto crescimento?* edited by João Paulo Velloso (Rio de Janeiro: J. Olympio, 2006), pp. 373–81. The work of Richard Nelson, Giovanni Dosi, and others was a significant influence. In Brazil the Campinas group and the São Paulo Foundation for Research Support were also active. From the first group, see Wilson Suzigan and João Furtado, "Política industrial e desenvolvimento," *Revista de Economia Política* 26, no. 2 (2006): 163–85; from the latter, see Carlos H. de Brito Cruz and Luiz de Mello, "Boosting Innovation Performance in Brazil," Working Paper ECO/WKP (2006)60 (Paris: OECD, 2006).

68. Paulo Gala, "Brazil's Development Conundrum," April 21, 2008 (http://rethinkingdevelopment.blogspot.com/2008_04_01_archive.html).

69. For a useful, brief summary on this matter, as well as on petroleum exploration, see *The Economist*, July 3, 2010, pp. 35–38.

70. There were numerous accounts of the sale, held on September 24, 2010, in the financial press. The gain did not fully satisfy the Left. They would prefer total government ownership of Petrobras, as in the past when the slogan was "O petroleo é nosso" (the oil is ours).

71. "Petrobras 'Slashes Pre-Salt Costs,'" May 6, 2010 (www.upstreamonline.com/live/article214258.ece).

Chapter Four

1. Federal transfers were allocated proportionately to population and inversely to per capita income.

2. Age-grade distortion measures the total number of students in a given grade divided by the population theoretically in attendance when there is no repetition. Here, for grade 4, that is equal to the number of ten-year-olds with attendance in the first grade, assumed to begin at age seven.

3. See, for example, Nora Gordon and Emiliana Vegas, "Educational Finance Equalization: Spending, Teacher Quality, and Student Outcomes," in *Incentives to Improve Teaching: Lessons from Latin America*, edited by Emiliana Vegas (Washington: World Bank, 2005), p. 151–86.

4. IPEA, *Brasil: O estado de uma nacão* (Brasília, 2006 and 2007), sections dealing with education in both surveys.

5. For an analysis of the establishment of the SAEB and the limited ability of state educational secretariats to take advantage of the resultant information, see Manuel Crespo, José Francisco Soares, and Alberto de Mello e Souza, "The Brazilian National Evaluation System of Basic Education: Context, Process and Impact," *Studies*

in Educational Evaluation 26, no. 2 (2000): 105–25. By 1997 the sample included 167,196 students, 13,267 teachers, and 2,302 principals.

6. These studies, many for postgraduate degrees, have availed themselves of the raw data generously and continuously made available over the years by the National Institute of Educational Studies and Research (INEP), a part of the Ministry of Education.

7. As quoted in Maria Inês de Matos Coelho, "Vinte anos de avaliação básica no Brasil: aprendizagens e desafios," *Ensaio: Availiação Politíca e Pública em Educação* 16, no. 59 (2008): 243.

8. Ibid.

9. Alberto Rodriguez, Carl Dahlman, and Jamil Salmi, *Knowledge and Innovation for Competitiveness,* (Washington: World Bank, 2008), p. 181, citing an unpublished 2006 World Bank policy note by G. Ioschpe.

10. See Angelina Barreto and others, "Subsídios para melhorar a educação no Brasil," in *Desafios e Perspectivas da Política Social,* edited by Anna Maria Peliano, Discussion Paper 1248, IPEA, 2006), 53–72. The original data come from the 2005 PNAD.

11. Claudio de Moura Castro, "O ensino medio: Orfão de idéias, herdeiro de equivocos," *Ensaio: Availiação e Políticas Públicas em Educação* 16, no. 58 (2008): 113.

12. Of the countries participating in the first Program for International Student Achievement in 2000, Brazil was one of two not from the Organization for Economic Cooperation and Development (OECD). There were thirty-two participating countries in 2000, forty-one in 2003, and fifty-seven in 2006. The test is applied to fifteen-year-olds, all of whom must be above the fifth year of education and currently in school. It covers reading, mathematics, and science. Another examination was given at the end of May 2009. As is the case with the SAEB results, there have been studies performed in Brazil utilizing the data. They find a combination of socioeconomic and school characteristics to be the important ones. See, for example, F. D. Waltenberg, "Iniqüidade educacional no Brasil. Uma avaliação com dados do PISA 2000,"*Revista Economia* vol 6, no. 1 (2005): 67–118.

13. World Bank, *Higher Education in Brazil* (Washington, 2002), p.29.

14. Completion of upper secondary education equally exceeds returns for primary schooling over this decade. Ibid., p. 34.

15. Calculated from Maria Helena Guimarães de Castro, "O sistema educacional brasileiro: Tendêcias e perspectivas," in *Um Modelo para a Educação no Século XXI,* edited by J. P. Velloso e Roberto Cavalcanti de Albuquerque (Rio de Janeiro: J. Olympio, 1999), p. 97, using an annual deflator from the Economist Intelligence Unit of 0.92 to convert to dollars.

16. Actual teaching costs per full-time equivalent in federal universities (in 1997) come out with a number only about equal to $5,100, compared to global expenditures that are more than twice as great. The reason is exclusion of outlays on pensions, medical facilities, and research, cost sources usually accounted for in several other countries. See World Bank, *Higher Education in Brazil,* p. 39.

17. OECD, *Education at a Glance 2008* (Paris, 2008), pp. 199–224.

18. See IPEA, *Brasil: O estado de uma nação, 2006,* ch. 3, pp. 144–82.

19. Such a large percentage of GDP for education, greater than found in any other country, also has political content: higher salaries for teachers, on the one hand, and criticism of the interest payments required on increased public debt, on the other. For

a sampling of such views, see the contributions of José Marcelino de Rezende Pinto, "Financiamento da educação no Brasil: Um balanço do governo FHC (1995–2002)," *Educação e Sociedade* 23, no. 80 (2002): 108–35; and Valdemar Sguissardi, "Reforma universitária no Brasil—1995–2006: Precária trajetória e incerto futuro," *Educação e Sociedade* 27, no. 96 (2006): 1021–56.

20. Organización de Estados Iberoamericanos para la Educación, la Ciencia y la Cultura, Madrid (www.oei.es/noticias/article 4459, February 24, 2009).

21. See André Cezar Medici, "Financing Health Policies in Brazil," Discussion Paper (Washington: Inter-American Development Bank, November 2002). Fifteen percent of those who completed college utilized the public health service exclusively or frequently; the comparable figure was 74 percent for those with elementary education (p. 3).

22. Patricia T. R. Lucchese, "Decentralização do financiamento e gestão da assistência à saúde no Brasil," *Planejamento e Políticas Públicas* 14 (December 1996): 79.

23. This list follows the presentation offered by André Cezar Medici, "Saúde: Modelos de gestão descentralizada," in *Políticas Sociais no Brasil*, edited by João Paulo Velloso and others (Rio de Janeiro: J. Olympio, 1995), pp. 124–25.

24. Sônia M. Draibe, "A reforma dos programas sociais brasileiros: Panorama e trajetórias," paper presented at the Twenty-Fourth Annual Meeting of Associação Nacional de Pós-Graduação e Pesquisa em Ciências Sociais, August 2000, p. 19.

25. Eduardo Levcovitz, Luciana Dias de Lima, and Cristiani Vieira Machado, "Política de saúde nos anos 90: Relações intergovernamentais e o papel das Normas Operacionais Básicas," *Ciência e Saúde Coletiva* 6, no. 2 (2001): 287.

26. Medici," Financing Health," p. 2. This seems too high for family outlays and too little for enterprises. Total public expenditure in 1996 comes to about 3 percent of GDP, which would imply a total health cost of 8.1 percent, which is about right. But indications are that enterprises, favored by tax provisions, must have spent more than a seventh of private outlays.

27. World Bank, "The Organization, Delivery and Financing of Health Care in Brazil: Agenda for the 90s," Report 12655-BR (Washington: June 1994), p 59.

28. Maria Elizabeth Barros and others, "Política de saúde no Brasil: Diagnostico e Perspectivas," Discussion Paper 401 (Brasília: IPEA, February 2001), p.81.

29. Carlos Octâvio Ocké Reis and others, "Financiamento das políticas sociais nos anos 1990: O caso do Ministério da Saúde," Discussion Paper 802 (Brasília: IPEA, June 2001), p. 10.

30. These estimates, as indicated, come principally from the World Bank. There is great correspondence with the series of André Cezar Medici, *O desafio da decentralização: Financiamento público da saúde* (Washington: Inter-American Development Bank, 2002), except for the year 1989, where he indicates greater federal expansion. There is a special data problem for 1993. Many sources—but not Medici—indicate great growth in federal receipts between 1992 and 1993, and subsequent decline in 1994. A 2001 IPEA paper has federal outlays about the same; see Reis and others, "Financiamento das políticas sociais." Note as well that Gauri indicates a major decline in average costs of hospital admissions between 1992 and 1993, which would make constancy in outlays more probable rather than an increase. See Varun Gauri, *Brazil: The Health System: Impact Evaluation*, World Bank Report 18142 (Washington: World Bank, 1998). There are also no state and local allocations for 1993; numbers here have been approximately interpolated.

31. World Bank, *The Organization, Delivery and Financing of Health Care in Brazil: Agenda for the 90s,* Report 12655-BR (Washington: 1994), pp. 40–41.

32. This tax had been passed in 1993, as the IPMF (Temporary Tax on Financial Transactions), in order to increase the resources available to the government during stabilization; it expired at the end of 1994. The tax was revived as a contribution, thus no longer requiring partial allocation to states and municipalities, by Law 9311, which was passed on October 24, 1996, and was to take effect in 1997.

33. Illustrative is an early article written in 1995 by the ex-municipal secretary of health of Riberão Preto. See Juan S. Yazlle Rocha, "Do caos mercantilista à racionalidade de saúde: A reconstrução do processo assistential," *Saúde e Sociedade* 4, no. 1–2 (1995): 123–25.

34. This is only a brief summary of the much greater quantity of information found in Levcovitz, Lima, and Machado, "Política de saúde," 269–91.

35. Ibid., p. 287.

36. Ibid., pp. 279–80.

37. *Veja,* April 1, 1998.

38. At the end of 1997, there were only 1,623 Programa de Saúde da Família groups in 567 municipalities; by the end of 2002, there were 16,698 teams in 4,161 municipalities, caring for what must have been more than 50 million people. The Programa de Agentes Comunitários de Saúde likewise expanded from caring for 55,000 people to more than 175,000 over this same period. As a proportion of expenditure, there was an increase from 16 percent of the ministry's budget in 1998 to more than 26 percent in 1993. These data come from the Primary Health Care Information System (SIAB), Ministry of Health.

39. Fabrício Augusto de Oliveira, "Fundef e saúde: Duas experiências (virtuosas?) de decentralização," in *Decentralização e Federalismo Fiscal no Brasil,* edited by Fernando Rezende and Fabrício Augusto de Oliveira (Rio de Janeiro: Konrad Adenauer Stiftung, 2003), pp. 245ff.

40. I have chosen these rather than the frequently used, but earlier, estimates of Ana Celia Faveret cited in Oliveira, "Fundef." The latter show a growth of 42 percent between 1998 and 2004, whereas those used here, starting from 2003, indicate a lesser expansion. In particular, state rates of expansion are much larger in Faveret. But both show the inferiority of Amendment 29.

41. A. Nunn, E. De Fonseca, and S. Gruskin, "Changing Global Essential Medicines Norms to Improve Access to AIDS Treatment: Lessons from Brazil," *Global Public Health* 4, no. 2 (2009): 131–49.

42. That did not prevent a wave of harsh criticism for Serra about his management of Health Ministry when he opposed Lula in the 2002 election. This extended to holding him personally responsible for some of the corruption later unearthed in the ministry. In May 2006, the *sangessuga* (bloodsucker) scandal emerged, involving allocations for ambulances purchased by municipalities at higher prices, enriching again some ministry officials and especially members of the congress. An ensuing congressional investigation in August exposed the involvement of numerous members of the congress. Lula avoided any blame, as a year earlier in the inquiries surrounding the mensalão bribery scandal, although his popularity was then affected, forcing a second round in the presidential election under way.

43. The basic questions relating to the mechanics of projection from the 1998 base are whether it should be fixed or compounded, including years when more than the minimal amounts are financed, and whether the expenditure base should be complete,

including items like retirement pensions, or limited to those related to health. The Health Ministry has always favored calculations that maximized its outcome, while the Finance Ministry—in both regimes—has favored minimizing the claim.

44. I therefore tend to disagree with the recent assertion that "the rush to decentralize health services to municipalities has, in the absence of sufficient financial and technical assistance from the federal and state governments, increased state-municipal conflict over the management of health policy, limiting municipalities' ability to increase bureaucratic capacity." See Eduardo J. Gómez, "A Temporal Analytical Approach to Decentralization: Lessons from Brazil's Health Sector," *Journal of Health Politics, Policy and Law* 33, no. 1 (2008): 54–91. The quotation is taken from the abstract (p. 51). The evidence seems to rely on sources dating back to the end of the 1990s and ignores the recent growth in state expenditures and transfers.

45. Calculated from Sérgio Francisco Piola and others, "Estado de uma nação: Textos de apoio [saúde]," Discussion Paper 1391 (Brasília: IPEA, February 2009), p. 31.

46. See, as an example of the SUS partisans, the treatment in Nelson Rodrigues dos Santos, "Política pública de saúde no Brasil: Encruzilhada, buscas e esolhas de rumos," *Ciência e Saúde Coletiva*, 13, suppl. 2 (2008): 2006–18. "Various non-foreseen expenditures for 2008 are occurring, like increases in public sector salaries. . . . Once more, the non-prioritization of public policy for health stands out" (p. 2016).

47. These are the arguments recently asserted by the World Bank on behalf of its new loan program of $235 million, QUALISUS-REDE. For an outline of its prospective engagement, see World Bank, *Project Appraisal Document*, Report 42359-BR (Washington, 2008). Counterpart Brazilian expenditure brings the total to $677 million.

48. The many works of the IPEA and of Francisco Oliveira and his collaborators have been invaluable on this subject.

49. World Bank, *Brazil: Social Insurance and Private Pensions*, Report 12336-BR (Washington, 1995), p. 63.

50. Francisco Oliveira and others, "Reforma da Previdencia," Discussion Paper 508 (Brasília: IPEA, 1997), p. 24. This result is for 1996, but as figure 4-4 shows, the same pattern prevailed earlier as well.

51. World Bank, *Brazil: Social Insurance*, pp. 46, 48, and Oliveira, "Reforma," p. 40.

52. For a report on possible privatization in Brazil, see Patricio Arrau and Klaus Schmidt-Hebbel, "Pension Systems and Reform: Country Experiences and Research Issues," Policy Research Working Paper 1470 (Washington: World Bank, 1995). The immediate cost of 5.3 percent of GDP presumes all retirements at age sixty-five, thereby ignoring the substantial issue of pensions offered at much earlier ages.

53. Ibid., p. 29.

54. World Bank, *Averting the Old Age Crisis: Policies to Protect the Old and Promote Growth* (Washington, 1994).

55. In the November 13, 1998, Letter of Intent to the IMF, articles 16 and 17 explicitly refer to the social security system and seem to suggest that Brazil was about to embark upon an explicit notional capitalization scheme: "The guiding principle of the complementary round will be the principle of actuarial balance. Notional individual accounts will be set up for the participants of both the private system and the public system" (footnote 41).

56. Fernando Enrique Cardoso, *A arte da política* (Rio de Janeiro: Civilizacão Brasileira, 2006), pp. 456–85. That sequence, while fascinating from a political perspective, need not be detailed here. For a more recent (and less personally engaged)

treatment, see Takeo Hiroi, "Timing and Outcome of Legislation: Brazilian Pension Reform in a Bicameral Perspective," *Journal of Legislative Studies* 14, no. 4 (2008): 394–420.

57. Notional capitalization ensures the continuing viability of a public PAYG (pay-as-you-go) system. Returns (at a low real interest rate) are calculated for individual accounts to ensure that the discounted present value of payments exactly equals contributions. This rate of return has a great influence on the replacement rate, that is, the percentage of receipts relative to payments. In Brazil, where the real rate of interest on savings accounts was 6 percent, the effect would be dramatic. See R. Holzmann and E. Palmer, eds., *Pension Reform: Issues and Prospects for Non-Financial Defined Contributions (NDC) Schemes* (Washington: World Bank, 2006).

58. This alternative is laid out in Francisco Oliveira and others, "Reforma estrutural da Previdência: Uma proposta para assegurar proteção social e eqüidade," Discussion Paper 690 (Rio de Janeiro: IPEA, December 1999). See also Sheila Najberg and Marcelo Ikeda, "Previdência no Brasil: Desafios e limites," in *A economia brasileira nos anos 90*, edited by Fabio Giambiagi and Mauricio Mesquita Moreira (Rio de Janeiro: BNDES, 1999).

59. The exact factor, multiplying the wage base, is $[(c \times P)/LE] \times \{[1+ (A + c \times P)/100]\}$, where c is the contribution rate; P, the contribution period; LE, life expectancy as updated by the Brazilian Institute of Geography and Statistics (IBGE); and A, the retirement age. For a male retiring at age sixty after contributing for forty years, the factor in 2006 was 1.03; for any earlier age, the factor was less than 1; for any higher age, the factor increases so that by age sixty-five, it is 1.27. The implicit interest rate is given by the second term: it rises from 0.07 for the base case to 0.08 at age sixty-five. Both are much higher than the 3 percent real rates utilized in the notional capitalization models. In this sense, Brazil did not follow this particular strategy, for it would have involved much lower returns.

60. See Guilherme C. Delgado and others, "Avaliação de resultados da Lei do Fator Previdenciário (1999–2004)," Discussion Paper 1161 (Brasília: IPEA, 2006).

61. See Maria Antonieta P. Leopoldi, "Reforming Social Security under Lula: Continuities with Cardoso's Policies," in *Brazil under Lula*, edited by Joseph L. Love and Werner Baer (New York: Palgrave Macmillan, 2008), pp. 232 ff.

62. Fabio Giambiagi and others, "Diagnóstico da Previdência Social no Brasil: O que feito e o que falta reformar," *Pesquisa e Planejamento Econômica* 34, no. 3 (2004): 372. Later revision of the national accounts reduces the change a bit.

63. Fabio Giambiagi and Isabela Estermínio, "Reforma Previdenciário no Brasil: Elevado investimento de capital politico, escasso resultados e desafíos não resolvidos," *Revista de Economia* 32, no. 1(2006): p. 144.

64. Eduardo da Silva Pereira, "A nova contabilidade da Previdência Social nas Projeções de longo prazo para o RGPS," *Informe de Previdência Social* 19, no. 11 (2007): 5.

65. See Fabio Giambiagi and others, "Impacto de reformas paramétricas na Previdência Social brasileira: Simulaçoes alternativas," Discussion Paper 1289 (Brasília: IPEA, July 2007); and Roberto de Rezende Rocha and Marcelo Abi-Ramia Caetano, "O sistema previdencíario brasileiro: Uma avaliação de desempenho comparada," Discussion Paper 1331 (Brasília: IPEA, December 2008). Some other recent contributions (like Graziela Ansiliero and Luis Henrique Paiva, "The recent evolution of social security coverage in Brazil," *International Social Security Review* 61, no. 3 (2008),

and Leopoldi, "Reforming Social Security under Lula") are much less troubled because they emphasize the gains in coverage accomplished and Lula's declarations in favor of further change.

66. Giambiagi and others, "Impacto," p. 218. One curious aspect of these results is the *greater* inequality that emerges between the sexes as a consequence of implementing all the reforms. Urban males within the private sector end up subsidizing everyone else. Another special feature is a presumed rate of increase of public sector wages of only 1.5 percent a year, making the public sector's participation within the total wage base fall considerably by 2050 and reducing annual increases in pensions.

67. Eduardo Silva Pereira, "A nova contabilidade," pp. 9,10.

68. Rodolfo Hoffmann, "Desigualdade da distribuição da renda no Brasil: A contribuição de aposentadorias e pensões e de outras parcelas do rendimento domiciliar per capita," *Economia e Sociedade* 18, no.1 (2009): 225.

69. Note that the 40 percent proportional reduction in poverty indicated for 1986 is not credible. Real income gains are exaggerated by the large number of goods for which prices were fixed at low levels but which were simply unavailable. See Francisco H. G. Ferreira, Phillippe G. Leite, and Julie A. Litchfield, "The Rise and Fall of Brazilian Inequality," Policy Research Working Paper 3867 (Washington: World Bank, March 2006), p. 11.

70. See Edward Amadeo and Marcelo Neri, "Política macroeconómico y pobreza no Brasil," in *Políticas macroeconómicas y pobreza en América latina y el Caribe,* edited by Enrique Ganuza, Samuel Morley, and Lance Taylor (Mexico City: Mundi Prensa Libros, 1998); and Sonia Rocha, "Renda e pobreza: Os impactos do Plano Real," *Revista Brasileira de Estudos de População* 13, no. 2 (1996): 117–33.

71. See Ferreira, Leite, and Litchfield, "Rise and Fall of Brazilian Inequality," for information and references.

72. The high level of importance of education in successive cross-sectional studies of income distribution is not replicated in the analyses undertaken over time. Other factors such as geographic location then have greater significance. It is also true that variability in occupational position continued to be important within the agricultural sector, as shown by the work of Rodolfo Hoffmann. See his two articles, joint with M. G. Ney, "Desigualdade de renda na agricultura, o efeito da posse da terra," *Economia* 4, no. 1 (2003): 113–52, and "Origem familiar e desigualdade de renda na agricultura," *Pesquisa e Planejamento Econômico* 33, no. 3 (2003): 541–72.

73. World Bank, *Brazil: Attacking Brazil's Poverty. A Poverty Report with a Focus on Urban Poverty Reduction Policies,* vol. 2: *Full Report,* Report 20475-BR (Washington, 2001), pp. 22ff. In 1973 I undertook a comparable analysis of poverty in 1960, finding somewhat greater costs: 6.1 percent of the income above the poverty line. The Gini coefficient then was a much smaller 0.44. See Albert Fishlow, "Distribuição da renda no Brasil: Um novo exame," *Dados,* no. 11 (1973): 67.

74. Calculated from Werner Baer and Antonio Fialho Galvão, "Tax Burden, Government Expenditures and Income Distribution in Brazil," *Quarterly Review of Economics and Finance* 48, no. 2 (2008): 349.

75. For an extensive, useful discussion of the introduction and early experience of the Comunidade Solidária, see Luis Fernando de Lara Resende, "Comunidade Solidária: Uma alternativa aos fundos sociais," Discussion Paper 725 (Brasília: IPEA, May 2000).

76. Ibid.

77. There was also the bottled gas subsidy begun in 2001, targeting families whose income per capita was less than half the minimum wage. It was intended to compensate for the rise in price of gas but eliminated the subsidy previously available to all users. This was a more modest supplement than the other two.

78. Sonia Rocha, "Impacto sobre a pobreza dos novos programas federais de transferência de renda," paper presented at the Thirty-Second National Meeting of Economics, João Pessoa, December 2004, p. 3.

79. The required income percentage comes from Ricardo Paes de Barros and others, "A importância da queda recente da desigualdade na redução da pobreza," Discussion Paper 1256 (Brasília: IPEA, January 2007), p. 16. I have taken the annual outlay in 2002 from World Bank, *Bolsa Família Project*, Report 28554-BR (Washington: May 2004), p. 16.

80. Jorge Saba Arbache, "Poverty and Markets in Brazil," in *Poverty and Markets in Brazil*, edited by Jorge Saba Arbache (Brasília: Comision Economica Para America Latina y el Caribe, 2003), p. 48.

81. The total expenditure reported for Bolsa Família varies somewhat among different sources, and even within a single one, such as Contas Abertas (a Brazilian nonprofit focused on transparency in government expenditures). This is due to the inclusion and exclusion of certain expenses. But even then, unless one includes some of the other outlays of the Ministry of Social Development for other purposes, such considerations do not alter the percentages of GDP by more than a tenth of a percentage point. Other parts of the program, like related medical services, are financed within the Ministry of Health and are not included; otherwise, they would increase reported outlays by about 20 percent.

82. For the study utilizing observations from all municipalities, see Monica A. Haddad, "A Spatial Analysis of *Bolsa Família:* Is Allocation Targeting the Needy?" in *Brazil under Lula*, edited by Joseph L. Love and Werner Baer (New York: Palgrave Macmillan, 2008), chapter 10. The article in favor of neutrality appeared first: André Carraro and others, "'É a economia companheiro!': Uma análase empírica da reeleição de Lula com base em dados municipais," Working Paper WP41 (Belo Horizonte: Brazilian Institute of Capital Markets, Minas Gerais, 2007). The two suggesting electoral consequences are by Elaine Cristina Licio and others, "Bolsa Família e voto na eleição presidencial de 2006: Em busca do elo perdido," *Opinão Pública* 15, no. 1 (2009): 31–54, and by Mauricio Canêdo Pinheiro, of the Fundação Getúlio Vargas, whose July 2009 paper was cited on the Internet.

83. Sergei Soares and others, "Focalização e cobertura do Programa Bolsa-Família: Qual o significado dos 11 milhões de famílias," Discussion Paper 1396 (Brasília: IPEA, March 2009). Unfortunately, this paper lacks an accurate measure of income volatility to go along with its sophisticated econometrics. The simple use of incomplete coverage reported in the PNAD directly yields the desired result.

84. For a summary of findings, see Centro de Desenvolvimento e Planejamento Regional, *Sumario executivo: Avaliação de impacto do Programa Bolsa Família* (Belo Horizonte, October 2007). There are other later evaluations currently being undertaken. Some can be found on the Internet by referring to the groups cited as well as to the Ministry of Social Development's website (www.mds.gov.br/bolsafamilia).

85. World Bank, *Brazil–Second Bolsa Familia APL Project*, Report AB2729, Project Information Document (Washington, June 22, 2009), pp. 2–3. Emphasis per original.

86. I have used the aggregate income gain reported in the national accounts, along with the poverty levels based upon the annual PNAD surveys and reported by Ricardo

Paes de Barros and others, "Markets, the State and the Dynamics of Inequality: Brazil's Case Study," UNDP Web, March 2009 (www.undp.org/latinamerica/inequality). There is a legitimate question about the comparability of these two different sources that serious Brazilian scholars have debated for a long time. Both Barros and Rodolfo Hoffmann, two of the three leading researchers on the subject of Brazilian income distribution—along with Marcelo Neri—have written extensively on this matter. They have concluded that the PNAD data are valid indicators of annual change in the distribution despite their exclusion of interest and profit that leads to understatement of the absolute level.

87. Sergei Soares and others, "Focalização," pp.18, 22; Fabio Veras Soares, Rafael Perez Ribas, and Rafael Guerreiro Osorio, "Evaluating the Impact of Brazil's *Bolsa Família:* Cash Transfer Programmes in Comparative Perspective," *International Poverty Centre Evaluation Note,* no. 1 (2007): 2.

88. Neri presents an assessment each year in January, using microdata from the PME/IBGE. This last one, as the economy was strongly progressing in 2010, projected this growth forward. See Marcelo Neri, *A pequena grande década: Crise, cenários e a nova classe media* (Rio de Janeiro: Center for Social Policies, Fundação Getúlio Vargas, 2010).

89. Degol Hailu and S. S. Soares, "What Explains the Decline in Brazil's Inequality," *International Policy Center for Inclusive Growth One Pager,* no. 89 (July 2009).

90. Barros and others, "Markets," p. 47.

91. Rodolfo Hoffmann, "As transferências não são a causa principal da redução da desigualdade," *Econômica* 7, no. 2 (2005): 335–41.

92. Sergei Soares and others, "Conditional Cash Transfers in Brazil, Chile and Mexico: Impacts upon Inequality," Working Paper 35 (Brasília: UNDP International Poverty Center, April 2007), p. 9.

93. IPEA, "PNAD 2007: Primeiras análises," *Comunicado da Presidência,* no. 10 (September 2008):19, 20.

94. IPEA, "PNAD 2008: Primeiras análises," *Comuncado da Presidência,* no. 30 (September 2009): 2–9.

95. World Bank, *Brazil–Second Bolsa Familia APL Project,* p. 2.

96. Barros and others, "Markets," p. 71.

Chapter Five

1. This discussion relies on, among others, Félix Peña, "Los grandes objetivos del Mercosur," paper presented at the conference "15 Anos de Mercosul: Avaliação e perspectivas," São Paulo, March 2006; Renato Baumann, ed., *Mercosul: Avanços e desafios da integração* (Brasília: IPEA, 2001); and José Augusto Guilhon Albuquerque, ed., *Sesenta anos de política exterior brasileira* (São Paulo: Cultura Editores Associados, 1996).

2. Francisco Thompson-Flores Netto, "Integração Brazil Argentina: Origem, processo e perspectiva," in *Temas de Política Externa Brasileira,* edited by Gelson Fonseca and Valdemar Carneiro Leão (Brasília: Instituto de Pesquisa de Relações Internacionais, 1989), p. 131.

3. Pablo Sanguinetti and others, "Trade Liberalization and the Dynamics of the Trade Structure in Argentina and Uruguay," preliminary paper for the 2002 World Development Report (Buenos Aires: Instituto Di Tella, August 2001), p. 3; Julio

Berlinski, "El sistema de incentivos en Argentina," Working Paper 179 (Buenos Aires: Instituto Di Tella, 1998).

4. Honorio Kume and Guida Piani, "Antidumping and Safeguard Mechanisms: The Brazilian Experience, 1988–2003," Policy Research Working Paper 3582 (Washington: World Bank, April 2005), p. 3.

5. Fabio Magalhães, ed., *Presidentes e o Mercosul: Reflexões sobre a integração* (São Paulo: Fundação Memorial da América Latina, 2003), p.118. Italics are mine.

6. David Rock, "Racking Argentina," *New Left Review*, no. 17, September-October 2002.

7. Paraguay and Uruguay, smaller and more open, were generally given longer periods of adaptation to avoid the immediate consequences of larger trade diversion.

8. Apparently neither Brazil nor Argentina had utilized the Mercosul technical committee initially set up to formalize the automobile agreement. For fuller discussions about this episode, see Andrés Malamud, "Presidential Diplomacy and the Institutional Underpinnings of Mercosur: An Empirical Examination," *Latin American Research Review* 40, no. 1 (2005): 144–47. Also see Andres Lopez, ed., *Complementación productiva en la industria automotriz* (Montevideo: Red Mercosur, July 2007), for a more technical treatment, as well as an update.

9. Alexander Yeats first raised doubts in a World Bank Working Paper in early 1997, later published as "Does Mercosur's Trade Performance Raise Concerns about the Effects of Regional Trade Arrangements?" *World Bank Economic Review* 12, no.1 (1998):1–29. A slew of critical articles can be found in the Inter-American Development Bank's journal *Integration and Development* during these years.

10. Alok K. Bohara and others, "Trade Diversion and Declining Tariffs: Evidence from Mercosur," *Journal of International Economics* 64, no.1 (2004): 65–88. They argue that the process was causal, from increased imports to lesser market power to lower protection. More likely, however, because they start with 1991, the decline in protection they observe was partially the result of the new commitment to imports associated with stabilization.

11. See Jeffrey Cason, "On the Road to Southern Cone Economic Integration," *Journal of Interamerican Studies and World Affairs* 42, no.1 (2000): 23–42.

12. As reported in *Clarín*, January 23, 2000. For more details, see Institute for the Integration of Latin America and the Caribbean (INTAL), *Mercosur Report No. 6, 1999–2000* (Buenos Aires: IDB, 2000), p. 31.

13. See, for example, Ricardo Rozemberg and Gustavo Svarzman, "El processo de integración Argentina-Brasil en perspectiva: El ciclo cambiario y la relación público-privada en Argentina," Disclosure Paper 17 (Buenos Aires: INTAL-IDB, 2002), pp. 37–48. See also Andrés Malamad, "Presidential Diplomacy and the Institutional Underpinning of Mercosur: An Empirical Examination," *Latin American Research Review* 40, no.1 (2005): 138-64; Mario Carranza, "Can Mercosur Survive? Domestic and International Constraints on Mercosur," *Latin American Politics and Society* 45, no. 2 (2003): 67–103; and Gaspare M. Genna and Takeo Hiri, "The Effects of Unequal Size: Costs and Benefits of Unilateral Action in the Development of Mercosur," *Journal of Developing Societies* 21, no. 3-4 (2005): 337–55. The country the authors implicitly favor influences the story told and conclusions emphasized.

14. Full information on the final agreement, filed with ALADI as an amendment to the original Article 14, can be found at the site of the Brazilian Automobile Industrial Federation (www.acrefi.com). Note, in table IX-1 on the website, that the 2001 ratio

of automobile imports by Argentina from Brazil relative to Brazilian imports from Argentina is the lowest in the years covered by the table. Penalties of over $100 million for trade imbalance were apparently forgiven.

15. His close associate, Adolfo Sturzenegger, put it directly, shortly after Cavallo's return to power: "Argentina must stop wasting its time with this absurd project called Mercosur. . . . It must immediately seek a bilateral negotiation with the United States." *New York Times*, March 24, 2001.

16. Afonso Bevilacqua and others, "Integration, Interdependence, and Regional Goods: An Application to Mercosur," *Economia* 2, no. 1 (2001): 153–99. The same concept is later used by IDB economists Eduardo Fernandez-Arias and others, "Trade Agreements and Exchange Rate Disagreements," Research Working Paper 1013 (Washington: March 2002), which was subsequently incorporated into the IDB 2002 Economic and Social Progress Report, *Beyond Borders: The New Regionalism in Latin America* (Washington, 2002). They test the model by looking only at the side of Brazilian imports, thereby ignoring the presumed effect there should have been on Brazilian exports.

17. Daniel Heymann's quarterly analysis of Argentine and Brazilian imports from each other is in accord, but it uses exchange rates vis-à-vis the United States rather than the relative Argentine-Brazilian rate. See Daniel Heymann and Adrian Ramos, "Mercosur in Transition: Macroeconomic Perspectives," Project Document (Santiago: Economic Commission for Latin America and the Caribbean, December 2005).

18. A measure of the extent to which Mercosul had faded is that none of the countries' four presidents attended celebration festivities of its tenth anniversary held in Montevideo in March 2001.

19. *Gazeta Mercantil*, July 23, 2002. Italics mine.

20. INTAL, *Informe Mercosur*, no. 11 (2007): 52–56; data for 2006 have come from ACREFI (Association of Financial, Credit and Investment Institutions).

21. Andrés López y Mariano Laplane, eds., *Complementación Productiva en el Mercosur: Perspectivas y potencialidades* (Montivideo: Red Mercosur, 2004), p. 35.

22. *Informe Mercosur*, no. 11(2007): 56–63, describes the mechanism. The report also points out, as of the end of 2006, that neither country had incorporated this mechanism into national legislation.

23. Fabio Giambiagi and Igor Barenboim, "Mercosul: Por uma nova estrategia brasileira," Discussion Paper 1131 (Brasília: IPEA, November 2005). Sometimes the authors' enthusiasm becomes excessive, as when they argue that access to the Argentine market through Mercosul bestowed a benefit of 9 percent of Brazilian national income in 2005. That calculation does not include the opportunity cost, which would allow for determination of the second-best alternative for utilization of the same resources. It is exactly such opportunity cost that is relevant.

24. Dante Sica, "Mercosur: Evaluación y perspectivas," paper presented at the conference "15 Años de Mercosur: Evaluación y perspectivas," São Paulo, March 2006, p. 48.

25. For a recent indication of mounting research in this area, see Maurício Mesquita Moreira, "Fear of China: Is There a Future for Manufacturing in Latin America," Occasional Paper 36 (Buenos Aires: INTAL-ITD [Integration, Trade and Hemispheric Issues Division], 2006). See also Moreira, *India: Latin America's Next Big Thing* (Washington: IDB, 2010).

26. Marcelo Abreu and Winston Fritsch, "Aspectos estratégicos da política comercial brasileira," in *Sesenta anos de política externa, 1930–1990*, vol. 2, *Diplomacia*

para o desenvolvimento, edited by José Augusto Guilhon Albuquerque (São Paulo: Cultura Editores Associados, 1996).

27. See the extensive discussion of the origins of the FTAA in Richard Feinberg, *Summitry in the Americas* (Washington: Institute for International Economics, 1997). Feinberg was in charge of Latin American relations during his tenure in the first Clinton administration National Security Council.

28. This discussion benefits from the work of Fernando Simas Magalhães, *Cúpula das Américas de 1994: Papel negociador do Brasil, em busca de uma agenda hemisférica* (Brasília: Instituto Rio Branco, 1999). This book takes direct issue with Feinberg's previously cited *Summitry.*

29. Feinberg, *Summitry,* p. 146; Simas Magalhães, p. 165.

30. This section is based on Andy Klom, "Mercosur and Brazil: A European Perspective," *International Affairs* 79, no. 2 (2003): 351–68. Klom at that time was Brazil desk officer of the European Union.

31. Ibid., p. 359.

32. My translation.

33. Cited by Richard Feinberg and Robin Rosenberg, "The Quebec Summit: Tear Gas, Trade and Democracy," *North-South Center Update,* May 2001, p. 2.

34. Quoted in "Tendencias e debates," *Folha de São Paulo,* July 8, 2003.

35. FTAA matters were hardly helped along by the interchange between Zoellick in the *Financial Times,* September 22, 2003, where he accused Brazil of leading the Won't Do countries, and Amorim, in the *Wall Street Journal,* September 25, 2003, asserting that Brazil sought simply to level the playing field.

36. J. F. Hornbeck, "A Free Trade Area of the Americas: Major Policy Issues and Status of Negotiations," Report RS20864 (Congressional Research Service, Library of Congress, January 3, 2005), p. 5.

37. Marcelo de Paiva Abreu reported computable general equilibrium results showing Brazilian exports to the United States going up 9 percent while imports would grow 23 percent, consistent with earlier partial equilibrium calculations by him and others. See Abreu, "The Political Economy of Economic Integration in the Americas: Latin American Interests," in *Integrating the Americas: FTAA and Beyond,* edited by Antoni Estevadeordal and others (Harvard University Press, 2004), pp. 435–36.

38. These studies are reported in Marta R. Castilho, "Impactos de acordos comerciais sobre a econômia brasileira: Resenha dos trabalhos recentes," Discussion Paper 936 (Brasília: IPEA, 2002).

39. The volume is edited by Alfredo G. A. Valladão, and bears the subtitle *The EU-Mercosur Agreement and the Free Trade Area of the Americas* (Paris: Sciences Po, 2003).

40. Ibid., pp. 32 and 50 for the quotation, pp. 84 and 113ff. for the basis for this brief summation.

41. The announcement occurred at the conclusion of the Fourth EU-Mercosur Summit in Madrid on May 17, 2010. See Spanish Presidency of the Council of the EU, "The EU and Mercosur Decide to Resume Talks about Reaching an Association Agreement (www.eu2010.es/export/sites/presidencia/en/cumbre_ue-alc/noticias/may17_mercosur.html).

42. There has been controversy over time surrounding Brazilian ratification, now achieved. Within the Federal Senate in 2007, there had been discussion of the Venezuelan decision not to renew the license of one of the opposition TV stations, RCTV.

Chávez asserted that the "Congress of Brazil . . . does not have the political or moral standing to decide our incorporation." He further called the members "United States parrots and oligarchs." *Mercopress,* July 4, 2007.

43. *Mercopress,* April 18, 2007.

44. There is a modest academic literature available on IBSA. FRIDE, the Fundación para las Relaciones Internacionales y el Diálogo Exterior, has been following the organization, and there are two books from Brazil: Alcides Costa Vaz, ed., *Intermediate States, Regional Leadership and Security: India, Brazil and South Africa* (Brasília: Editora UnB, 2006); and Fábio Villares, ed., *India, Brazil and South Africa—Perspectives and Alliances* (São Paulo: Instituto de Estudos Economicos e Internacionais, 2006).

45. As mentioned at the beginning, the BRICS are another grouping, first given notice in 2001 for their increasing weight and importance within the world economy. They have moved to a first meeting in Russia in 2009, followed up by one in Brasília in 2010, and in China in 2011. At the latter, South Africa will also attend, increasing the overlap with IBSA.

46. These and subsequent paragraphs rely heavily on Ricardo Wahrendorff Caldas, *Brazil in the Uruguay Round of the GATT* (Farnham, United Kingdom: Ashgate, 1998).

47. Paulo Noguiera Batista, the Brazilian ambassador to GATT through 1987, was opposed to inclusion of the new subjects and remained critical of subsequent Brazilian concessions. He maintained that separate negotiation on services would mean that decisions would not be binding on all countries. For a fuller sense of his commitment to *desenvolvimentismo,* see his last essay, "O consenso de Washington" (humbertocapellari.wordpress.com/2006/06/20/o-consenso-de-washington).

48. See Marcelo de Paiva Abreu, "O Brasil na Rodada Uruguai de GATT, 1982–93," Working Paper 311 (Pontifícia Universidade Católica do Rio de Janeiro, 1994); and Rubens Ricupero, *Visões do Brasil* (Rio de Janeiro: Editora Record, 1995), pp. 299–321.

49. Those initial projections showed global welfare gains of US$265 billion in 2015 from free agricultural trade. They were subsequently revised downward, using a new base year and model, to US$182 billion. The latter still was greater than the estimated welfare gain of little more than US$100 billion for manufactures free trade. For the earlier estimate, see World Bank, *Global Economic Prospects: Realizing the Development Promise of the Doha Agenda* (Washington, 2004).

50. For a fuller discussion of these points and still others, see Kym Anderson, Will Martin, and Ernesto Valenzuela, "Why Market Access Is the Most Important of Agriculture's 'Three Pillars' in the Doha Negotiations," *World Bank Trade Note,* no. 26, March 21, 2006.

51. The discussion here is based on Albert Fishlow, "The Doha Round: Has It Now Expired?" in *The WTO: Governance, Dispute Settlement, and Developing Countries,* edited by Merit E. Janow, Victoria Donaldson, and Alan Yanovich (New York: Juris Publishing, 2008).

52. See Arvind Panagariya, "Liberalizing Agriculture," and William R. Cline, "Doha and Development," *Foreign Affairs, WTO Special Issue* (December 2005): 56–66 and 67–76, respectively, for these statistical details and many more involving the four subsidy categories.

53. Daniella Markheim, "Moving Forward after Hong Kong," Backgrounder 1915 (Washington: Heritage Foundation, February 22, 2006), p. 1.

54. "What Happened in Hong Kong," Briefing Paper 85 (Oxford: Oxfam, December 2005), p. 2.

55. As reported in the manuscript version of Kym Anderson and Will Martin, eds., *Agricultural Trade Reform and the Doha Development Agenda* (Washington: World Bank, 2005).

56. Sandra Polaski, *Winners and Losers: Impact of the Doha Round on Developing Countries* (Washington: Carnegie Endowment for International Peace, 2006).

57. Ibid., chapter 4, compares the alternative models used. At an aggregate level, there is not that much difference: 0.67 percent of world income gain from full free trade based on World Bank estimates, 0.53 percent from Carnegie estimates. But there is a great distinction in composition: the World Bank finds two-thirds of the gains from agricultural liberalization, while the Carnegie figure is about one-third.

58. Ken Haydon, "After the WTO Hong Kong Ministerial Meeting: What Is at Stake," Trade Policy Working Paper 27 (Paris: OECD, 2006), p.4.

59. See L. Alan Winters, "The Temporary Movement of Workers to Provide Services," in *A Handbook of International Trade in Services,* edited by Aaditya Mattoo, Robert M. Stern, and Gianni Zanini (Oxford University Press, 2008), 498ff.

60. Kym Anderson and Will Martin, "Scenarios for Global Trade Reform," in *Poverty and the WTO,* edited by Thomas W. Hertel and L. Alan Winters (Washington: World Bank, 2006), p. 35.

61. For a breakdown by country, see Polaski, *Winners and Losers,* p. 35; for the World Bank model, see Anderson and Martin, *Agricultural Trade Reform.*

62. José Goldemberg, "Current Policies Aimed at Attaining a Model of Sustainable Development in Brazil," *Journal of Environment and Development* 1 no. 1 (1992): 110.

63. Susanne Feitelberg Jakobsen, "The Determinants of the National Position of Brazil on Climate Change—Empirical Reflections," Working Paper 97.1 (Bonn: Center for Development Research, May 1997), p. 6.

64. Ibid., p. 12.

65. Ken Johnson, "Brazil and the Politics of the Climate Change Negotiations," *Journal of Environment and Development* 10, no. 2 (2001): 188.

66. Andrew Hurrell, "Brazil and the International Politics of Amazonian Deforestation," in *The International Politics of the Environment,* edited by Andrew Hurrell and Benedict Kingsbury (Oxford University Press, 1992), p. 405.

67. Jakobsen, "Determinants," p. 12.

68. See the recent work of André Aranha Corrêa de Lago, *Estocolmo, Rio, Joanesburgo: O Brasil e as três conferéncias das Nações Unidas* (FUNAG: Brasília, 2009). Like Itamaraty as a whole, he stresses greater continuity than difference between the Brazilian positions at the Stockholm and Rio meetings.

69. See Intergovernmental Panel on Climate Change, "Reports" (www.ipcc.ch/publications_and_data/publications_and_data_reports.shtml).

70. "A Special Report on Forests," *The Economist,* Sept. 25, 2010, p. 14.

71. Ibid.

72. World Bank, "WB Support Grows for Brazil's Environment," March 25, 2009 (http://go.worldbank.org/YT0WTPF2E0).

73. World Resources Institute, "Brazil's Global Warming Agenda," March 1, 2010 (www.wri.org/stories/2010/03/brazils-global-warming-agenda.)

74. Brazil served in the years 1946–47, 1951–52, 1954–55, 1963–64, 1967–68, 1988–89, 1993–94, 1998–99, and 2004–05. The country's selection in 1966 came

during a period when it seemed that the military regime would be brief. Only Japan has served comparably.

75. In 1997 there had been a positive report regarding modification of the Security Council by the president of the General Assembly, Razali Ismail from Malaysia. It called for an increase in size, the presence of developing countries plus two developed country permanent positions, absence of veto for the new permanent members, and revision after a period of time. New permanent members would be selected by the General Assembly but only with approval of the present five permanent members.

76. *The Economist*, January 4, 2007.

77. Celso Amorim in an interview with BBC Brasil, June 3, 2006.

78. Edward C. Luck, "How Not to Reform the United Nations," *Global Governance* 11, no. 4 (2005): 412.

79. Tullo Vigevani and Gabriel Cepaluni, "Lula's Foreign Policy and the Quest for Autonomy through Diversification," *Third World Quarterly* 28, no. 7 (2007): 1313.

80. See Samuel Pinheiro Guimarães, *Desafios brasileiros na era dos gigantes* (Rio de Janeiro: Contraponto, 2006), pp. 321–22, for this characterization. He was second in command at Itamaraty until forced to retire because of age.

81. Guimarães, as cited by Vigevani and Cepaluni, "Lula's Foreign Policy," pp.1314–15.

Chapter Six

1. *The Economist*, October 2, 2010.

2. See Ministry of Finance, *Brazilian Economic Outlook*, Special Edition (Brasília, 2010), p. 19, where an investment ratio of 24.1 percent is judged necessary by 2014 to achieve an annual growth rate of 6.5 percent a year. Unfortunately, there is no indication of how the large increase is to come about.

3. Banco Itaú shows negative public savings of 2.4 percent of GNP in 2010; that ratio declines over time but remains negative in 2020. Itaú Unibanco, *Macro Visão*, February 15, 2011, p. 7. The investment ratio never gets above 23 percent, and growth correspondingly is at an average rate of 4.5 percent.

Index

ABECEB (consulting firm), 157
ABN (bank), 62
Abreu, Marcelo, 158
Absolute poverty. *See* Extreme poverty
Ação direta de inconstitucionalidade (ADIN, direct action of unconstitutionality), 16
Account deficits, 47, 80, 147, 150
Act of Buenos Aires, 143
Adaptable Program Loan, 134
ADIN (*Ação direta de inconstitucionalidade,* direct action of unconstitutionality), 16
Aerus (pension fund), 21
Age-grade distortion rates, 89, 92–93
Agricultural sector, 169–72, 174–77
Ahmadinejad, Mahmoud, 164, 183
AIDS. *See* HIV/AIDS
AIG, failure of, 82
ALADI. *See* Association of Latin American Integration
ALBA (Bolivarian Alternative for Latin America), 164
Alckmin, Geraldo, 75
Alfonsín, Raúl, 141, 143, 147
al Qaeda, 49
Amadeo, Edward, 129
Amazon: deforestation of, 180–81; and global warming, 178–79; investment in, 76

Ambev (beer company), 73
Amendments, constitutional. *See* Constitutional Amendment
Ames, Barry, 13
Amorim, Celso, 161, 171, 181, 182, 183
AMRO Real (bank), 62
ANAC (National Civil Aviation Agency), 20
ANATEL. *See* National Telecommunications Agency
ANEEL (National Electricity Regulatory Agency), 29, 30
ANP (National Petroleum, Natural Gas, and Biofuels Agency), 29, 30
Antidumping, 145, 159, 161, 177
Antiretroviral medicines, 112
Aracruz (financial firm), 83
Arbix, Glauco, 79
Argentina: economic crisis in, 49–50; and exchange rates, 47; and exports, 73; higher education in, 99; inflation models in, 35, 36, 38, 41; rapprochement with Brazil, 140, 141–58, 191
Arida, Pérsio, 35, 42, 43–44
"Arinos" (Constitutional Studies) Commission, 7
Association of Latin American Integration (ALADI), 142, 143, 151
Atomic Agency, UN, 184